TARTE TATIN

Susan Herrmann Loomis was born in Orlando, Florida. Her childhood was spent moving from country to country and state to state as she followed her military father. She graduated first from the University of Washington in Seattle in 1977, then from La Varenne Ecole de Cuisine with a Grand Diplôme in February 1981. She met and married Michael Loomis, a sculptor, in 1983 and together they lived in France for a year and a half before moving back to Seattle. In 1993 the Loomis family moved back to France so that Susan could write *French Farmhouse Cookbook*, which was published in 1996. She then went on to write *Italian Farmhouse Cookbook*, which was published in 2000, after two years of research in Italy. In 2001, HarperCollins published *On Rue Tatin*, the first instalment of life for the Loomis family in Louviers.

TARTE TATIN

More of La Belle Vie on rue Tatin

SUSAN LOOMIS

HarperCollins*Publishers*

HarperCollins*Publishers*
77–85 Fulham Palace Road,
Hammersmith, London W6 8JB

www.harpercollins.co.uk

A paperback original 2003
1 3 5 7 9 8 6 4 2

A catalogue record for this book
is available from the British Library

ISBN 0 00 714351 6

Set in New Baskerville by
Rowland Phototypesetting Ltd, Bury St Edmunds, Suffolk

Printed and bound in Great Britain by
Clays Ltd, St Ives plc

I dedicate this book to our children Joseph and Fiona, whose love, humour, and energy suffuse life with a very special richness. I also dedicate this book to the memory of André Taverne whose jokes and ready smile are missed, to his wife, Marie-Odile, and to his sister-in-law Marie-Claire, for their friendship.

ACKNOWLEDGMENTS

Any book, even a narrative about one's own life, owes its existence to a handful of helpful people. I would like to give particular and heartfelt thanks to my editor, Susan Watt, who has a true love for words and a story, for her punctual and careful editing, her encouragement, and her vivid laugh, and to my agent Angela Miller, for her insistent and quiet support. I would like to thank, too, the delightful Katie Espiner who keeps things running and responds quickly and efficiently, and Rachel Nicholson who gets the public eye to read the right books! In Australia I would like to thank Shona Martyn and Helen Littleton for their cheerful support.

I want to thank the editors who have, over the years, encouraged me by publishing my work, including Lisa Higgins at Metropolitan Home, Barbara Fairchild at Bon Appétit, Jill Melton at Cooking Light, Gabi Tubbs at House and Garden, and the many others over the years who have been so helpful and supportive.

Closer to home I want to thank Edith and Nadine for their sisterhood, and Chantal, Anne-Marie, Annie, Babette, Antoinette, Miche, and Dalila for their wonderful friendship, the friendship of women! And I don't want to leave out the men, including Bernard, Christian, Michel, Patrick, Johan, Jean-Lou, and Jean, for they are more than wonderful too!

And finally I thank Michael Loomis, without whom none of this wonderful life would be possible.

CONTENTS

The Opening up of On Rue Tatin 1

The Kitchen and the Cooking School 19

A French Poodle in the House 53

An Ode to the Market in Louviers 73

The Florists 101

Be Careful of Me, I'm Dangerous 125

The Place for a Party 159

There's an '*Ado*' in Our Midst 187

Driving *À La Française* 215

Paris 237

While Louviers Sleeps 255

Shopping and the Cart 267

Michael's Studio and the Gentrification of
 Louviers 279

Bi-Culturalism and Play Ball! 295

Cultural Differences/Cultural Sameness 311

Home Away from Home – September 11 325

Afterword 349

List of Recipes 355

The Opening up of
On Rue Tatin

It had been five years since we'd moved to rue Tatin in
Louviers, northwest of Paris. The house was habitable,
though hearty draughts still tugged at the curtains, and
attic rooms remained as they were when we bought the
place: dry but in sad repair. We used them to store things,
like the dozen or more beautiful antique doors that were
in the house when we acquired it, building materials and
electrical supplies, as well as the general flotsam and jet-
sam that collectors such as Michael and I accumulate.

We had pretty much adjusted to the schedule of Joe's
school, accepting that – just as we'd feel we were getting
into our individual rhythms – it seemed to be time for
another vacation. Professional demands dictated that we
rarely went on holiday, so we would divide our days in
two. Michael would generally be with Joe in the morning
while I worked, and I would take Joe in the afternoon
while Michael worked. Joe would have friends over now
and then, but the French don't share their children in
the way Americans do, so it was less often than either we

or Joe liked. We had put Joe in a local school, thinking he'd make friends in the neighbourhood but, as luck would have it, most of his friends lived in other towns, and the few boys his age who lived locally were kept hidden somewhere; we'd see them only on their way to school.

Michael and I were settling in with a close group of friends that included Edith and Bernard, Christian and Nadine, Babette and Jean Lou, Chantal and Michel, our neighbour Patrick and Anne-Marie and Patrick. We'd even met two Franco-American families who lived in towns nearby, which provided us with some comic relief when we got together and shared evenings, laughing at each other's jokes because – for a change – we understood them. We had friends in Paris, too, which occasioned going there regularly for dinner, driving back in the wee hours when the roads were empty. I always say it takes an hour to get to Louviers from Paris, but at 1 a.m. it's an easy forty-five minute trip.

We were, all in all, beginning to understand how things worked in France, and to feel comfortable as the only American family in Louviers. Louviers, and France, were beginning to feel like home.

My *French Farmhouse Cookbook* had been published, and I was currently involved in developing and testing recipes for an important American cookbook that was a collaborative effort by many of my colleagues. I was also doing research and testing for the *Italian Farmhouse Cookbook*, which for two years took me to Italy for long periods of time. I loved doing both projects, particularly the Italian book, since it gave me an insight into a country, people and culture with which I was unfamiliar. I wanted it to be my last farm book, as I felt I'd said what I could say about farming, and I knew that just writing books would no longer be enough to support our family. I began thinking about what would be next. I wouldn't stop writing books, because it is something I am made to do. But I wanted to use our home for a business, and the business I'd always imagined operating was a cooking school. Way back when we had lived in Seattle I'd wanted to do the same sort of thing, but the situation there hadn't been right. This time, it just might be.

My inspiration to open up our home came initially from the time Michael lived on a farm in the Dordogne with the Dubois family – nearly twenty years ago. Danie Dubois, in an effort to augment her income and give herself an interest outside their isolated little village, decided she would take in paying guests for meals and the night, and would offer 'cooking weekends' using local specialties as ingredients. By the time Michael went to live with them, Danie's business was prospering. She not only made endless meals to satisfy her guests, but she also offered pig and foie gras weekends.

For her '*weekend de cochon*', she and her guests turned an entire pig into delectable pepper- and salt-cured hams, rillettes, blood sausage, head cheese, roasts, chops and more. For the '*weekend d'oie*' she transformed geese into untold marvels like confit, stuffed gooseneck, foie gras en terrine and a wonderful local delicacy called '*demoiselles*': goose carcasses grilled on a wood fire. Everything Danie made was sumptuous: her foie gras was so delicate and buttery that it made any other of little interest; her confit was beguilingly crisp on the outside and mouth-melting inside. The confit went so well with her creamy pumpkin soup, the wonderful dandelion salads, made from leaves picked in the field next door and dressed with her own walnut oil, the crisp country breads, her homemade cheese, the grapey wine her husband Guy made from their own grapes . . . Danie would grill country bread over the fireplace coals and spread it with fresh foie gras. She served this as an aperitif, and what an aperitif it was.

Everything Danie did was first-rate, and every dish she made was better than the one before it. Because of this, her enterprise was enormously successful, her table so sought after that she eventually expanded her dining room and turned it into a restaurant, which is still thriving today.

Michael and I loved the ambience that Danie's business gave to the farm; the flow of appreciative guests from around the world; the sharing of traditions; the way the house and their life encompassed everyone; the seamlessness of it all. I'd always wanted to create that at our own home, and I realized that we had the potential on rue Tatin. We wouldn't house people – the house isn't large enough – nor would we grow all our own food. We didn't need to – local farmers would do that for us.

We had one problem, however, and that was the kitchen. It was far from suitable for a cooking school in its present state. We'd planned to build a new one, but Michael was still embroiled in the dining room. When we sat down to discuss the idea of the cooking school we realized that it would be at least two years before we could consider bringing the idea to fruition. How, we wondered aloud, could we make the house work for us now?

With our friends Pat and Walter Wells, who were over for lunch one day, we came up with the idea of offering lunches to paying guests, tourists who would like a moment of delicious luxury and an opportunity to get a more intimate view of French culture. We all decided, looking around at the dining room and the view out of the window, that it didn't matter that the house was half finished, or that our 'forever' kitchen wasn't yet built. All I needed for this idea was a kitchen where I could cook fabulous food. 'This house, this room, this whole place is gorgeous; people will love it as it is,' Pat said, and Walter concurred.

Once the idea had been articulated, I began to get excited. It could be so perfect. I could easily imagine greeting small groups of friendly Americans with meals made from the best of local and mostly organic ingredients, and delicious wines. I could imagine us discoursing on the local community, agriculture, the state of the European Union, and we could answer their questions about life in France. One of my favourite parts of this plan was that we could justify buying beautiful dishes and glassware (which I love) to make lunches the luxurious experience I imagined.

I was scheduled to go on a book-tour in the United States not long after our lunch with the Wellses. I decided to take a stab at marketing the lunches as I went, and to that end brought it up during every interview. I enlisted a friend in the US, Marion Pruitt, to be the contact person, knowing that she was so organized she wouldn't let one detail fall through the cracks, and that people who called would love her. She'd been to visit, too, so she could speak knowledgeably about us and about our location. Before I knew it, a group of five women had signed up as paying guests.

When I returned from my book-tour I looked at the house with fresh eyes, and I wondered if I'd been crazy to think we could have strangers here. The setting and the bones of the house were gorgeous, no doubt about it, but would people mind the stacks of crooked old timbers and stones? Would they be as charmed by the unfinished dining room as we were? Would they think the sheet rock wall in the kitchen that Joe used as an easel as cute and practical as we did? 'We'll see,' I thought. Then I began to plan the menu.

The group would come in October, one of my favourite times of year. How to decide what to serve? I put myself in the shoes of the person thinking of Norman cuisine: what would they want to eat? Apples, of course. Duck, for there is nothing like it to whisper 'Normandy' on the palate. Shellfish, cream, wonderful cheese.

Whenever people come to eat I want to offer them all the good and wonderful things we have available to us, but of course in one meal I can't. So I use the aperitif to offer a multitude of small tastes and flavours that will give a hint of the meal to come, and of the wealth the region offers, as well as a sense of what is typical. I decided that, in this instance, oysters from the cold waters of the Normandy coast were a must. I personally love them plain: just well chilled and without sauces or condiments. As a compromise, to cater to tastes that might not be so pure, I would serve lemon wedges and a sauce mignonette alongside.

Anyone who has ever dined in a French home knows how vital pistachio nuts are to the aperitif hour. I have a source for slender, dark pistachios from Turkey, the kind my father used to bring back from there by the laundry bag full when I was a child. I developed a passion for their crisp, rich nuttiness then, and I still love watching others taste them for the first time. Their eyes widen and pretty soon they are back for more, for these pistachios are so much more flavourful than any other. So, duck, oysters, pistachios. The menu needed work.

I make a sweet, salty olive cookie from an old Provençal recipe, and I added that to the aperitif – no one can resist them. Now, I needed a crisp vegetable to round out the selection, and I decided it would be sticks of fresh fennel. It is the only vegetable aside from celery with a natural saltiness, and it is round, fat and crisp in October. I would serve my homemade orange wine, too: its intense, caramel-orange flavour beguiles everyone who tastes it.

I decided on confit tomatoes for the first course, since Normandy tomatoes are rich and sweet in early October. To make these, I cut them in half and bake them long and slowly in olive oil with rosemary, thyme, thinly sliced shallots, whole cloves of garlic and sea salt. When they emerge from the oven they taste and smell like concentrated sun. With the roast duck I would serve autumn turnips glazed with cane sugar. Just thinking about it made me hungry.

Salad would come from the garden – arugula and baby beet greens, sorrel and snipped sage leaves. I settled on a trio of Normandy cheeses – Livarot, Camembert and Neufchâtel. I would carefully caramelize apples for a tarte tatin. After all, we live on rue Tatin – how could I plan a meal without it?

As good fortune would have it, a visit from my parents would coincide with our first lunch. Friendly, warm and well-travelled, they are the perfect lunch companions any time. For our first lunch they would be our trump card, carrying the conversation while Michael and I attended to the details.

This lunch would resemble a theatre performance as we hid the worst of the remodelling messes and created a captivating, luxurious ambience. We began cleaning up the dining room, garden and courtyard three days before our guests were due to arrive. Michael moved and stacked materials; we both worked furiously to get the garden cleaned up. I bought and planted flowers and we trimmed and tidied the window boxes. The exterior had looked pretty good before we started. By the time we were finished it looked magical. As for the interior, we cleaned, polished and dusted, and I put bouquets of flowers everywhere. We didn't have an official bathroom downstairs, but a toilet hidden behind a wall. I hung a pretty curtain over the door and hoped for the best.

Finally, it was market day before the big lunch. Accompanied by my parents and Joe, I went to buy all the ingredients, loading myself down with the best butter and milk, the finest tomatoes and oysters, gorgeous little turnips and even some late-season raspberries that smelt like heaven. I wasn't sure where they would fit in, but how could I resist?

I went home and began to prepare the meal, then was up at 6 a.m. the following morning to continue cooking. With my mother's help I covered the table with an antique monogrammed white linen sheet, then curled a strand of ivy down the centre. Michael almost killed me when he saw the ivy; he had been at great pains to make our one ivy plant climb up a small section of brick wall near the ancient wooden door in our courtyard, and I had just trimmed off the longest pieces. He needn't have worried, however, as the ivy on the brick still looked good. I knew his reaction resulted from being as nervous as I about this first lunch.

I printed up menus on parchment paper and set one at each place, along with sprigs of bay leaves, which guests could take home with them, silver cutlery, our amber and turquoise water glasses from Portugal, crystal wine glasses. I had recently found a stack of blue and white vintage Sarreguemines plates tucked away in a local *brocante*, second-hand market, and with these on the table it looked fit for royalty.

Our guests arrived at 12:30 p.m., right on time. They came into our courtyard exclaiming over the view, and over the aromas issuing from the front door. 'We could smell this all the way down the street,' said one of them. 'We were hoping it was coming from here!'

The day was perfect: sunny and warm with that lovely autumn coolness that makes it perfect for sitting outside. We had put a lively cloth on our round, wrought-iron table in the garden, and set up the parasols so that we could sit outside for the aperitif. Michael gave each guest a glass of orange wine and we all toasted the day and each other, then our guests asked if I would give them a tour of the garden.

Michael had recently completed a low, curved stone wall that enclosed the largest part of my herb garden. It held a border of thyme plants, and behind them a trio of different sages. There was salad burnet and sweet cicely, summer savory, bronze fennel and garlic chives. An old-fashioned climbing rose was in its second stage of blooming, covering the house with its bright red flowers. At its foot was one of its favourite companions, tarragon, which had grown into a lacy bush.

Further away from the house was another herb garden. To get there we crossed a narrow brick walkway Michael had made with beautiful old, worn bricks, which divided the gravel and grassy portions of the courtyard. The grass was for Joe to play on and we had had to declare it sacred; otherwise it would have been so easy to keep expanding the herbs and flowers until they covered everything.

A small, ancient apple tree stood at one side of the grassy patch and an old pear tree stood at the other. We'd planted a rosemary hedge against the metal fence near the pavement, to afford us some privacy. Under the pear tree I'd planted an antique variety of strawberry that was still white when it was ripe, a handful of lily varieties, an ornamental sage whose tiny, fuchsia flowers bloomed almost all year, and a row of dahlias which lent their colour and spirit from mid-June through to November. We were planning to put in a row of espaliered apple trees as soon as the temperature dropped a bit, and these would shield us from our neighbours next door. A *laurel nobilis* reigned in the corner of the garden, supplying me with bay leaves to perfume sauces and soups, and I had both red and green sorrel in front of that, along with a rhubarb plant. The very foreground of this patch of garden was devoted to lettuces and tomatoes, and a handful of basil plants that were offering their last. I realized, with this tour of the garden, how I'd gathered all my botanical friends around me in the five years we'd lived in Louviers. The house wasn't finished – and maybe it never would be – but the garden told me I was home.

We sat down to our aperitif and could easily have whiled away the afternoon as we nibbled and sipped, but lunch awaited. I excused myself to prepare the first course and get the turnips cooking, remove the duck from the oven so it could rest, and slice Michael's loaf of freshly baked bread. Michael opened the St Véran, a golden and buttery white Burgundy, and my parents ushered our guests into the dining room. That occasioned more oohs and aahs and more photos. Michael and I were bubbling with excitement as we saw the reactions these strangers had to our home.

We ate our tomatoes confit, then I presented the whole ducks before returning to the kitchen to carve and arrange them in traditionally symmetrical fashion on a warmed platter. I arranged the golden turnips around them, garnished the plate with sprigs of salad burnet and garlic chives, and presented it. Michael poured the wine, a Sablet from the Côtes du Rhône.

As I knew they would be, the duck and the turnips were a marvellous success. In fact the lunch, from start to finish, was so friendly and delicious that we were all sorry when it was over. When our guests left, just before 6 p.m.,

Michael and I and my parents looked at each other with satisfaction, knowing it had been a stunning success. The house worked, the meal had been a real insider's look at French country cuisine and the wonderful products available, and the conversation hadn't stopped for a minute. Having people come for lunch as strangers and leave as friends was exactly the right use for our house and our talents.

A series of lunches followed, as interest was sparked by an article in the *San Francisco Chronicle* by Patty Unterman, who came to test one of our lunches, as well as mentions in other top magazines. Each meal required as much work as the first one, since we stopped our lives to clean and organize both garden and house, but we did it with pleasurable anticipation. We ended up doing a dozen lunches over the next twelve months, for groups as large as twelve and as few as two, as we tried it on for size.

One of our favourite groups was made up of three generations of the same family. The grandmother organized the meal as a gift to her children and grandchildren, and she worked with me to make sure it was perfect. She wanted the youngest children in the group – who were about eight – to be occupied in some way, as she suspected they would tire of a long meal. I agreed, and arranged for them to be taken in hand by a young man I knew who babysat, spoke a modicum of English and had a driver's licence. I called the Louviers *pétanque* club and asked if the children could watch a game; very kindly, the president offered to teach them how to play. I arranged a visit to a local farm to end the afternoon. The grandmother was delighted, and wanted to know if Joe would be interested in joining her grandchildren. She thought it might be nice for them to meet an American/French boy. I don't push Joe into these situations, so I said we would wait and see. When the family arrived and he saw how boisterous and fun the children were, he joined right in.

The children sat down with us for the first course of pumpkin soup with freshly baked rolls, then they left with the babysitter and returned in time for dessert some four hours later. The lunch was a success except for the fresh chestnuts I'd carefully peeled and braised which are, to me, as prized as truffles. I was happily enjoying mine when I looked around and noticed that several of the guests hadn't touched theirs. Maybe they didn't know what they were, I thought, so I began talking about hunting the local chestnuts, about how to prepare them and how happy I was to have been able to offer them. This helped a bit, but many of the chestnuts were still on the plates when they returned to the kitchen. The grandmother confided to me later that not only did her children know what they were, but that they had always refused to eat them. She'd seen them at least try them today, which for her was a huge victory!

I had another lunch scheduled with two delightful women from Seattle. They arrived and we all sat down to lunch. I'd marinated a leg of wild boar for three days in a rich mélange of red wine and spices, then roasted it. I served slices of this as a first course, drizzled with the marinade that I'd reduced to a syrup, along with a small mound of wild boar rillettes that I'd made as well. Following that was a delectable dish of guinea hen roasted with oranges and lemons, a freshly picked garden salad, and poached pears with honey ice cream. There were other little dishes here and there, and everyone had a wonderful time. Joe was home from school that day and he ate with us, which was an exception. For him, I'd purchased a large slab of pâté as a first course, since wild boar rillettes weren't yet among his list of favourite dishes. He tucked into the pâté with gusto, cutting small chunks to eat on bread, interspersing bites of this with nibbles of tiny cornichons. When one of the women wrote to thank me for their experience later, she said, 'I loved it all, but what I couldn't get over was watching that little boy eat that pâté. An American boy would never have done that.' It hadn't occurred to me that it was odd for Joe to like pâté: it is my sure-fire success dish for him – and now for Fiona too.

I had a near-disaster on my hands one day. I'd decided to make pot au feu, a festive, delicious dish that brings people together. I used a recipe from my neighbour, André Taverne, which calls for the finest beef cheeks and oxtail, rump roast and ribs – which I ordered from my favourite butcher – and a host of vegetables including gorgeous leeks, carrots, celery root and onions from the market. When I set out the ingredients on the cutting board it was enough for an army, and I had not one single pot large enough to cook it in.

I had allowed myself just enough time to prepare and cook the pot au feu and not one minute more. What had I been thinking? What was I going to do? I considered dividing the ingredients in half and cooking them in two pots, but that wouldn't really do. I got out every pot I had, including my lightweight couscoussier for making couscous. Nothing was big enough. I knew Edith had a big pot, but she wasn't at home. Who else did I know who might have something? 'Aha,' I thought. My friend Martine at the *ferme-auberge*. I called, and her husband Patrick assured me they had something. Meanwhile, Michael had called a friend who cooks huge meals for the people who stay at his camping site. Within an hour we had three huge pots sitting in our kitchen, each large enough to hold the pot au feu. I was saved.

*   *   *

13

I continued to schedule lunches that year, with the twelfth one in November, just over a year after our first. We looked back over the year in amazement. We'd actually realized a small part of our dream with very little publicity. True, the lunches were far from a goldmine, but they accomplished a great deal – we met very interesting people and were becoming accustomed to welcoming strangers into our house. I was having the time of my life creating menus and offering the best that I could possibly find, and watching people really enjoy it. And I was setting up a small infrastructure of people who could help me do everything from babysitting to serving at table. I considered it some of the most enjoyable on-the-job training I'd ever done.

We offered lunches from spring through to autumn for the next two years, as Michael finished the dining room and moved on to the huge task of building the kitchen. They continued to be interesting and enjoyable and they were leading us where we wanted to go, which was to the cooking school. It was taking on a real dimension. All I needed was a kitchen.

OLIVE COOKIES FROM THE DROME
Les Scourtins des Vieux Moulins

———————— ❧ ————————

These sweet and salty bites are a very old recipe from Jean-Pierre Autrand, whose family produced olive oil at *Les Vieux Moulin* in Nyons, an ancient olive mill, until 1952. M. Autrand found this recipe in his family's archives, updated it, and sells the results at the gift store adjacent to the olive mill. *Les Vieux Moulins*, 4, Promenade de la Digue, 26110 Nyons, France.

9 tbs (125g) unsalted butter, softened
¾ cup (100g) confectioner's sugar, sifted
1 tbs extra-virgin olive oil
1¼ cups (200g) all purpose flour
1 generous pinch of fine sea salt
½ cup (100g) cured olives, preferably from Nyons, pitted
and coarsely chopped

1. Preheat the oven to 350°F (180°C). Line two baking sheets with parchment paper.
2. In a large bowl or the bowl of an electric mixer, cream the butter until it is soft and pale yellow. Mix in the sugar until blended, then drizzle in the olive oil and mix until combined. Add the flour and sea salt, and mix gently but thoroughly until the dough is smooth, then add the olives and mix until they are thoroughly incorporated into the dough.
3. Place a piece of waxed or parchment paper on a work surface, and place the dough in the middle. Cover it with another piece of waxed or parchment paper and

roll out the dough until it is about ¼-inch thick (½ cm)
– (the dough is very sticky, and the paper makes it
possible to roll out). Refrigerate the dough for at least
30 minutes, and up to 24 hours.

4. Cut out 2-inch rounds of dough and place them about
½ inch (1.3 cm) apart on the prepared baking sheets.
Gather the trimmings into a ball and roll it into a 1-inch
(2.5 cm) diameter log. Wrap well and refrigerate, and
when you are ready to bake, cut off ¼-inch (½ cm)
thick rounds (this avoids over-rolling the dough).

5. Bake until the scourtins are golden, about 15 minutes.
Remove from the oven and cool on wire racks.

Yield: about 34 *scourtins*

ORANGE WINE
Vin d'Orange

This wine is so simple to make, and to enjoy! Be sure to
use organic oranges, and make this in the winter
when the fruit is at its best. Though this wine is very
drinkable after four weeks in the bottle, it mellows with
age. I make it one year to serve the next, and suggest you
do the same.

10 good-size oranges, preferably organic and well scrubbed
8 cups (2 l) dry white wine, such as Sancerre
2 cups (500 ml) pure fruit alcohol, or vodka
1 vanilla bean
1 tbs arabica coffee beans
2 cups minus 2 tbs (375 g) sugar

1. Peel the oranges right down to the fruit, including the pith. Put the fruit aside for another use.
2. Place the skins with the pith in a large nonreactive pot or bowl. Add the wine, vodka, vanilla bean, coffee beans, and half the sugar. Stir.
3. Caramelize the remaining sugar: place the sugar in a small heavy saucepan over medium-high heat. The sugar will melt and begin to bubble, then gradually liquefy, turning a golden colour. This will take about 7 minutes. Continue cooking, swirling the pan occasionally if it colours unevenly, until the sugar is a deep golden colour, like light molasses, about 5 minutes.
4. Remove the pan from the heat and pour the caramelized sugar into the orange mixture, scraping as much of the sugar as possible from the pan with a wooden spoon. The caramel will sizzle and send up steam, and it will instantly harden. Don't be concerned – it will gradually dissolve. Loosely cover the bowl and let the mixture ripen in the bowl for two weeks, stirring it occasionally.
5. Strain the orange mixture through a sieve lined with a double layer of dampened cheesecloth or a dampened cotton tea towel. Discard the orange skins, the vanilla bean and the coffee beans and decant the liquid into sterilized bottles. Seal with corks. Let sit for at least 1 month before drinking.

About 2 ½ quarts (2 ½ l)

The Kitchen and the Cooking School

Before Michael started on the kitchen he added a long, narrow room at the back of the house and just off the now-finished dining room. Our friends though he was crazy: he had all this other work to do on the house and now he was adding more? But he knew it made sense, and so did I, for it was a very clever way to get privacy. We weren't allowed, under the terms of our mortgage, to build any kind of wall between ourselves and the parish house next door, but we were allowed to put an addition onto the house. The addition, then, became our wall.

I should explain that our property abuts that of the parish meeting hall, an active spot where parishioners came for catechism, communion classes and evening prayer vigils. All too often we found people peering in through our small-paned windows at what we assumed they thought was an abandoned house. We didn't understand how they could have thought that, since all the windows were clean, the garden was landscaped and the chimney in active use, but it had been empty for a long time, and presumably they just couldn't resist being nosy. Their surprise when we caught them at it was amusing – they would stare and ogle, not realizing that we were in there, since it was usually early evening when they were there awaiting their classes or vigils, and the light was quite dim. When their eyes adjusted and they realized they were looking right at us, horror and embarrassment would flit across their faces as they abruptly pulled back, and hastily walked away. We would giggle slyly, knowing that they now felt more uncomfortable than we did. Still, it wasn't the most pleasant of situations – what if we'd been walking around naked? Or eating off the floor? Or . . . ?

The long room, which Michael put up quickly, consisted of an outer timbered wall, a glass ceiling and a floor of bricks laid in sand rather than on a foundation, a long window at one end and a door at the other. It would ultimately be turned into a passageway to the courtyard and I, dreaming of our own little orangerie, wanted to plant lemon trees along the warmest wall, with the glass ceiling acting as solar heating.

Home grown citrus fruit would not materialize until years in the future, however. For the duration, this unheated room with its unheated floor would be my temporary kitchen, while Michael socked his way through the building of the permanent kitchen which, we now knew, would be the heart of our cooking school.

Michael installed a large, shallow ceramic sink around the corner and at one end of the room, lined the walls with shelving, and once my two small gas stoves, the refrigerator and all my kitchen equipment were installed it was cosy and efficient, like a kitchen on a boat. Everything was out where I could see it and within easy reach, the way I like it, and the blue and ochre timbered walls, the old brick floor and my copper pots hanging above the stove gave it a certain style.

The day Michael began work on the kitchen was one of those red-letter moments. I know he dreaded the job because it was massive and would require not only super-human strength, but super-human patience as he turned a series of sixteenth-century rooms into one, cohesive kitchen. He carefully sealed off the space with plastic, tape and curtains and proceeded to go at it with satisfy-ing hammer-blows as he bashed down walls and the old, crumbling fireplace, pulled up tiles and generally turned the space into a shambles. A wall with two beautiful long windows that had divided the former kitchen from Michael's workshop disappeared, as did an angled wall at the back and another one to the side. The result was one huge space that stretched from the street to the back court-yard. Destruction, the easy part, took weeks. Once every-thing was a mound of rubble the real work began as Michael hauled it out, tons of it, dustbin by huge dustbin. He found someone who needed landfill, which helped enormously, as the city dump allows just one visit per person per day.

It took months of backbreaking labour to get it all cleaned out. Then Michael ran pipes and wiring through the floor before he poured a concrete pad at the end of the room: this would remain his workshop. With nothing in the space but Michael's tools it looked large, airy, wonderful. Joe was soon in there on his roller blades, swirling around the obstacles of Michael's paraphernalia.

Michael had completed kitchen plans before he began demolition, and he pored over them at night after working in the space all day, tweaking them as it opened up. The planning stage had been a torturous process for me: I don't have the gift of being able to visualize space. When I look at plans on paper I see flat drawings on paper.

When I look at an empty space I see just that – an empty space. But I do know what I need in a kitchen to work well and efficiently: a big centre island with a butcher block and a sink; my knives handy without being in the way or accessible to small fingers; pots and pans and certain utensils hung where I can reach them; lots of full-extension drawers; enough room to accommodate a crowd.

I have ideas about the way I want a kitchen to look, ideas which have to do with colour and warmth and being able to display some of my favourite things like the gorgeous wedding cookies tied with pale blue ribbon that were a gift when I was in Sardinia, the jar of jewel-like candied fruit from Apt, photographs of the children at work in the kitchen, strands of garlic and Espelette peppers, a frothy bunch of pink peppercorns, bay leaves, shallots. I communicated all of this to Michael, who knew it all already, and beyond that I was pretty hopeless. Oh, I read kitchen design books but found most spaces in them cold and impersonal. Flipping through French magazines I found some design elements I loved, and these went into a file for Michael, along with my ideas and observations. He referred to them all when he drew up the plan, going so far as to making a paper '*maquette*', or model, so that I could see, in three dimensions, what he was talking about.

A year of demolition and cleaning up, of concrete-pad pouring and figuring had passed before Michael began the construction phase of the kitchen. He worked on it slowly and steadily, his brow knitted most of the time as he puzzled out the intricate details. It was very slow going, but fortunately one of Michael's many gifts is persistence. He worked and worked for months, grumbling and cursing, hammering and sawing, measuring and figuring. There was a point where I could see it was getting the

better of him and, one night, after Joe was in bed, I suggested we rethink the plans. I'd had my doubts about a
bank of cabinets he'd drawn in on each side of the stove
in a ziggurat pattern. He was trying to give me maximum
storage and light at the same time, but each time I looked
at them on paper they seemed top-heavy and complicated.

I suggested, gently, that I didn't need the cabinets,
knowing that Michael had spent a lot of time figuring,
measuring and planning to fit them in. Surprisingly, he
agreed easily, and with a swipe of his eraser the cabinets
were gone and the kitchen lightened up. It is very hard
to work on a project such as the one we had naively
embarked upon – and to live in it as well; to have the
husband be the contractor and the crew while the wife is
the dreamer and the breadwinner. Anyone who has been
through a similar situation will sympathize – it is one of
the ultimate tests of marriage. Throw in a foreign country,
metric measurements, a toddler and my frequent absences
for work, and the situation becomes even more like dry
tinder.

Michael and I were managing, but it required extreme
delicacy on my side and extreme organization on his. He
is a master at keeping construction messes separate from
our living area through his system of plastic, tape and
curtains, so that as little dust and noise as possible escape
into our lives. I have always appreciated this about him. I
am very good at keeping out of his way, both when he is
designing and when he works, something he appreciates
about me. Still, there were times when I wanted to scream
at the noise and puffs of dust that inevitably escaped, and
there were times when he wanted to, I am certain, walk
out and close the door behind him. But each time we lost
patience we stepped back, took a deep breath and really
looked at what was happening. Progress was being made,

spaces were changing, the bones of the kitchen were in place and it was all taking shape. Observation like this gave each of us renewed energy.

One of the most exciting things about the project was a back porch that Michael had incorporated into the kitchen. To do this, he'd pushed out the back wall and put in glass doors, and pushed up the ceiling then roofed it with glass, which pulled light into the whole room. He'd removed a battered old small-paned metal window that I loved, and painstakingly built two replicas using wood and wavy, antique glass. Michael's brother David, a frequent visitor, helped finish them, and when they were installed they looked as though they had always been there.

Michael rebuilt the fireplace into a cooking fireplace, with a shelf in front wide enough to hold a dinner plate, and a beautifully graceful mantel and chimney. It was a tense job because, even though he'd already remodelled a fireplace that worked, he was building this one from scratch and he didn't know how to guarantee it would draw. We asked friends who'd had fireplaces installed, and all their suggestions pointed in one direction – make the fireplace itself deep enough to build a fire towards the back so the smoke has nowhere to go but up. A book about chimney-building confirmed this and, using calculations he found there as his compass, Michael constructed an entirely smokeless fireplace.

Michael was about to do a final plastering on the fireplace when a friend called to ask if he wanted an old coal stove. Michael went to take a look, only to discover that what he was being offered wasn't any old stove, it was a vintage Aga cooker in mint condition. Our friend just wanted to get rid of it, and said if Michael would take it off his hands, he could have it. Michael jumped at it.

I was in the United States on a book-tour at the time,

and when I called that day and Michael told me what he'd just been given I was so excited I could hardly stand it. Both Michael and I had spent significant years of our childhoods in England, where each of us had eaten oatmeal, soups, stews and breads cooked in the oven of an Aga, and heard our mothers extol the virtues of this heavy, cast-iron stove. We'd both wanted one for years.

Our friend needed the Aga out of the apartment building and Michael called three friends to help him move it. They took a sturdy dolly that Michael had built, hoisted the heavy stove up on it and pushed it uphill from our friend's building to the house, a journey of about five blocks. One of them played traffic policeman as they huffed and puffed and somehow shimmied and wrestled it into our courtyard, then into the house. I took a photo of them from my office window as they pushed and guided this ungainly stove up the middle of the street – they were working hard and laughing at the same time, knowing they were a spectacle, and I just hoped they wouldn't laugh so hard that they would let go of it and send it rolling back down the street.

Michael couldn't install the Aga before he made room for it, which meant that he had to deal with our immensely tall and spindly chimney, which looked as if a strong puff of wind would topple it. Michael had checked it when we moved in and determined it was secure, and the last thing he wanted was to take the time and resources to rebuild it. The addition of the Aga meant he couldn't avoid it; the oven needed a separate flue.

He gritted his teeth, bought the materials and enlisted the help of a Sicilian friend who is a mason. Together, they managed to build an even taller chimney with two flues, one for the Aga and one for the fireplace. This proved providential when an epic windstorm blew through

Normandy just months later: the new chimney withstood the storm, whereas the old one wouldn't have; it would almost certainly have crashed right into the kitchen below it, destroying months of work.

The kitchen was about half-built when I was contacted by a restaurant chain with whom I'd done some promotion, who asked if I would design a five-day programme for fourteen of their managers that would include hands-on cooking classes. 'Of course,' I said. We'd been serving lunches to paying guests from a temporary kitchen in an unfinished dining room, why shouldn't we go ahead and let fourteen cooking students come too?

Michael and I studied our options, trying to figure out how to make this a reality. We resorted, once again, to theatre. We would transform the now-finished dining room, next to the temporary kitchen, into a 'laboratory', where all of the *mise-en-place*, or recipe preparation, would be carried out. We wouldn't have water, but the sink wasn't far. Then, all the cooking would be done in the long, narrow kitchen, which was basically arranged for one person, so I would need to organize the menus carefully to make it work efficiently. We would set up the dining table in our hallway, which is just large enough to hold a long table and has the house's best view of the church's main façade.

Meanwhile, I became pregnant with Fiona. When I'd agreed to do the class I hadn't expected this. She was due in February and the class had been scheduled for April. That gave me two good months to recover, which I figured would be plenty.

The closer the date for the class got, the more nervous I became. I had organized the week as best I could before Fiona was born so that my mind was at ease, but I still needed to work out the menus and figure out where and how to procure ingredients. I would buy everything I could from local farmers, and rely on Chez Clet, the *épicerie* – grocery – next door, for the rest.

I have taught many, many cooking classes, but never in my home, never with a two-month old baby, and never a hands-on class for fourteen people with little or no cooking experience. I knew I'd need some help and I turned to Bruno Atmani, a friend and professionally trained chef. He had recently returned to France from Sweden where he'd worked in restaurants for ten years. His English, which he'd perfected by watching English-language movies, was fluent and his humour of such quality that it is hard to look at him without giggling. I'd never worked with him, but I knew he'd be perfect for the job.

I also enlisted a young American woman, Allison, who had worked for me previously, to help organize things, take some of the trips with us, and generally keep things in order. With Michael, we formed the heart of the 'cooking school'!

The day before the group arrived Michael and Bruno set up work-stations in the dining room. One of the stations was the butcher's work-bench we intended to move into the kitchen when it was finished, a beautiful piece of furniture we'd picked up at a *brocante* for next to nothing. The others were sturdy tables that Michael had quickly built. I set out cutting boards, tea towels and knives, bouquets of herbs and salt and pepper. I lined several dustbins with plastic bags, and set large bowls of water in strategic positions, for rinsing knives and hands. When we were finished we stood back: with the church looming through the windows in the background, it looked incredibly romantic!

The group arrived, starstruck with being in France and

with coming to our house. The group leaders had prepared them well: each manager had a beautiful little book that described their tour, and included a biography of me. They'd all read my *French Farmhouse Cookbook,* so they had a sense of the food they would be asked to prepare.

I gave them each a long white apron, a *toque,* or chef's hat, and a book of the recipes we were going to prepare. They went to settle into their hotel while Bruno, Allison and I set out ingredients and prepared for them to return.

I'd planned a simple menu for the first meal, which included tapenade as an appetizer, asparagus with a fresh goat's cheese and herb sauce, chicken with cream and sorrel sauce, salad and cheese, and lemon cake with fresh strawberries and cream.

My first step was to take them through all of the ingredients, to explain what they were and where they had come from. When I got to the chicken there were a few shrieks, for its head was still attached, and one of the students almost fainted. I had been warned that these people weren't cooks. Despite working for a restaurant chain, they were people-managers and number-crunchers, and it turned out that most of them had almost no hands-on experience with food at all. Their 'restaurants' were really bakeries that served food, and they all knew a lot about how to sell breads and cakes, tarts and cookies, how much wood to order for the wood-burning ovens and how to manage the people who actually did the cooking. But they couldn't navigate their way through a recipe. This made my job that much more interesting and important, and more fun, because I had them captive for a week and could imprint upon them my own standards of quality and freshness!

What this group didn't know about cooking they made up for in willingness to learn and to work, and the experience was more fun than I could have imagined. I was organized down to the last clove of garlic, but considering the variables – not the least among them the fact that I was nursing an infant Fiona – the results of the first session were near miraculous. The temporary kitchen, intended for one cook, at one point had seven people in it laughing, sautéeing, tasting as they went. There was just one French person with the group, a chef employed at the company's central kitchen, and he had decided that he would go off on his own. He'd run out to the butcher while I was giving my talk about ingredients – being French, he didn't need to hear it – and bought some lamb brains. As everyone worked and jostled in the kitchen, he'd carved out a little space to prepare the brains, which, I was certain, he would eat all by himself. I could have strangled him, but I held back. In any case, everything went so smoothly that we were all ready to sit down and begin our inaugural meal at 8 p.m., as I'd planned.

We had a terrific week going to markets and visiting artisan food producers, farmers, and pottery makers. We even visited an ancient wood-fired bread oven and everyone had a chance to wear the baker's traditional Norman wooden clogs with their turned-up toes, slide loaves around in the oven, then see them emerge from the oven's heat, their crusts popping and crackling. The baker opened jars of homemade jam and bottles of cider, and we had an unexpected feast in the small, timbered building. As we left, the baker gave a warm loaf to each person and we rode the bus back to Louviers in a haze of toasty aroma.

Our week culminated in a meal that Bruno and I prepared for the group, who had gone on a day-trip to the D-Day landing beaches. They returned just as we were putting the finishing touches to the seafood stew we'd

prepared, but before we sat down Michael had some enter-
tainment planned. He called everyone into the kitchen,
opened champagne and poured glasses. He was preparing
to install the centre island in the kitchen, and that afternoon had poured the small concrete pad where it would
sit, which was still soft enough to take an imprint. After a
toast to the group and the week, he asked each person to
autograph the concrete. 'You will be immortalized at On
Rue Tatin,' he said, and everyone cheered, then dropped
to their knees and covered the concrete with their fanciful
signatures. One day, should our house be excavated, the
archaeologist will surely scratch her head over the signatures in the concrete pad!

The dinner table was set. On it were bottles of Côtes
de Blaye and big baskets of Michael's freshly made bread.
Because this group was service-oriented, they jumped right
into helping out, insisting that Bruno, Michael, Allison
and I be waited on. It was a fitting end to an unbelievably
warm, enjoyable week, and it heralded a happy future for
a cooking school at On Rue Tatin.

After the group had gone, Michael returned to working
on the kitchen, and I to writing and recipe testing. Michael
installed the butcher's work-bench, then proceeded to
expand on it for the centre island. The butcher block top,
which was about five feet long, had fissures in it the size
of the Grand Canyon. We had bathed it with water for
months, hoping the wood would expand, but the spaces
remained. Michael cut the block into three pieces, which
he trimmed and evened off, then stuck back together to
make a shorter, smoother cutting surface. It still had small
cracks in it, which Michael filled with beeswax, a food-
friendly, aesthetically pleasing solution.We wanted the
front of this graceful piece of furniture, with its two deep,

curved drawers, to be what people saw when they entered the kitchen, so Michael put them facing forward. He built a frame that widened the piece and set the butcher block atop it at the back, on the stove side.

We hadn't determined what our counter-tops would be. We'd tried poured concrete for the surfaces in the temporary kitchen, but it hadn't held up as well as we'd hoped, and we'd also tried tile, which I found an un-friendly work surface, and hard to clean. We were con-sidering all kinds of things when Michael came home from a materials buying trip one afternoon, excited about some end-lots of marble he'd seen. We went to take a look.

Here again, a limited budget worked in our favour. We wouldn't have tried so many surfaces, nor looked so hard if we could have just gone out and purchased what we wanted. Thanks to Michael always looking for ways to make the budget stretch, here was a beautiful solution in the form of huge, polished squares of a marble that was luminous with ochre, dark pink, grey and a tinge of bluish green.

With the marble chosen, Michael could continue with the centre island. He first rounded the edges of the squares, then installed them opposite the butcher block. He incorporated a small sink to the right of the butcher block for washing vegetables, and underneath it he built two drawers, one for rubbish and the other for compost. He incorporated other drawers into the island, too, to accommodate all the paraphernalia of a family kitchen, from first-aid kit to napkins and bibs. In the centre of the island, between the wood and the marble, Michael inserted a wooden knife-holder that was flush with the surface. My knives fitted down into it, their blades separ-ated by adjustable wooden pegs. Over the island he installed a beautiful, art deco chandelier we'd purchased several years before, which was, we discovered when we got it home, signed by the Frères Mueller from Lunéville, in Alsace.

We wanted to tile the entire twelve-foot-long back wall of the kitchen, as a backdrop for the gas stove. I wanted to use handmade tiles we'd seen in the Marais area of Paris, which came in a beautiful *blanc cassé*, soft white. We brought two of them home and set them on the counter, more as a tease than anything else, for their price would eat up the whole of the rest of our kitchen budget. Michael came home with many other tile samples, but none of them looked good next to those from the Marais. One day, though, he found some industrially made tiles he liked, and I went with him to take a look. They were nice and irregular, with a good shine and rich colour. We decided to use them, and Michael made the wall look as good as it would have with the tiles from the Marais, by mixing white and off-white to give the wall depth and subtle texture.

I wanted my copper pots to hang somewhere in the kitchen, both for the warmth their colour would add and for practicality, but we couldn't figure out where to put them. I didn't want them over the butcher block because they would block the view of the stove and the mantel, and our chandelier looked so graceful there. I couldn't hang them against the tile wall because the counter top was too deep for them to be within easy reach.

I stood at the stove and reached up, as though reaching for a pot. I realized that if they hung inside the hood Michael had built, along the sides, they would not only look beautiful but would also be accessible to me yet out of the way. This is where they hang today, a perfect solution.

Michael built all the cabinets in the kitchen, which include twenty-two long drawers, each of which slides out to its full length. One of my favourite and most useful drawers is the tall, narrow one that sits next to the stove and is used to store baking sheets and odd-shaped baking pans. In this kitchen I would have the luxury of space and storage that I could only have imagined in kitchens of yore.

Michael laid a beautiful floor in half the kitchen that consisted of the ancient tiles he'd pulled up from the original kitchen floor, some old six-sided terracotta tiles called tommettes that had come from the hallway behind the kitchen, and small squares he cut from the marble that covered the counter-tops. The area where I would spend most of my time, between the stove and butcher block, the refrigerator and the sink, was floored with buttery old pine planks he'd lifted from the house's original sitting room. They would be much kinder than tile or stone to my legs and back.

I'd wanted stone sinks like those in old farms and chateaux, but we didn't find one easily and I wasn't so devoted to the idea that I would go to any lengths to have one. I've always liked stainless steel, so Michael went about looking for a stainless steel sink that fitted the dimensions we wanted, long and wide enough to hold the removable pan under the stove burners, and shallow enough for ease and comfort. Needless to say, such a sink was nowhere to be found or ordered.

This was a puzzler. I didn't want to compromise on the shape of the sink – it had to be practical and easy to use. I didn't want porcelain because it is fussy to maintain. Michael heard about a place where he could get any size stainless steel sink, and a friend of ours said that he could intervene and get it wholesale. Michael handed in the sink's dimensions and got a call back the following week with an estimate that sent him through the roof. 'Five thousand dollars for a stainless steel sink?' he said, shaking his head. Apparently, the sink would have to be custom-made, which is what made it so costly. Like the handmade tiles, the handmade stainless steel sink would have to go.

How would we get around this one? Michael had lined a wall in our downstairs bathroom with zinc, just for fun, and he'd loved working with it. One night I heard him soldering in his workshop and I looked in to see him fashioning a zinc box. 'It's a sink,' he said shortly. The next day he brought it to show me. 'If this thing holds water, this is what our sinks will look like,' he said. 'It should work – zinc lasts forever. Just look at all the zinc bars in French cafes.' He filled it with water and it was watertight. Our sink problem was solved, sort of. He had to figure out how to put in a plug and how to support it, which he did, and the upshot is that we have three custom-made zinc sinks in our kitchen, which are burnished and lovely, and easy to maintain.

With the sinks in place, the drawers all built, the floors laid, Michael could install the yards of marble. He studied all the squares to choose those with the most ochre in them, and the most harmonious patterns. He tried them out on the counters to see how the light fell on them, then carefully rounded their edges before setting them in place. He had fashioned a narrow ledge at the back of the counter-tops on either side of the stove for condiments, timers, knick-knacks, all the little things that clutter a work surface, and he cut small pieces of marble to fit that. When all was installed he had to figure out how to polish and treat it so it would hold up to kitchen use.

We both got on the phone to do some research. Mine led me to an Italian family of masons in Paris; they were very generous with information and offered to have Michael come in so they could give him a marble-treating demonstration. Michael's research led him to the head-stone makers in Louviers. Between these sources, he got the information he needed. The results turned the marble smooth and luscious, and made the colours, which are warm and complementary to food, flowers and people, emerge. A visitor, looking at the marble, said, 'Do you realize people go to school just to learn how to cut and polish marble and he just did it?'

I had heard that marble was hard to maintain and very delicate, and I wondered how it would hold up to the kind of use I would give it. I needn't have worried, as it has proved to be low maintenance and very forgiving. Even acid, which eats away at its surface leaving a rough white spot, isn't as much of a problem as I feared, for those rough spots go away with regular wiping.

The stoves were installed, the counter-tops finished, the drawers ready to fill. I wanted to move in, or at least to decorate. One night, while Michael was at his weekly sculpture class, I opened up some kitchen boxes, trying to figure out what I could put on the mantel that would surprise him the next day. I stumbled onto teapots and soup terrines; it turned out that over the years I'd amassed a small collection in varied bright colours. These I set on the mantelpiece and said nothing. I knew they would get covered with dust as Michael continued to work, but I wanted to see how they would look and I mostly wanted him to see that I was paying attention. He loved seeing them there the next day, giving truth to the adage that it is the little things that make a difference.

I was concerned about hiding in drawers all the many little tools I use a hundred times a day, from measuring spoons to whisks, mixer attachments to fish-bone pullers, because I could see myself getting very frustrated with the time lost opening them, closing them, keeping them orderly. As I stood in the kitchen trying to figure out how I would solve this, my eye hit upon an unmatched pair of brass shelf-supports sitting in the corner, beautiful pieces that Michael had found at our friend Magaly's second-hand shop. I picked up one and set it on end on the raised shelf at the back of the counter-top, right near the stove. Then I hung measuring spoons, whisks, skewers and tongs on its various levels. I set the other one up on the other side of the stove and did the same. They looked gorgeous without being cluttered. When Michael came in and saw them he said, 'They're perfect.'

I'd come up with a schedule for cooking classes, thinking it would be good to hold the first one in June, the beginning of summer when produce is at its most gorgeous, gardens are fresh and growing, markets are taking on their festive summer air. In order to publicize the classes, I did a mailing to all of our lunch guests, to editors I'd worked with over the years, and to various other friends, colleagues and acquaintances who constituted my nascent mailing list. This must have been in February, and I figured that by June I would be well settled in the kitchen, accustomed to where everything was, ready to teach and share. I asked a young American woman who had worked with me before if she would come again for two months to help me settle into the kitchen and do the class. I planned out the schedules.

With the weeks planned and the possibility of people actually coming to take classes, I assessed my cooking equipment. I have a great deal of utensils, but I reckoned I would need more knives and more things like vegetable peelers and melon-ball makers, stiff plastic scrapers and wooden spoons, measuring cups and spoons. I would also need more cooking pans and baking sheets and more wine glasses, and I would need to find beautiful aprons and a multitude of tea towels to match.

I investigated all of the hotels and a bed and breakfast in the area to determine which were best for my 'guests'. I settled on four places. My favourite hotel is a rambling place in the country, with charming bedrooms and a lush garden just outside the limits of Louviers, in a village called Le Haye le Comte. The most convenient, however, is a hotel in the town, five minutes on foot from our house. It is very comfortable, and it is where most people choose to stay.

I have had to work with the people at this hotel, whose attitude reflects that of shopkeepers I used to meet when I first moved to Paris twenty years ago. Those were the days when you walked into a shop and were greeted with hostility, as though your very presence was an insult, an affront. The people who run the hotel were the same. Though they agreed on a special price for anyone who reserved through me, every additional request – whether it was a reservation for two double rooms, a faxed reservation confirmation, an unlocked front door on Sunday afternoon so guests could get into the hotel, or whatever – was met with almost laughable rudeness and hostility. I suggested to the owner that we meet, thinking that if there was personal contact it would melt the ice, but she brushed me off, telling me that her assistant took care of everything. One would have thought she was the manager of Le Bristol in Paris the way she acted, though I've had better luck there. I spoke with the assistant who wasn't much better. I couldn't work it out. I sent more than thirty people to them in the first year, all of whom stayed for five days at a time. I knew they were very busy with business groups, but I also knew that they liked having the business I sent their way. I asked a well-placed friend if he knew them, and if he could help me out. 'I'll do what I can,' he said, 'but I'm not sure if I can help. He – the owner – is all right, but his wife, who takes care of the hotel, is awful, just awful.' When I heard that, I figured there was little hope.

I haven't pursued it any further because there has been a perceptible thaw which, in this case, amounts to enormous progress. I still haven't had a formal meeting with the owners, but I don't care if I do. What I care about is that everyone who stays there has a good experience and thankfully, thus far, that has been the case.

Sometimes guests choose to stay in a charming bed and breakfast in the village of Heudreville, a ten-minute trip by car. Run by a friendly and energetic woman who takes great pride in fine linens and homemade jams for breakfast, it is a little spot of country finery in the midst of a charming village.

Michael and I had discussed the dates of the first classes, thinking it was possible. But May came and he was still working in the kitchen. It looked nearly finished to me, but he said there was a long list of things to finish. By mid-May I knew that it was unrealistic to hold a class, yet I had a small group signed up. What should I do? I tossed and turned over it, then one morning when I opened up my emails I found a message from Marion, who now handled the organization of the school as well as the lunches. 'They can't come,' she wrote. 'One of them is ill so none of them are coming.' I was relieved to hear it wasn't a life-threatening illness, but at any other time this would have been disastrous. In the circumstances, though, and as sorry as I was that they were kept from coming, I heaved a sigh of relief. Someone was watching over me.

By this point I was getting impatient to move into the

kitchen. My appetite was whetted for more space, functionality, ease. I needed to increase my productivity, too, as I had deadlines looming. How could I speed the process along?

I offered to help, suggested we hire someone to help, said I didn't mind if all the details weren't finished. Michael resisted and calmly went about his work. One day I walked into the kitchen to find him on his knees, calmly, carefully polishing the twenty-two brass drawer-handles we'd gone to great lengths to order. I stood there watching, realizing this was, in part, keeping me from moving into the kitchen. I asked him why he was polishing them. 'Because they're too shiny, they'll look too new and the rest of the kitchen is burnished and comfortable looking,' he said.

I left him to his polishing, and went and cried. I was convinced, then, that I would never move into the kitchen; the cooking school would never happen; Michael would always have one more detail to attend to, calmly, as if nothing but time stretched out before him.

Michael finished the series of drawer-handles, and we never said another word about them until many years later, when we could laugh about it. I had learnt, through the process of creating the kitchen, that Michael becomes so intensely involved in projects that he forgets real life is going on around him. I had seen his sense of aesthetics and perfection dictate that all drawer-handles be burnished in exactly the same way. He is right about them in one way – it's a tiny detail that makes a difference. But the alternative would have been all right, too. After all, life is a series of compromises, isn't it?

Michael finally pronounced the kitchen ready. I was so excited, and so nervous too. Michael had given two years of his life to creating this beautiful kitchen; we'd made many compromises, we'd argued about it, we'd changed it many times on its way to completion. When it was finished it had to work, and I had to love it. The pressure was enormous. It's interesting how one's basic self is challenged by something so insignificant as a kitchen remodel. I feared having to change my cooking habits, having to put things in drawers instead of on shelves or on the walls, yet I had agreed upon a 'tidier', more elegant kitchen. The idea of change made me very anxious, as I've based a lifetime of cooking and a career on my swift, sure movements in kitchens where everything is out and accessible. Then I stopped myself. I vowed to loosen up.

I put off the actual move until the American woman I'd hired joined us. She was going to be helping me test recipes and I wanted her to know from the start where everything was stored.

After she'd settled in we got to work hauling boxes and filling drawers and shelves, in a process that took two days. Unbelievably, there wasn't enough storage for every single thing, and it was then I realized how much kitchen equipment I had. If this kitchen couldn't accommodate it all, no kitchen ever would. It was a good excuse to weed out things I didn't use.

With most things in place, I prepared to cook our first meal in the kitchen, which we would all eat at the central island. It was exciting, wonderful, completely disconcerting. I grated raw beets and tossed them with a vinaigrette, then made a simple, herb-rich potage with leeks, carrots and potatoes, garnished with minced parsley and garlic from the garden. It took me twice as long as usual because I couldn't put my hands on anything quickly, but how luxurious it felt to work in a place where I could stretch out my arms and not touch the wall, where the sink was handy and there was ample counter space, where the wood floor was easy on my legs and back, and where I didn't have to use any of the economy of motion I'd mastered in my other kitchen. Here, everyone in the neighbourhood could come and cook and we'd all have our own spot.

I served the salad on my side of the island as Michael, Joe, Fiona and Paige, the American woman, sat and watched from the other side. It was wonderful to be so easily together in such a huge space with a gorgeous stove to cook on. Michael and I looked at each other. It had been a long and difficult process for both of us to get to this point. We'd left our country with, on my part, a dream to live in France and raise our children, write books, even open up a cooking school, and on Michael's part a willingness to put his career aside for the time it took to make it happen.

We'd had several kitchens in our life together, most of them either designed and built by Michael or remodelled by him, but this was our first that was intended for teaching, and included every detail that we could possibly have thought of to make that efficient, comfortable, pleasant. The struggle to get this kitchen built was still fresh in our minds, but we both knew that it would fade and that we were in for some wonderful times and delicious meals. I, who love the kitchen more than any spot on earth, knew I was in for some exhilarating moments, which, I hoped, I would be able to share not just with my family and friends, but with people eager to learn the secrets of French cooking. Here we were, unbelievably, all of us together, in the heart of our beautiful new kitchen.

I had decided to give myself about six months in the new kitchen before teaching any classes, because I figured it would take me that long to become accustomed to working in it. I couldn't risk any fumbles for the classes – I had to be smooth, at ease and professional. So I established the dates for two classes the following spring, and I sent out another mailing to publicize them. I also investigated getting a website, but I found the venture beyond my budget. Besides, I was sceptical about websites. Internet access in France was problematic, and every single thing took so much time that I didn't have the patience for it: sitting and staring into a screen has never been my forté. I supposed that most people were like me, and that websites were a 'must have' because of their novelty, not their real usefulness.

My ideas were changed by two wonderful lunch guests who came, ate, and fell in love – with the house, with the food, with what we were trying to do, and with baby Fiona. Both high-level professionals, they were alight with ideas on how to market the school, and both were adamant that it, and I, needed a website. I told them my opinions. They disagreed, vehemently.

Glo, one of the women, fixed me with a gaze as stern as that of an owl and said, 'Susan, I'm here to tell you that if you don't have ".com" after your name in the States you are nothing.' I flinched, told her thank you, and said I still didn't think I needed a website.

She badgered me about it for a while, then let the subject drop for the remainder of our lunch together. On her return to the United States she started sending me emails. 'Susan, you need a website, you've got to have one, you are no one without one,' she would write, along with her cheery messages filled with news and jokes. She was a great person and I appreciated her enthusiasm and concern, but I couldn't have cared less. I didn't have the wherewithal to develop a website, and I didn't think I needed one. If that made me a nobody, so be it. Then one day I opened my email messages to find the following from Glo. 'Susan, since you are so stubborn, I'm doing a website for you. My friend Geoff will design the site. He charges $4000 and he says he'll trade you for cooking classes. I will too. We don't care if you don't want it, we're doin' it.'

I was flabbergasted. I read on. She explained how it would go, how she would help design it and write the copy. She would pass everything to me for approval before it went 'live'. Glo had pinned me to the floor. I capitulated, succumbing to the force of her energy.

I ended up spending a month working on the website with Glo and Geoff, answering a million questions, writing and rewriting, choosing photographs and graphic styles. It was exciting, like writing and publishing a book, with all the attendant satisfaction and anticipation. By the end of the process the three of us were fast friends, and I had a gorgeous, user-friendly website. I couldn't imagine who would go there, but now at least I could put a '.com' after my name. I was somebody!

I now had a key marketing tool in place to test with the restaurant group, who had asked if I would host more of their managers. Naturally I agreed, and when they came back to me with questions about myself, my work, the school, where they could stay (I had posted photographs and information about my chosen four places on the site), I sent them to susanloomis.com.The response was miraculous; I didn't have to spend any more time answering questions, and when they arrived they were fully informed about my work, the cooking school and me.

I felt extremely fortunate to be trying out the new kitchen on these restaurant managers who would, I was sure, be as open and easy-going as the first group had been. That group had loved working in the makeshift kitchen; this group would have all the advantage of working in the finished kitchen. If there were a few stumbles or some head-scratching about where to find this or that, it wouldn't matter.

By the time they arrived I'd augmented my equipment. A friend of mine, Barbara Tropp, a wonderful Chinese cook who lived in San Francisco, sent me a dozen great, light-weight chef's knives. I found some very good quality copper pans at a shop near Louviers for ridiculously low prices, and purchased multiples of the most useful sizes. I'd augmented my utensils and cutting boards, and I'd found beautiful long white aprons as well. I was all ready to go.

There were sixteen managers and I paired them up to cook. I couldn't believe how well we all fitted in the kitchen: there was room to work, room for me to circulate among the couples and guide them, room to arrange the cheese tray off in a corner, to roll out pastry, to open wine. Not only was there room, but the lighting Michael had installed could be modulated to fit the occasion. We went from laboratory bright while preparing the meal to cosy intimate while we stood around the tidied-up island with our aperitifs, a fire roaring in the background.

From cooking in the new kitchen to eating in the dining room, everything worked so well, so smoothly and so effortlessly. No one could possibly know all the planning, dreaming, and plain hard work that had gone into the smooth flow of food from kitchen to table. I was so proud of Michael, and I knew that our cooking school was going to be a well-organized and luxuriously comfortable success, thanks to the setting he had provided.

Filled with confidence, I scheduled a class for the following spring, and hoped it would fill. I knew I had to do some marketing, so I had a brochure printed up that explained the school, and sent it out to friends, colleagues and the editors I'd worked for over the years, hoping they would all get behind the project and spread the word. I announced the opening of the school on the website, then I crossed my fingers. Meanwhile, we had to celebrate the kitchen and *'pendre la crèmaillère'*, or 'hang the soup pot', the French expression for a house-warming. Everyone we knew had become intimately acquainted with this massive project, and they all wanted to experience the results. I invited our friends, our neighbours, Fiona's various baby-sitters, Joe's friends and their parents, who had kept an eye on progress while they dropped off or picked up their children, until we had at least fifty people on the guest list. The party was to be casual, and I wanted it to be a surprise for Michael. I made lots of appetizers, among them a favourite of Michael's: wild boar rillettes. My vege-tarian friend Babette had offered to come cook with me, and when Michael saw her in the kitchen helping me with the rillettes he began to suspect that something was afoot, but he said nothing.

Babette and I also made tapenade, anchovy toasts and strips of air-cured ham wrapped around chunks of feta and fresh sage. Because this wasn't a sit-down affair, I decided I would make thin crusted pizza with many different top-pings, from olive oil, sea salt, rosemary and garlic, to Sicilian tomato sauce with capers, and onions with bacon and cream. For dessert I slathered dough with crème fraîche and sprinkled it generously with brown sugar and cinna-mon. Our neighbour, Patrick Merlin, diverted Michael with an invitation for a drink at his house.

Joe was in charge of lighting the hundred candles out front in the courtyard, and as our friends arrived I set them to other tasks – making sure the music was organized, arranging platters, putting away coats. Some washed dishes and put things away.

I'd asked everyone to bring something sparkling, with-out being specific. Had this been the States, I suspect that offerings would have ranged from boxes of glitter to sparkling items of clothing, but here in France it meant one thing and one thing only: champagne. I assigned five men to open bottles, and instructed them that the minute Michael and Patrick came in the front gate they were to pop the corks.

I'd told Patrick to bring Michael at 8.30 p.m., and by then all our friends were assembled and everything was ready, but there was no Michael nor Patrick. I called Patrick. He'd forgotten about the party because he and Michael were having such a good time drinking whiskey, listening to music, talking. Fortunately he lived three minutes away and, much chagrined, said they would leave immediately. I alerted everyone and it went just as planned: the minute Michael walked in the door, corks popped and flew, and he was as surprised as if someone had put ice cubes down his shirt. It was a terrific party, one of our best.

I had a group signed up for a class in May 2001, and it would be my first, official class. By this time I had a terrific assistant, Kerrie Luzum, who has degrees in cooking and nutrition, as well as years of restaurant experience. She lives in Paris and comes out two days a week to help in the office and the kitchen.

I planned that first week over and over and over, with Kerrie making phone calls to set up farm visits and wine tastings, restaurant meals and visits to artisans. Establishing the mix of recipes that we would all make during the six hands-on classes was the most difficult part of planning, and the most important. I take my role as cooking teacher very seriously, and I want people to leave my classes not only with a reinvigorated passion for cooking and a sheaf of recipes they can't wait to make at home, but with confidence in their technique and a keen understanding of how to balance flavours. To that end I was up at all hours tweaking the menus, changing recipes, testing details until I came up with a perfect mix which incorporated the right blend of techniques, methods and ingredients. When the recipes were finally printed and bound, I realized why it had felt like so much work – I'd produced a small book.

I look forward to the classes as a whole, but the Sunday evening when guests tap gently on the old, wavy glass of the front door for the first time is almost the best part, for it is like a reunion. We've never met anyone before they arrive, but the communication and arrangements that have gone into making this moment a reality mean that we are, on some level, already acquainted.

I've thought, planned, and cooked my way to this first meal with each guest in mind, sparing no detail so it will be perfect. Like all the recipes and meals that we encounter during our time together, this first is based on what is best and freshest at the market. It's a fête, too, because Michael and I – and the others who help out at On Rue Tatin – are just as excited as anyone that our five days together are beginning.

We greet each other, we share the meal I've prepared, we linger over dessert, then the participants leave with their recipes in hand. They return to our home the next morning, put on their monogrammed On Rue Tatin aprons, and cook their way up to lunch.

After the first evening, the weeks speed by in a blur of cooking classes and meals at home, visits to artisans and restaurants, wine tastings, cheese tastings and drinks outside in our courtyard, in the shadow of Nôtre Dame in Louviers. I can never believe, when the last meal rolls around, that another week is ended: it always goes by so quickly. Yet it has been long enough to bond with great people, to get involved; not only to instruct but to learn and share.

I imagined many things when we decided to go ahead with lunches, then with a cooking school, but what I didn't anticipate was the friends we would make. We've had the most special people cross our threshold, from the wonderful New Yorker who presented me with an apron her grandmother had embroidered with the name On Rue Tatin, and which I treasure (she also sent us her special Christmas cookies after the week she spent with us), to the duo of dentists who kept us laughing from Sunday night through to Friday noon, then gave both kids a quick dental examination and advice, followed up by packages of fluoride in the mail; from the school librarian who made a list of 'must read' books for Joe, to the retired university professor who keeps me up to date with all manner of interesting food items. Nor will I ever forget our first Australian guest, who kept saying, as she fastened her apron and picked up her knife, 'I didn't know we were going to cook!'

All of this, and we've only just begun!

My goal with this cooking school is simple, aside from providing an income for us all. I want everyone who comes to On Rue Tatin not only to gain a practical knowledge of French culinary techniques but also to get a real, authentic flavour of France, to experience the rare relationship people here have with food producers and artisans, and to taste the difference in food that is grown locally with care, and eaten within just a few miles of where it was grown. I want them to leave On Rue Tatin with a sense that they 'know' France through all of us, and I want them to go home and share what they have learned.

CORN LOAF
Pain de Maïs

⎯⎯⎯⎯⎯⎯⎯⎯⎯ ⊂⟊⟎ ⎯⎯⎯⎯⎯⎯⎯⎯⎯

This rustic bread is a delight with any meal, though I particularly like it with roast pork. Make sure you keep some for breakfast, to toast, for it is sublime with a touch of salted butter and a drizzle of honey!

3 cups (750ml) lukewarm milk
2 tsp active dry yeast
1½ tsp sugar
4 cups (535g) fine cornmeal (or semolina), preferably yellow
1 tbs sea salt
5 to 6 cups (705g) unbleached, all-purpose flour

1. Place the warm milk in a large bowl or the bowl of an electric mixer. Stir in the yeast and sugar, then the cornmeal (or semolina), 1 cup at a time. Stir in the salt, then add the flour, 1 cup at a time, until you have a soft dough. Turn out the dough onto a lightly floured work surface and knead it several times, adding a bit of additional flour if necessary so it doesn't stick to your fingers.

2. Let the dough rest for 15 minutes on the work surface, then knead it until it is smooth and elastic, about 8 minutes, adding more flour if necessary to keep it from sticking to your hands. Don't use more than 6 cups of flour – the dough should be soft and slightly wet, not firm.

3. Place the dough in a bowl, cover with a damp towel and let it rise in a warm spot until it has doubled in

bulk, about 1–½ hours. Punch it down, and divide it in half.

4. Sprinkle two 9½-inch (23.5cm) pie plates with cornmeal (or semolina). Shape each half of the dough into a round and place them, seam-side down, in the prepared pie plates. Press down on the rounds so they fill the pie plates, cover loosely with a towel and let them rise in a warm spot until they are nearly doubled in bulk, about 30 minutes.

5. Preheat the oven to 425°F (220°C).

6. Using a very sharp knife, cut a large spiral in the top of each loaf, then bake in the centre of the oven until the loaves are golden and sound hollow when tapped, 40 to 45 minutes. Remove from the oven, turn out of the pie plates and let cool to room temperature on wire racks.

Two large loaves

RAW BEET SALAD
Salade de Betteraves Crues

———————— ∽⊸ ————————

I love beets any way I can get them, though this salad is a favourite. I make it often at home, and serve it as a little extra during cooking school weeks, so that everyone has a chance to sample beets at their crunchy finest!

I serve very small portions of this, as its flavour is intense. It looks beautiful in the centre of a small plate garnished with a sprig of green!

1 tsp sherry vinegar
Sea salt and freshly ground black pepper
2 tbs extra-virgin olive oil

¼ tsp cumin seeds
1 shallot, peeled and cut into paper-thin slices
4 medium beets, trimmed, peeled, and finely grated
Small bunch of chervil, flat-leaf parsley, or arugula

1. Whisk the vinegar with salt and pepper to taste in a large bowl. Add the olive oil in a thin stream, whisking constantly. Taste for seasoning; then stir in the cumin seeds and the shallot. Add the beets and toss so they are thoroughly coated with the dressing. Let the beets rest for at least 15 minutes before serving. Just before serving, mound the beets in the centre of 6 small plates, and garnish them with the parsley or the arugula leaves. Serve immediately

6 servings

A French Poodle in the House

Every day for three years, while Joe and I were walking to school in the early mornings, he used to ask me if he could have a little sister, as though this was something we would buy at the charcuterie we passed each morning. The first time the request came up I didn't know what to say. Joe didn't know that Michael and I wanted another child – boy or girl – and had been trying to have one for several years. It wouldn't mean a thing to him if I said, 'We're trying, Joe, we're trying, we don't want you to be an only child any more than you do.' So, I put him off by saying, 'Well, maybe you will one day,' sheepishly knowing this probably wasn't true.

Michael and I weren't desperate to have another child, but we thought it would be great for Joe to have a sibling, and for our family to be one person bigger. We assumed I would get pregnant, but two years had passed and I hadn't. I decided I would take the first steps to check into adoption, to see how serious we wanted to get. I didn't get far in my research before I learned that there are few if any babies available for adoption in France: pregnant woman of any age and situation are encouraged to keep their babies, and financial assistance from the state makes it very possible for them to do so. This explains the number of babies wheeling around babies; some of the mothers I see look no older than thirteen and, for all I know, they may be.

The only couples I knew in France who had adopted babies had gone to South America or China to find them, and I knew that we wouldn't go that far. We didn't want to, nor could we afford to purchase a child. Secondly, our passion for a child didn't go to those lengths. Maybe we were selfish – we wanted our own baby, and if our own baby wasn't going to happen, we'd stay a happy little family of three.

Finally we did what any sensible couple whose son wants a sibling would do. We considered getting a dog. Joe wanted a dog. Michael wanted a dog. I'm not much of an animal-lover, but I figured I could live with a dog. I'd grown up with a dachshund and loved her, but she was a yippy little attack dog who would go after crawling babies if she couldn't find the moles she was bred to chase, so I didn't think we wanted that sort. Michael had grown up with and loved golden labradors, but they needed lots of space and exercise, and our house and garden weren't appropriate. What we really needed was a robotic dog that acted like a real dog and needed no space (or maintenance).

Joe's plaintive request for a sister continued. One of his favourite stories was *The Little Match Girl* and he would get so sad at the plight of the little girl. He wanted to bring her home and make a little bed for her in his room so he could protect her. He was obviously ready for the care and feeding of a living creature. We continued to mull over the dog idea until we finally decided that was what we would do. It would be Joe's 'little match girl', his sibling.

Joe was ecstatic and promised to do his share of taking care of the dog. I was clear from the start that, while I would go along with the idea, I wouldn't take care of it full-time. We all agreed the dog would be a family project. Knowing that the best way to find a great dog was *de bouche à oreille*, by word of mouth, I mentioned it to our neighbours the florists. The very next day there was a knock on the door. Michael opened it to a rotund boy of about eleven with the thickest, most lush crew-cut I'd ever seen. '*Bonjour Monsieur, Madame,*' he said, politely. 'I believe that you are looking for a dog. The florists sent me over here.' That was fast, I thought. He went on to explain, in very adult language, about a dog he had found and that he loved, but that his father, a fireman, insisted he get rid of because their apartment was too small. Tears welled up in his eyes. 'I love this dog,' he admitted, hiccuping a sob back into his throat. 'My mother loves it, too, but my father says no, we must not keep it.' He closed his eyes and two little tears popped out.

We were taken in by the drama, and told him we would think about his offer and call him. We were only vaguely interested, though, since we didn't want a fully grown dog with someone else's bad training habits. The boy, whose name was Anthony, turned away, shoulders sagging, and slowly walked out through the courtyard door. Not two hours later he was back, dog and mother in tow. This time, when Michael answered the door, Joe was right behind him.

'*Monsieur, –dame,*' he said brightly. 'You seem like such nice people, I just had to bring this little dog over to meet you.'

The dog turned out to be an *abricot caniche*, a mid-sized, full-grown, fuzzy poodle the colour of dirty reddish straw, or unripe apricots. A male, his eyes were invisible under his unruly curls, and he wiggled all over, obviously delighted to be around people. Anthony, the boy, was holding him by a leash. 'He is so adorable I know you'll love him immediately,' he said artlessly, and with a slight quaver in his voice.

'Oh brother,' I thought. Deciding to get a dog was one thing. Being presented with a warm and full-grown one that wiggled was another. We had never imagined getting a poodle – they are reputed to be as silly as they look. To prove our point the dog, held firmly by the strong Anthony, began little arcing jumps to nowhere, nearly choking himself and pulling over Anthony simultaneously. He wanted to get away, to move, to be free. He finally arced so hard that Anthony let go of the leash and he bounded into our front yard as though shot out of a cannon. He ran stupidly around the apple tree a couple of times, then back through the gravel, spraying pieces everywhere, until he stopped right at Joe's feet. Well, he sort of stopped. He actually bashed right into Joe's leg, startling Joe, and hurting his own nose.

Michael bent down and beckoned, and the dog plastered himself against Michael's leg. Joe, who likes dogs in theory but is afraid of them, stood behind Michael and bent over to stroke the dog's back. He and Michael had turned into pools of melted butter in the face of this dog.

Like a horse-whisperer with horses, Michael knows just how to get a dog to respond, where to scratch, pat, tickle and rub. This dog responded by lying flat on his back on the bricks, and shaking all over. Joe crouched over him. I stood by, watching the scene. Anthony and his mother were in a half-embrace, tears running down their faces. Joe and Michael were rapt. Molière couldn't have written a better farce.

I was lukewarm about the dog. He was a little messy for

me, a little too rambunctious, a little too – well – dog-like. I'd imagined something smaller, cuter, calmer; something that resembled a stuffed dog a little more. The more Michael teased him, the more the dog slobbered all over him and the closer Joe got to him. I knew he would soon be moving in.

Michael released the dog. Anthony called him, and the dog responded. We formed a family huddle while Anthony and his mother mooned over the dog. 'Oh mama and papa, he's so cute,' Joe said.

'He really is cute,' Michael said. 'And he seems really nice and not too wild.'

We agreed to give the dog a try, but on a trial basis. If the dog turned out to be awful, we'd return it to Anthony and his mother. We looked at Joe. 'Does this make sense to you?' we asked him. He nodded, eyeing the dog with desire. 'OK,' Michael repeated. 'We take the dog on a trial basis. If he's perfect, we keep him. If he's not, out he goes.' I looked at Michael, the animal-lover. I don't think he's ever met an animal he doesn't like, and he has infinite patience with them. I doubted that if the dog got into our home and life it would ever leave.

We told Anthony and his mother our conditions, and they just stared at us. '*Oh monsieur, –dame*, and you, little boy, you will love this dog so much you'll never want to get rid of him,' Anthony said. 'The one thing I do ask you is that I be able to visit him once in a while. The transition will be hard on him, and I will miss him so.'

Who was this boy who spoke like a French politician? We agreed, of course, to regular visits for as long as he liked, and he handed over the leash to Joe. He turned to kiss the dog, but as far as the dog was concerned, Anthony and his mother were history. Of much more interest was our garden, our apple tree, our dahlias. Anthony began crying his eyes out and he and his mother, who held him around the shoulders, sobbed their way out through the door.

I was exhausted by all the emotion. I looked at Michael, who shrugged. 'We'll see,' was all he said.

The dog bounded over to us and Joe leapt out of the way. Michael scratched the dog's ears and he lay down, calmed. Joe eased in; I patted him, too. He was awfully cute, and he seemed very sweet, just like Anthony and his mother had said. They had assured us he was house-trained, had no bad habits, didn't sleep in their beds – one thing I deplore – and that he was very calm. This all sounded good to me.

I went into the house to cook. I was working on recipes and the menu included avocado with pistachio oil and shallots, braised oxtail with cinnamon, baked potatoes with bay leaves and ginger madeleines with allspice ice cream. With all this dog business, I was behind schedule.

Several hours later Anthony returned with a dog dish, some dog toys, and another leash, this one bright red leather. The dog was all over him, and he all over the dog, and they played for a moment. Then the waterworks began again. 'You can come visit him whenever you want,' I reassured Anthony, who seemed close to a nervous break-down. 'I will do that, *Madame, merci,*' he sniffed, backing out of the courtyard.

We went about finding a place for the dog to sleep, and a place to set his bowls. We had decided the dog would eat leftovers and dry food, since both Michael and I are morally opposed to feeding dogs food that could logically be given to hungry humans, and most canned dog food fits into that category. So, Michael and Joe went off to buy him some dry food.

We got the dog set up. He was asleep by this time, on the entranceway rug, right in the middle of the traffic pattern. We all stood there and looked at him. He was pretty darn cute.

He needed a name. I wanted to give him a literary French name, like Aristide or Gionot, since he was a French poodle. Michael and Joe settled on calling him LD, for Little Dog. I'd renounced responsibility for the dog – how could I intervene?

Dinner that night was a resounding success – we loved all the recipes – and there were few leftovers, but what remained went into the dog's dish. He immediately dragged the bones into the middle of the kitchen floor and noisily chewed on them, then left them right there when he wandered off to fall asleep again.

We transferred LD to a clean blanket in the kitchen, and we all turned in. Sometime after we'd all fallen asleep we heard excited barking. It was LD reacting to something outside – a light going off, a car going by, we didn't know what. Michael quieted him down and we went back to sleep. The next day Joe came down the stairs and wrinkled his nose as he walked into the kitchen. 'Where's LD?' he asked and, simultaneously, 'What is that smell?'

LD and the smell were in the same spot. He hadn't left any untoward packages anywhere; he just smelt like a not-very-clean animal. We hadn't noticed it the night before, most likely in the excitement of having him in our home.

'When you get home from school we'll give him a bath,' Michael said to Joe.

But Michael and I couldn't make it through the day with this fragrant dog, who smelt as if he'd rolled in something dead. How had we not noticed this the night before? Michael bathed him, rubbed him dry, and put him outside on a long tether. He was fluffy, clean and very cute. We both went back to work.

LD began to bark, at moving objects – people, cars,

birds flying by. I went out to tell him to be quiet, in English. He stopped barking, but gave me the most quizzical look. We stared at each other for a full minute before I realized he hadn't understood the words I'd said. So, I wondered, how does one tell a dog to be quiet in French? *'Tais-toi'*? Impolite. *'Calme-toi'*? Ineffectual. I settled on *'Shhht!'*, the sound most often heard in a French classroom, which can be uttered with a great deal of authority.

By the time I'd climbed the flight of stairs to my office he'd started up again. I brought him inside, and he stopped. I showed him his blankets and he lay down and immediately fell asleep. 'Whew,' I thought, but I was wary.

I went back to my office. Pretty soon I heard LD leaping up the stairs. He nosed open my office door, came in, sat down under my desk and rested his head on my foot. 'Aw,' I thought, 'he's really cute.'

But he still smelt, and he twitched. Then he got up and left. I heard Michael lead him to his blanket, after which I heard no more.

Later on, Michael put LD on a leash to go and pick up Joe from school, and off they went. I looked out of the window after them. There was Michael, tall, well-built, masculine, with this fluff-ball on a leash that walked in an odd, gimpy way down the street. The scene looked good, unlike the hysterically funny scenes of the Frenchmen I see who walk their dogs. There they go, normal, virile-looking men, in handsome business suits or newly pressed jeans, walking mincing little dogs who stop and sniff at every piece of gravel. Whenever I see one I try not to stare, which is hard because they look so ridiculous. I can't believe they actually go out in public with their dogs. Why don't they have labradors, or huskies, or something more befitting their sartorial splendour?

When Michael and Joe returned, Joe was holding the

leash, petting LD, completely enraptured. 'This experiment seems to be working,' I thought.

Several days passed and, aside from LD barking constantly when he was outside, he easily settled into our lives. He was obviously an inside dog, and he seemed used to making himself at home. Anthony and his mother had been right – he didn't jump on the furniture or make any messes inside. He didn't eat leftovers or dry dog food, either. 'He'll get used to it,' Michael promised. 'It's a matter of time.'

Lulled into a feeling of security, I let him out through the front door one day, sure he'd stay close to the door. How wrong I was. He bolted immediately, so far and fast that I lost him. Oh dear, I thought, that was short and sweet. Within an hour he was back, however, docile as could be. He headed to his blanket and fell asleep. When he woke up, he immediately threw up, a lot, in the middle of the floor. He looked perplexed for a minute, then bounded around, the picture of good health. He hadn't eaten anything at all since morning, so how, I wondered, was he able to throw up so much?

We developed a routine. LD stayed in the house during the day, more often than not in my office, his head on my foot. I didn't love the dog, but it was kind of sweet that he'd chosen my foot as his pillow. And he was quiet enough. We learned that he would bolt immediately if he got out the front door, so we tied him to the apple tree with a very long leash a couple of times a day so he could get fresh air. He barked, but we ignored him and hoped the neighbours did, too.

Despite our efforts, he ran away often, always returning an hour or so later. He would circle his bedding, lie down and sleep for a while, then rise and throw up. After the first few times we concluded he had found someone who fed him a lot of meat. 'This,' Michael said looking at LD, 'is a hobo dog.'

Michael put up wire mesh around our fence to keep him in, and asked the priest and the office workers at the parish house to be sure and keep the gate closed on their side – something they'd resisted doing when we'd claimed an open gate was dangerous for our son, but something they seemed very willing to do for a dog. Secure in the knowledge that he was fenced in, we let LD out. He bounded around the garden, tried to wiggle through the iron grating and found it closed. Then he just stood there, head cocked, as though he was thinking. I went back to work, and LD disappeared. Michael found that he'd pushed up the heavy wire mesh and crawled under it. Maybe he wasn't as dumb as he'd first seemed.

One night Joe begged for LD to sleep in his room, and we didn't object. We moved his bedding up there and he settled in, the 'little match' dog. Sometime later, Joe called out my name. When I went into his room, he said, 'Mama, LD stinks. Can you take him out of here?'

I almost choked with laughter, yet it was sad, too. Joe's dreams about having a dog to keep him company hadn't included a smelly animal that ran away all the time, came home and threw up, barked too much. LD was beginning to be a disappointment.

The next day LD got out of the house, ran away, and didn't return. I answered a knock on the door and it was a young woman who worked at one of the shops in the neighbourhood. 'I saw the police pick up your dog,' she said in a sly sort of way. 'When, where?' I asked.

'Oh, it was a while ago. He was really annoying everyone with his barking,' she said.

'I'm sorry, you should have signalled me somehow, I would have gone to get him,' I said.

'Well, you know it is illegal for a dog to be wandering around without a leash,' she said, righteously. I realized that she had called the police about LD.

I went to the police station and described LD. Sure enough, they had just transported him to the animal shelter in Rouen. Michael, horrified, jumped in the car and went to retrieve him. Fifty dollars and two hours later, he was back with a lively, unapologetic LD.

'This dog is really dumb,' Michael said, locking him into the house. 'We cannot *ever* let him out without a leash. If he runs away again like that, I'm not going after him.'

By then, LD had been with us about a month. I kept trying to convince myself to like him. He seemed to love us, wiggling all over when he saw us, snuggling up if one of us sat down. He wanted to be near us all the time, but he didn't really want to play. I don't think he understood the concept of play. Life to him was running free, sleeping, eating, being walked on a leash that he could pull against. And he had so many bad habits: incessant barking when he was outside, or when he heard a noise inside; his running away; his aroma. His eating habits hadn't adapted to our rules, either. He didn't like vegetables or dry dog food. Michael caved in and got him some canned food, which he inhaled. Michael bathed LD practically every day, but it didn't help much: he was just a smelly dog. Joe liked him, but they weren't bonding. In fact, none of us were bonding with LD. Poor thing – he was a travelling dog with bonding issues, not a family dog.

Two months had gone by, and we were sure the statute of limitations on dog borrowing dictated that we had owned him too long to return him to the emotionally distraught Anthony. In fact, we now wondered if Anthony and his mother hadn't been rehearsing for a drama project with their Oscar-winning sobfest, as neither of them ever came to visit the dog.

Now and then, I would take LD on a walk in town, thinking perhaps he and I would bond. Besides, I figured that I would look really French if I had a *caniche* on a leash. I'm taller than most French woman, have reddish hair, freckles, blue eyes and blonde eyebrows, which means I don't look French in the least, so maybe LD would be my ticket to Frenchness. But it didn't work. Friends and acquaintances stooped to give him a pat but mentioned nothing different about me. Their only reaction was a certain sympathy when I explained why I was walking LD down the pavement. I guess I didn't look any more French than usual as I struggled to keep him from running into every shop we passed, and from stopping to sniff every tiny little thing.

Then there were those terribly embarrassing moments when LD had to '*fait ses besoins*'. I gently tugged him to the gutter, but he resisted, so I had to pick him up and deposit him there, then stand on the other end of the leash, waiting. It was excruciating. Where was I supposed to look? How was I supposed to act if someone I knew came up to greet me?

I love to bicycle, and I go for a ride through the fields several times a week. Invariably, LD would wind up flapping along behind me and I would stop, grab him, go home and lock him up, then start again. This happened so many times it became part of my bicycle ride. I would have loved his company on my rides, but he was too undisciplined: at the first opportunity he'd run into someone's house, or jump over a fence into a yard full of chickens, or make a mess on someone's front path, or knock over an elderly lady; it was impossible to let him run free.

The more we had LD, the less we all liked him, but no one wanted to admit it. It was nearing summer and the

French government had launched its yearly pre-holiday campaign to discourage the French from abandoning their dogs, which they do in huge numbers each year. Plaintive doggies looked out from posters everywhere, while the words, 'You wouldn't be able to abandon *him*?' stretched like a reproach above his head. It was as if they were reading our minds, though we certainly weren't the kind of people to abandon a dog, even a tramp dog, rubbish-eating, meat mercenary like LD.

Michael, the lover of all animals, agreed that he was a sorry excuse for a pet. 'This dog is an apartment dog,' he said, the worst judgement he could lay on an animal. 'He should sit on a chair all day and be fed with a silver spoon.' Joe liked him but didn't really want to be around him much, either, but we were stuck with him and we were attached, sort of. So we settled into accepting him, the way one does dopey neighbours or quirky plumbing. He didn't chew up things, he wasn't mean, he didn't wet in the house, he wasn't ruining anything but the peace and quiet of the neighbourhood. But he certainly wasn't the playmate Joe had envisioned.

We'd had LD for about two months when I discovered I was pregnant. I couldn't believe it, and Michael's disbelief surpassed mine. I looked at LD, long and hard, perplexed. I try for three years to get pregnant, then decide it's impossible. We decide to get a dog, get one within moments of our decision, and within two months of its acquisition I'm pregnant? What did it all mean? If we'd known pregnancy was imminent, we wouldn't have had to go through this dog thing. On the other hand . . . I couldn't entertain that thought: the same one which holds that couples who want to get pregnant and can't suddenly manage to do so the minute they decided to adopt a child.

I was determined to stay fit and healthy during this pregnancy, and stepped up my regular bike rides. One day I set off to ride to the supermarket. For once, LD was nowhere to be seen, until I began to go around the roundabout several blocks from the house. Then, out of the corner of my eye, I spied him behind me. I felt as if I could just let him keep running behind me until he lost me and was too far away from home to find his way back. This seemed a rather heartless way to end our relationship, but it showed me that LD needed a new home.

Michael, Joe and I later had a family discussion about LD as the dog snuggled under our feet until its head was resting in its accustomed place. We all agreed that we really liked him, but that he wasn't the right dog for us. We all knew that lots of people would love him, but that being part of our family must have been like reform school for him: he had rules to follow, regular baths, no fresh meat and was prevented from rampaging around the neighbourhood. 'What kind of a life is this?' he must have asked himself. The animal shelter seemed like the best solution, so we took him there

One day, not two weeks later, I was walking to pick up Joe from school when I saw a *caniche* not far ahead, running in a funny, familiar, gimpy way. I gained on him and looked him in the face. It was LD, sticking close to the walls, stopping every five seconds to sniff, fat and happy. He'd been adopted by a new owner who was walking some way in front of him: a middle-aged, nicely dressed woman. They looked good together.

Since then we've seen him often. He's a lot fatter than he was with us, and he's clipped now, an uptown dog. But it is obvious that his heart and soul are still free and on the run. Old LD is having the best of it all!

CHICKEN WITH SORREL
Poulet à L'Oseille

———— ⌘ ————

This recipe is a family favourite, and perfect in spring or fall when sorrel is at its lemony best.

1 tbs extra-virgin olive oil – optional
5 oz (150 g) slab bacon, cut into 1 × ½-inch (2.5 × 1.3cm) pieces
1 medium free range chicken (3½ pounds; 1¾ kg), cut into
6 pieces (2 wing/breast pieces, 2 thighs, 2 legs)
Fine sea salt and freshly ground black pepper
1 lb (500 g) onions, peeled, cut in half, and
sliced paper-thin
1 cup (250 ml) dry white wine, such as a Sauvignon Blanc
2 imported bay leaves
4 cups (loosely packed) sorrel leaves, rinsed and patted dry
1 cup (250 ml) crème fraîche, or heavy, non ultra-pasteurized
cream

1. If your bacon is very lean, you will need to use the olive oil. Heat the oil, if using, in a large heavy skillet over medium-high heat. When it is hot, add the bacon and sauté until it is just golden on all sides, 3 to 5 minutes. Remove the bacon from the skillet with a slotted spoon and set it aside on a plate. Drain all but 1 tablespoon of the fat from the skillet.
2. Add as many pieces of the chicken as will comfortably fit in the skillet without being overcrowded. Sprinkle them with salt and pepper and brown until golden, about 5 minutes. Turn, sprinkle with more salt and pepper, and brown the other side, 5 minutes. Repeat

until all of the pieces are browned. Remove the chicken from the pan and reserve.

3. Add the onions to the skillet and cook, stirring, until they are softened, about 8 minutes. Then add the wine and scrape any browned juices from the bottom of the skillet. Return the chicken and the bacon to the skillet, along with the bay leaves, pushing the chicken down among the onions. Bring to a boil, then reduce the heat to medium. Cover and cook at a simmer until the chicken is tender and nearly cooked through, about 30 minutes.

4. While the chicken is cooking, stack the sorrel leaves on top of one another and cut them crosswise into very, very thin strips (chiffonade).

5. Remove the chicken from the skillet, place it on a serving platter, cover it loosely with aluminum foil, and keep it warm in a low oven. Stir the crème fraîche into the cooking juices, raise the heat to medium-high and bring to a simmer. Add the sorrel, stirring as it melts down into the sauce. Reduce the heat if necessary so the liquid remains at a lively simmer and cook until the sorrel has wilted and turned an olive green, and the sauce has reduced by about one third, 5 to 7 minutes. Taste for seasoning.

6. Remove the chicken from the oven, and pour the sauce over it. Serve immediately.

4 to 6 servings

BELGIAN ENDIVE WITH LEMON AND GARLIC VINAIGRETTE
Endives a la Vinaigrette Citronnée

———————— ೲ ————————

This is a fresh, winter salad that chases away the chill! I often add cured black olives to this salad, for a wonderful counterpoint in flavour and texture.

For the vinaigrette:
½ tsp minced lemon zest
2 tbs freshly squeezed lemon juice
Sea salt and freshly ground black pepper
1 medium shallot, halved, peeled, cut in paper thin slices
1 small clove garlic, green germ removed, minced
6 tbs (90ml) extra-virgin olive oil
6 large Belgian endive, trimmed

1. In a large salad bowl, place the zest then whisk together the lemon juice with the salt, pepper, shallot, and garlic. Slowly whisk in the olive oil until the vinaigrette is emulsified.
2. Cut the endive into crosswise slices. Add it to the vinaigrette and toss until it is thoroughly coated. Season to taste sand serve.

6 servings

ROASTED COCKLES WITH SAFFRON AND LEMON

Coques au Four à la Sauce Safrane

———— ᎒Ꮒ᎒ ————

Try this recipe with tiny manila clams as well. There is no salt in the dipping sauce, and none is generally needed.

The zest from ¼ lemon, minced
1 scant tbs freshly squeezed lemon juice
½ tsp saffron threads
3 lb (1.5 kg) small clams, degorged*
¼ cup (60 ml) extra-virgin olive oil

1. At least one hour and up to four hours before serving, place the lemon zest and the juice in a small dish and crumble the saffron into it. Stir so the saffron is completely moistened and reserve.
2. Preheat the oven to 450°F (230°C).
3. Place the clams in one layer in a large baking pan. Roast them in the centre of the oven until they open, 8 to 10 minutes.
4. While the clams are roasting, transfer the lemon juice and the saffron to a small bowl and whisk in the olive oil. Evenly divide the mixture among six tiny ramekins, and place the ramekins in the centre of six warmed plates.

* To degorge the clams, place them in a large container of heavily salted water. Stir in 1 tablespoon of semolina or fine cornmeal, and refrigerate them for at least 4 hours and up to 8 hours, changing the water at least 3 times, adding semolina or cornmeal each time.

5. Remove the clams from the oven, discarding any that haven't opened. Evenly divide the clams among the six small plates, carefully arranging them around the ramekins. Serve immediately.

6 appetizer servings

An Ode to the Market
in Louviers

I love waking up on Saturday morning; even from inside my bedroom I can feel the lilt in the air because it's my favourite day of the week, market day.

I like to get to the market by 8.30 a.m. If I go any earlier the vendors won't have their stands fully set up; much later and the crowds who at that hour are still at home taking their last sips of coffee and wiping the crumbs of baguette from the corners of their mouths, will descend to block the passages, chat with the vendors and stand in long queues in front of the most coveted produce. By getting there before them I can do all of these things at a leisurely pace, and still be home in time to put in a good, full day of cooking.

I have a prescribed order to my marketing, which rarely varies. I walk out of our courtyard and head right down the main street of town to the bank's cash machine. I am already in heaven as I watch the street wake up: the florists are putting out the last plants and buckets of flowers on the pavement; Brigitte, the owner of Laure Boutique is arranging the precarious stacks of baskets and postcard racks that announce her store; and one of the women who works at the charcuterie is carefully spelling out the daily specials on a sandwich board outside the shop. I always, every time, admire her slightly Victorian handwriting and the way she manages to produce a perfectly straight, perfectly justified list.

Brigitte looks up as I pass, takes off her glasses and we kiss twice on each cheek, then I go on. When I turn the corner from the main street I can hear the hum of the market, which will build to more of a crescendo as it swings into its full, mid-morning rhythm.

When I turn again, into the market, I get the same feeling as when I set foot on the dance floor: the rhythm takes over and I pick up my pace, straighten my back and hold my head a bit higher as I meet the sounds and colours.

I refer to this street as 'goat cheese alley' because the goat's cheese producer is here with his soft, creamy fresh cheeses. I don't dare buy any now because they're so fragile they need special handling or they'll turn to mush, but I smile and nod to the producer, who is usually sharing a rillettes sandwich with his neighbour, the *produits de luxe*, or luxury products man across the way. I'll buy cheese from him just before I leave the market to return home.

I smile at the *produits de luxe* man, too. He has the most exquisite smoked herring, fat, luscious fillets of salt cod, dried and peppered mackerel fillets, gorgeous smoked salmon and trout. I buy the herring and the salt cod most often – the first to serve with boiled potatoes and fresh onions, the latter to serve in dozens of different ways, though my favourite preparation is a silken, garlicky purée called *brandade*.

Next to him is the plant man who, each year, has the most beautiful pansies and petunias. I always buy royal blue pansies for the autumn and winter window boxes, which I like to mix with white, or white and salmon. Come spring and I plant pots with his deep purple petunias, which fill our courtyard with their vanilla aroma. Along with the fuchsia and white and mauve petunias in the window boxes, they make a riotous display of colour that lasts right into autumn.

The long farm-stall next to him is manned by a trio of young farmers who laugh and make jokes all morning long. The mother of one of them is there sometimes, too, and she is just as jovial as they. I check out their produce as I walk by, cataloguing it in my head in case they've got something I'll need when I return. The market is full of quirky personalities, and across the street is one of them: a woman with an assortment of fruits and vegetables that she grows herself and that she claims are all organic. She's got that honest, country look that can't help but be attractive; I bought most of my vegetables from her when I first began shopping at the market years ago. But I learned to pass her by, because each time I returned home I would find something rotten, unripe or otherwise inedible in the bottom of my bag. Then I began hearing others complain about her. How she stays in business I'll never know, but she seems to do just fine. Kitty corner from her is a snaggle-toothed man with unkempt hair who sells very few items, all of them slightly smudged and grubby. I cannot imagine anyone actually buying the smashed pats of butter he says he makes, or the boxes of nuts that are surely from several years ago, judging by their allure. He is a distant cousin of people we know, and all they can say is that he was put on this earth to be mean. Mean he may be and a cheater to boot, if what they say is true, but he certainly seems to enjoy himself at the market, and is always in conversation with one of his neighbours.

The Portuguese stand at the corner scents the air with peppers, garlic and lemon from a dozen varieties of seasoned olives. The charming proprietor and his carbon copy of a son smile shyly as they spoon them into small plastic bags, then knot them tightly with a quick flip and turn. They also sell strings of gorgeous sun-dried figs, white and yellow cornmeal, deliciously salty air-cured pork loin called *luomo*, candied fruits including kumquats – which I buy at Christmas – and an assortment of Portuguese wines, cheeses and spices.

Once past this stand I make a beeline for Jean-Claude and Monique Martin, the undisputed reigning family of the market. Oh, there are many other wonderful producers and much delicious produce, but none have the finesse of character and produce that Jean-Claude and Monique possess. My mouth waters as I stand there looking at their crates full of violet-flavoured *mâche* (lamb's lettuce), delicate cauliflower, sweet carrots, earthy potatoes and celery root.

Jean-Claude is small and wiry with intense blue eyes that burn with humour and intelligence. Monique is small and much calmer, with a steady, direct gaze. Their daughter Myriam, with her choppy punk haircut and her slim 1950s glasses doesn't say much, but she's got a lively glint in her eyes, as does her older brother Xavier, who speaks with a charming lisp. They both work hard at the market stall with their parents, though each holds a full-time job during the week.

It pays to get to the Martins' stall early, as they are extremely popular. Jean-Claude is full of mischievous comments, and when he sees someone he knows well he booms a greeting of '*Ça va ti?*' which is the local patois for 'How're you doing?' Monique gives a kiss on each cheek to customers, some of whom the couple has served for the twenty years they've been coming to the market in Louviers. I've learned over time that Monique has a quick wit. I was reminded of it most recently when I was struggling to find exact change in my purse full of euros and cents. France had changed its currency from francs to euros about two months before, in what had been an amazingly tranquil transition. There were some complaints, particularly about the size of the small denominations of coins, the kind I was trying to locate so that I could give Monique exact change. 'Oh, I'm just like an old lady digging in my purse,' I said, frustrated with the sameness of all the coins.

'Suzanne,' Monique replied with a straight face, 'the old ladies have a lot less trouble than you.'

I first struck up a friendship with the Martins over recipes. Monique is a good country cook who loves to talk food, and I have several of her recipes in my *French Farmhouse Cookbook*. Jean-Claude is a good country eater who couldn't care less about technique, but loves to eavesdrop and add his two cents worth. I'm not really sure which recipe was the first Monique shared with me – I believe it was for a salad tossed with apples sautéed in butter – but ever since then we've been friends. I've been to their home to cook with Monique and I've shared meals and aperitif hours with them, too, sitting at an outdoor table that overlooks their rectangular farmyard.

Monique and Jean-Claude live in the lovely old farmhouse that sits at one end of the farmyard, while Monique's parents' house stands at a right-angle to it, and Myriam's house is across the patch of green lawn with its big flower pot in the centre. Beyond, completing the rectangle, are hangars filled with farm equipment, hutches for dogs and refrigerators for storing produce.

I've seen the Martins prosper in the ten years I've known them. When I first visited them at their large farm

it was dusty and in desperate need of some loving attention. The big storm at the end of 1999 caught them
unawares and their chimney crashed to the ground,
destroying a good part of their roof with it. They used this
unhappy event and the repairs it required as impetus to
redo the entire façade of their farm in *trompe l'oeil* timbers,
which brightened it up immensely.

I believe one of the reasons the Martins have prospered
is because they added an extra farmers' market to their
week. For once, in a moment of seriousness, Jean-Claude
took the time to explain to me the marketing of vegetables, helping me see how much more advantageous it
is for them to sell directly to the consumer than to go
through a middle person. The organization required to
sell at several different markets is daunting, and it means
that Jean-Claude often stays at the farm to harvest while
Monique and their children sell. But it makes their hard
work and the long hours they put in worthwhile. For the
consumer like me it means that I'm getting produce that
was harvested just hours before I buy it from the person
who grew it. The only thing better than this would be if
I grew and harvested the produce myself.

It is relationships like the one I have with the Martins
that results in the intensely flavoured food I have the
privilege to cook and eat. I am so thankful to farmers like
the Martins and consumers like the French who demand
the quality of goods they produce, for they are responsible
for the network of vibrant markets throughout France.
They are the country's soul, and no one would want to
live without them.

The Martins raise basic produce on fertile fields that
are scattered around the area. There are some behind the
farm, and some down a lane and across a bridge to a
bucolic island in the River Eure. Further down another

road is yet another field. The Martins are fortunate to have their fields nearby; I know farmers who travel many kilometres to work their land, which makes their days long and inefficient.

The alluvial soil of the Martins' fields makes for sweeter-than-average carrots, crisp, tender lettuce with a delicate flavour, spicy shallots and lush, sweet spinach. They sell many other vegetables including gorgeous tall leeks, incredibly delicious cauliflower and tasty broccoli, celery root, sweet and hot '*jaune paille*' onions, courgettes, tomatoes, squashes and fat round beets as well as long slim ones.When I first began buying from the Martins' they sold only cooked beets, a custom that dates from the Second World War when fuel was scarce. Farmers had a more generous fuel allotment than other citizens then, so they cooked beets in huge vats at the farm and sold them cooked to save their customers fuel. I prefer to cook my own beets, and I also love them raw, tossed in a cumin vinaigrette, so I asked Jean-Claude if I could buy some raw beets from him. He brought a crate the next week and found that other customers liked them raw, too. Now the Martins always have raw beets along with the cooked.

I noticed that each week the Martins would sell crate after crate of black radishes, and I asked Jean-Claude what people did with them, for I had only ever come across black radish grated and tossed with rice-wine vinegar. Jean-Claude opened his eyes wide and looked at me as if I was an imbecile. 'Suzanne, you don't know what to do with black radishes?' he said in an exaggeratedly surprised tone. 'Monique, *viens dire à Suzanne ce qu'il faut faire avec les radis noir*. Come and tell Susan what to do with black radishes.'

She laughed and said, '*C'est simple.*' She told me to slice them thin and serve them on fresh bread slathered with butter, or toss them in a shallot-rich vinaigrette. I do both and we all love their nutty, slightly hot flavour. It turns out they have medicinal properties, too, the most common being a cure for a sore throat once they've been cooked with sugar to a golden purée.

The Martins periodically invite me to stop by the farm, which is a twenty-minute drive from Louviers. Most recently I took Fiona, and with Monique we ambled along the '*chemin de halage*', the towpath that was used by horses to drag barges down the River Eure. Almost every riverside town and village in France has such a road, and it provides an insight into the life of the community, as it is hidden from the main streets behind homes, farms and factories. In this particular farming village it runs along behind tidy productive gardens and small fields, a restored manor house and little fishing huts that have been turned into vacation homes. We saw flowers and vegetables, rabbits and chickens, people having drinks under huge parasols, fishermen reeling in their small, wiggly catch. We even picked some redcurrants that hung over a fence into the pathway. Our return to the Martins' farm, which is in the centre of the village, coincided with Jean-Claude's return from the fields, and it gave us a chance to take a drink together at the large table outside. Monique's parents joined us too, and it was a warm, friendly time.

When I've finished at the Martins' stall at the market I pack everything carefully into my basket and they tell me what I owe. How, I always wonder, is it possible to get so much for so little? I would be willing to pay so much more for all this gorgeous produce that my family, my luncheon guests and my cooking school students enjoy so much. I walk away from the stand thinking that I'm getting much, much more than I've paid for.

When I'm shopping for my cooking classes or for a

special lunch I buy a lot of produce, and take no end of teasing. After I've chosen multiple heads of lettuce, enough carrots and leeks to make soup or turn into a garnish, radishes and baby potatoes for an appetizer, aubergine and tomatoes to accompany something from the grill, my basket is overflowing. One week I was asking about the keeping qualities of their shell beans: I needed them on Friday morning to serve as a garnish on sautéed foie gras, and our market is on Saturday morning. 'Xavier can deliver them to you on Friday morning: he goes to Louviers every day,' Monique said. Xavier nodded in acquiescence. I looked at him a bit sceptically. 'Are you sure that this is convenient for you?' I asked. 'If you don't mind getting them at seven-thirty in the morning, I'll do it whenever you want,' he responded. Imagine: farm-fresh vegetables delivered to my door. I accepted, gratefully, realizing that this might change my shopping habits forever.

I walk right by the gorgeous loaves of sourdough bread that are displayed at a stand next to the Martins', and which beckon like a siren's call. I've succumbed before to this bread, which is sold by the pound, and each time I've been disappointed. The crust is dark and shatteringly crisp, the '*mie*', or crumb, is filled with irregular holes, just like good bread should be, but there is an aftertaste of chlorine. I assume it is from the water used in the bread since, according to the man who sells it – who I don't think is actually the man who makes it – the only ingredients in this bread are the sacred triumvirate of flour, water and salt. Unfortunately, not everything at the market is as it seems.

Baptiste's stand is next. The farm he works with his uncle must be in a microclimate, for while he has just about the same variety of produce that the Martins do, his is always a bit in advance, which gives him an edge – he's got the first tomatoes, aubergines, peppers, courgettes, and a variety of strawberry called Mara des Bois that produces from early spring into autumn with a flavour and aroma so musky and sweet it should be bottled. I always think I'll serve them with a cake or a crème brûlée, but we usually end up eating them all before I can do anything with them.

In the winter Baptiste makes his fortune, a word I use as hyperbole, on Belgian endive. This he cultivates in soil, unlike most endive in France, which is cultivated hydroponically. It is in season from November to March or April, depending on the year, and he sells every single endive that he harvests.

I get milk across the way from Baptiste, then continue on down the row of stalls to a vendor who specializes in Hass avocados which, depending on the time of year, are either from Spain or Israel, and are unparalleled in flavour. On my way I bypass Guy-Guy, the charcutier, despite the delicious aromas emanating from his huge pan of bubbling choucroute, or sauerkraut, his fat sausages, his smoked hams and his enormous, garlicky pâtés. I shopped at this large, colourful stall until I discovered a charcutier whose products are finer, more richly and carefully flavoured, less mass-produced than Guy-Guy's.

I don't know why it took me so long to discover him, for his pork products are head and shoulders above anyone else's at the market, or in the town of Louviers, for that matter. A dapper little man with pomaded hair and a tidy white coat, he and his plump, blonde-haired wife are old-fashioned and gracious, products of a different era. On Saturdays they have two young men working alongside them, one of which, I'm almost certain, is their son. Though they are all very pleasant, they have no time for

chit-chat, since the queue at their stand is long and insistent. As I wait I watch people load up for the week on pâté,
sausages, garlicky *saucisson à l'ail*, ham, tripe, head cheese,
jellied pigs' feet. I buy '*jambon à l'os*', ham on the bone,
which the charcutier hand-cuts into sumptuous, uneven
slices, which I like to serve along with a green salad dressed
with chive vinaigrette. I'm not even a ham lover, but for
his boiled ham I make a huge, almost gluttonous exception. We all love his garlicky sausages, which I serve with
vinaigrette-dressed green beans and potatoes, or atop a
salad. His lightly smoked bacon, which, like all bacon in
France, is lean and delicately flavoured, is delicious too.

Beyond the charcuterie truck and past the honey man,
his card table loaded with several kinds of honey and
handmade beeswax candles, is the quiche truck. Here
Madeleine, Monique Martin's cousin, and her husband
Jean-Pierre sell quiches, cakes, pizza and a few fruit tarts.
They make everything themselves at home, except for the
quiches – their specialty – which they cook in the two gas
ovens inside the truck. I always wonder, when I watch
Jean-Pierre put a baking sheet crowded with quiches into
his oven, where I can see the blue flame burning, why the
whole thing doesn't explode. I would have thought it
would act like an incendiary bomb, but so far as I'm aware
there has never been a mishap. And the quiche truck is
hardly a threat compared with the pizza truck and its
wood-burning oven that parks in one of Louvier's car
parks every Friday night – but that's another story. In any
case, Monique and Jean-Pierre make the most delicious
little quiches I've ever had. The crust is crisp and tender,
while the filling – which is seasoned with Gruyère or a
classic blend of Gruyère and bacon, with salmon and leeks,
or with tomatoes and garlic – is just the right creaminess.

Often Fiona and I go to the market together, and when

Monique sees us coming she's already got a quiche that's not too cold, not too hot, all ready. '*Bonjour Mademoiselle,*' she says, and hands it down into Fiona's waiting hand. Sometimes I'm so hungry I'll eat mine right there, too, along with all the other people who are doing the same thing. Like them, I'll go ahead and get myself another one for lunch, along with those I'm buying for the rest of the family. Madeleine and Jean-Pierre's quiches are one of our Saturday lunchtime treats.

My *périple*, or route, through the market is not as quick as it may sound, for I've undoubtedly run into several people on my way. Xavier Rousseau who, with his wife Virginie, makes the beautifully delicate Rouennais-style pottery across town from us, which they paint in the trad- itional seventeenth- to eighteenth-century decor, is an early market goer too. We buss each other on the cheek, then do a quick catch up, our conversations usually revolv- ing around the same subject. 'How's work?' I ask him. 'Fine,' he says. 'Too busy, *mais qu'est-ce que tu veux?*' 'Too busy, but what do you want?' I often visit them at their studio and they are always there, sitting on tall stools by their big front window, painstakingly painting the dishes they so carefully throw and mould.

I usually see Patrick Coquelin, too, who, with his wife Martine and his brother-in-law Jean-Pierre, owns Le Ger- moir, a handsome ferme-auberge about ten minutes from Louviers, deep in the heart of farming country. Martine used to dream about cooking during the years she was a farmer, as she followed the long crop rows in the family tractor. When farming became tough, she and Jean-Pierre decided to open a restaurant on the farm, taking advan- tage of funds provided by the state for just this sort of development. They chose as location a beautiful old build- ing that was once used for germing potatoes, hence the restaurant's name 'Le Germoir'. The brick and timbered building looks out on the farmyard and the game-rich forest and fields beyond. The food that Martine prepares is a seductive blend of traditional dishes and inspirations from books and magazines, and it has made the restaurant a success ever since it opened more than four years ago.

I might run into my friend Chantal, too, at the flower lady's stand, buying one of her beautifully wild bouquets. Chantal, who is Michel-the-baker's wife, looks like one of the bouquets she is buying, for she is always dressed stylishly in cool, refreshing colours and fabrics. We both love the bouquets that the energetic, white-haired, freckle-skinned lady puts together, from nosegays of bachelor buttons and statice, calendula and sweet peas, marigolds and cosmos, to much larger bouquets of lupin, dahlias, hydrangeas, daisies, Echinacea and chrysanthemums, which she lightens with delicate fronds or herbs so that each is wispy and graceful.

I always buy her bouquets in the spring and autumn when my own garden is naked. Come summer I don't need to because I've purchased so many of her flowering plants over the years that they garnish my garden well. Michael visits her stall regularly in the spring, too, and many of the plants in his garden at the studio have come from her.

If I do buy a bouquet, like the willowy Calla lilies of early summer, I'm never sure where to put it. If I tuck it into the basket and head out into the fray of the market, it is likely to get bumped and battered. I often leave it with the flower lady – I have never learned her name – to hold for me until I come back to get it.

My next stop is the egg lady across the aisle. There used to be half a dozen egg producers at the market, but little by little they've given it up because it isn't remunerative, the effort involved being more than the money earned. This little lady, with her kind face, is a retired farmer, and she finds it more than worth her while. 'Like all farmers, my husband and I have a small retirement income, so this helps out a lot. Besides,' she says conspiratorially, 'it keeps us busy, we don't see the time pass, and it gets me out to the market.'

I pay her two euros (about £1.30) a dozen, which again seems like highway robbery on my part for such gorgeous, tasty eggs, but it's the asking price. I bring my own egg cartons; if I don't there is the danger that she will put them in a plastic bag and they will be good for nothing but omelettes on my return home.

From time to time next to the egg lady there is an Algerian man, who sets up a card table on which he places white boxes of nut-filled, powdered-sugar-dusted Algerian pastries. He's like a mirage with his magical pastries, his tweed sports coat, crisp white shirt, dark tie and '*baratin*', or sales patter, and his irregular appearances. If I hadn't actually eaten his pastries I'd think he might not be real. He's a fabulous salesman, seducing passers-by with a taste of buttery, nutty '*corne de gazelle*', the crescent-shaped cookie that is a hallmark of the genre, or a date-filled, honey-rich confection. I love every single thing he has to offer, but I love more to participate in the drama of the sale.

'Oh, Madame, we used to own an *auberge* where all the actors and actresses came,' he says with a flourish. 'We don't have it any more, and our children – one is a doctor, the other a dentist – are gone and my wife, my wife, she makes these pastries just for fun.' He holds up a crown-shaped pastry. 'Simone Signoret, oh how she loved this one, it was her favourite,' he says, then tucks it into a small white box he happens to have ready.

The last time I stopped by I was with a visiting young American, Fiona, and Brinn, our au pair. I turned to speak with a passing friend, and when I turned back they were all munching on one of his pastries. He continued his sales pitch, holding up the pastries, telling me how they contained no fat, just almonds and a bit of butter, how they were made that morning, how tender and delectable they were. After he described each one he carefully set it in the small white box. When he was finished he held up the box. '*Pour vous, Madame?*' I bought the box, narrowly avoiding having to take out a second mortgage on the house to pay for it, and he thanked me profusely. 'Madame, if you ever need to hire someone to come to your house to make couscous, you call me,' and he handed me a piece of paper with his name and phone number on it. '*Merci, Madame,* give my best to your husband.' How does he know Michael? Well, Michael is as easy a mark as I am, and one day he came home with the same assortment in a similar box, having succumbed to the same charm!

Next in line is Cristelle the duck lady, with her delicious herbed duck sausages, duck pâtés, foie gras and fat, meaty duck breasts, as well as whole ducks, rabbits, guinea hens and chickens. She also sells golden, thick crème fraîche and eggs. It was her farm-fresh eggs that attracted me initially, and it was while waiting in the queue that I was tempted by her other products, each better than the next. She doesn't sell eggs any more, but I still stop by for the duck sausages, which I slowly braise in water then brown at the last minute and serve with a green salad.

My next stop is Solidaire, the only market stand to officially announce its products as organic. It is run by an organization developed to help people who have fallen by the wayside to re-establish themselves in the workplace. They work in the fields, then sell products from the stall, and after a year of such 'on-the-job-training', are let loose to find a job. It's a terrific programme and I always check the stand carefully. I may buy potatoes or kohlrabi – which we all love drizzled with lemon juice and seasoned with pepper and sea salt – spaghetti squash or *potimarron* – squash that tastes like chestnuts. Depending on the time of year they might offer beans or patty-pan squash, small beets or bunches of stalk celery, raspberries or strawberries.

Though Solidaire is the only produce stand to announce itself as organic, most of the locally grown produce at the market is either organic or very close to it. The tradition for *maraîchers* – or market gardeners – is to husband their soil carefully with a nod towards the future, and to sow and reap according to the lunar cycle. No one in their right mind treats fields or produce any more than they have to, and most use nothing at all but '*bouille bordelaise*', or Bordeaux mixture, a sulphur treatment that is permitted to organic growers. I am very careful about what I feed my family and my guests, and I have asked every producer I buy from about how much of their stock is produced through organic cultivation. They scoff at the word organic, '*biologique*' in French, but they go on to talk about the health of their soil and the high cost of synthetic treatments, and how they'd rather not use them. Many of them practise what Baptiste describes as '*culture raisonée*': thoughtful agriculture. When done honestly, this means they treat only when they absolutely must, and I know the farmers at my market well enough to know that they are sincere in their efforts to produce the cleanest, most chemical-free food they can.

Following Solidaire is a handful of small stalls that come and go. They mostly go in winter and come with spring, as they tend to be gardeners with a very few things to offer. I love to see what they have each week and am likely to buy anything from healthy zinnia plants to basil, miniature lettuce plants to bunches of shallots ready for drying.

Beyond these is an elderly woman who looks like a friendly witch, with her scarf tied around her head, her squinty eyes and gap-toothed smile. She sets herself down in a folding chair and places a basket of live chickens next to her, one of their legs attached so they won't run off, perhaps a rabbit or two, berries in summer and hazelnuts and walnuts in the autumn. She never has much, and everything she sells is very expensive.

During asparagus season an odd, slightly hunched and very garrulous woman shows up with a trailer-load of green and white asparagus tied into one-kilo bundles, and little baskets of the most delicious strawberries. She's like another mirage, for her presence at the market lasts for only five weeks each year and then she is gone. While she is there I, along with dozens of others, make the most of her wonderful produce. We stand in a queue and listen as she lets each person pick their bunch of asparagus, then painstakingly explains exactly how to prepare it. By the time I get up to her to make my purchase I could recite her suggestions verbatim. Now and then a waiting customer will sigh or roll her eyes at the careful rep-etitions, but always with a certain tolerance, for this lady is like a garden sprite with only the good of her customers in mind. I cannot wait to get home and steam the aspara-gus and serve it either with homemade chive mayonnaise, or simply unadorned. The children don't yet care for it, which is just fine with Michael and me, because we will easily eat the entire bunch. To me, a meal of freshly picked white and green asparagus is about the finest I can think of.

Across from the asparagus lady is the organic dairy lady. Young, short, cheerful, she moves in a very deliberate manner, so that if you are in the least bit of a hurry there is no point in waiting to be served. I go crazy watching her scoop cream into a container so slowly it almost turns to butter as she does it. If there is no queue or just one person I go, though, because her butter is sweet and the milk she sells is delicious, particularly in winter when it stays cold and fresh. In summer or when the day is stormy the milk sours almost before I get it home; some people like it that way, but we don't.

One day a man in front of me asked her about the Norman cows she milks. A look of rapture came over her face as she talked about her cows as though they were her children, laughing about their foibles, their good points, the incomparable richness of their milk. The man seemed embarrassed at the intensity of the response and said, 'Oh, but they are so stubborn.' The young woman rose to defend them. '*Oh non, non, elles sont superbes, simplement merveilleuses,*' 'They are superb, simply marvellous,' she said gently. I almost had tears in my eyes at this affectionate testimony, and when I glanced behind me at the people who were now waiting, many had smiles on their faces.

Next I stop at my friend Annique's stand. I say that Annique is my friend because she feels like a friend, but we have never spent any time together outside of the market, where she is the vendor and I am the customer. There is a complicity between us, though, which comes in part from mutual acquaintances, so that we know much more about each other than we ourselves have let on, but also because we both have firm goals in mind, we love quality when we see it, and we love local food produced on a small scale. Annique raises ducks to make foie gras, and hers is the best at the market. She is also a tireless promoter and is present at every specialty market, produce fair, or any other gathering where locally produced food is for sale. Beside the golden, buttery livers she sells are gorgeous, fat, meaty duck breasts called '*magret*', which I like to sear, cook to medium-rare, then deglaze with balsamic vinegar, or Calvados, or a blend of apple cider and apple jelly. She has luscious, thin-sliced, air-cured duck breast which I like to lay on top of a salad of bitter greens dressed with walnut oil, or on warm toasts, and mouth-meltingly tender duck gizzards.

Annique is always trying something new and one of her more amusing creations is a sliver of raw duck breast, called an *aiguillette*, which she gently pounds then rolls around a nugget of foie gras. These, sautéed to golden on the outside, are heaven. Annique stuffs whole *magret* with foie gras, too, makes terrines and pâtés, blends ground duck with stinging nettles to turn into sausages – her experiments are endless and most of them are exquisite. She also offers a whole selection of canned items like cassoulet and rillettes, the *aiguillette* stuffed with foie gras, foie gras terrine. I see Parisians line up at her stand to buy as though they were preparing for a famine.

One day Annique handed me a bottle of cider to try. 'We're going to begin making cider,' she said. 'Try this and tell me if you like it.' We did, of course – who wouldn't? It was so light and fruity it tasted like apple champagne.

After Annique's I am about to begin my homeward journey. First, though, I stop at the chicken lady's on my right, whose chickens are the best at the market. This is saying a lot, since all chickens raised in Normandy are amazingly richly flavoured. I almost always roast one of hers for our Sunday night supper, stuffed with as many bay leaves as it will hold, and with Baptiste's potatoes roasting along with it. We never tire of these delicious, crisp-skinned birds.

I might vary the menu by roasting one of her guinea hens, or once in a while a rabbit, both of which are also delicious. She also offers pigeons, which are sumptuous when macerated overnight in cream and roasted with fresh figs, or tiny quail, which I braise with garlic. Now and then I will buy a bucket of chicken livers, a rarity in France where chickens are sold with all of their parts intact. I dredge them in flour the way my grandmother did, for frying, then heat up goose fat and plunge them in.

The chicken lady recently began roasting chickens on a huge, upright, revolving rotisserie behind her stand. I decided to try one, and her assistant was just putting a plump little chicken in an insulated bag when she rushed over. *'Oh non, pas celui-là,'* she said. And she forked a large, meaty bird into the insulated bag, put her face close to mine and whispered, 'Those small ones, they're not my birds, they're industrially produced and you won't like them. I have to have some for people who won't pay the price of my own chickens.' Then she turned to her assistant. 'Don't ever try to sell her a little one, she won't like it.' I was touched by her attention.

I am now on my way home, stopping to buy fresh goat's cheese which I will shower with freshly minced shallots and cracked white pepper, then drizzle with extra-virgin olive oil, perhaps some flowering plants, and an additional vegetable or two from the friendly farmers such as bulbous fennel or firm, snaky cucumbers. When I'm shopping for classes my baskets are so full and heavy that I can't possibly buy much more at this point: my purchases are so precariously balanced that if I'm not careful I'm likely to have an accident. I pull my trolley-basket, which usually has another basket balanced on top of it and a bag or two hanging from its handle, down the middle of the street, which is smoother than the pavement. Should a car come around the corner towards me I must negotiate the kerb, a feat that – when I'm loaded down like this – feels not unlike scaling Mount Everest.

I rarely purchase anything at the market but food, though I could easily fit out the entire family there from the racks of market fashion on display, or load up on popular French music for Joe, hair baubles for Fiona, or the latest purse in its pirated version. I could buy a new mattress, have my chairs recaned, buy an assortment of sheets or used clothing, get the latest miracle cleaner or a cosy winter hat for my children. But I don't do any of that. For me, the market is food.

Despite the fact that all I ever bring home is food, the family is still eager to see what comes out of my basket once I roll into the house. Joe and Fiona hover over the quiches or tuck into a banana or an apple in winter, a nectarine or plum in summer. Michael carefully unwraps everything and I put it away. The chicken comes out of its plastic bag and is wrapped in a tea towel before being stored in the refrigerator along with the crème fraîche, the fresh milk, the duck sausages or foie gras. Any cheese I've purchased goes into a screened-in 'cheese house', which I put outside in winter, or down in the *cave* or cellar in summer. I put vegetables and fruit outside in winter, too. In summer we eat them up quickly.

When all is carefully packed away I contemplate the recipes that I've lined up for the day, which may be destined for luncheon guests, or for the cooking school (which always begins on Sunday evening), for friends who might be coming for dinner, or simply for the family. Then, I set out our market lunch and we have a real feast of steamed potatoes and cauliflower tossed with garlic and extra-virgin olive oil, or a tomato, shallot and fresh basil salad, warmed quiche, perhaps some sugar-studded choux pastries called *chouquettes* from the boulangerie. It's a lunch unlike any other, for it's the best and freshest from producers at the market whose names I know, many of whose farms I've seen. Most are young and will be producing for a long time to come, which is as restorative a notion as the food. Yes, our post-market lunch is just about the most delicious meal of the week.

PEAR AND CREAM TARTE FROM THE MARKET IN LOUVIERS
Tarte aux Poires à la Crème, du Marché de Louviers

※

This recipes comes from a woman who buys her pears from Vincent at the market in Louviers. It is wonderfully simple and delicious!

1 recipe for On Rue Tatin pastry (see page 97)
3 tbs fresh breadcrumbs, lightly toasted
3 large (about 7 oz; 210g each) Doyenné de Comice, Beurre Hardy, Conférence or other flavourful and not-too-ripe pears, peeled, cored and cut in sixths
5 tbs (62g) vanilla sugar
¾ cup (185ml) crème fraîche or heavy, non ultra-pasteurized cream
2 large eggs
Pinch fine sea salt

1. Roll out the pastry and fit it into a 10½ inch, removable bottom tart tin. Refrigerate for at least 1 hour.
2. Preheat the oven to 450°F (230°C). Prick the pastry, line it with parchment paper and fill it with pastry weights and bake until the edges are golden, 12 to 15 minutes. Remove the parchment paper and the weights and continue baking until the bottom of the pastry is pale gold, 3 to 4 more minutes. Remove from the oven. Sprinkle the bottom of the pastry evenly with the breadcrumbs.
3. Arrange the pear slices with the narrow end towards

the centre of the tart, like the spokes of a wheel, as close together as possible without overlapping. Coarsely chop any remaining pear and mound it in the centre of the tart. Sprinkle the pear evenly with 1 tablespoon of the sugar and bake until the sugar begins to caramelize slightly on the pear and the pear is partially baked, about 15 minutes. Remove from the oven and reduce the heat of the oven to 400°F (180°C).

4. In a medium bowl, whisk together the crème fraîche, the eggs and the remaining sugar and the salt. Pour the mixture evenly over the pears and return to the oven to bake until the custard is golden and set, 20 to 25 minutes. Remove from the heat and remove the ring from the edge of the tart tin. Serve warm.

8 servings

QUICHE FROM THE LOUVIERS' MARKET
Quiche du Marché de Louviers

———— ଓଓ ————

This is simple and delicious!

One recipe for On Rue Tatin pastry*
6 large eggs
⅔ cup heavy cream or crème fraîche
1 cup milk (preferably whole)
8 oz Gruyère, Emmenthal, or other Swiss-type cheese
¼ teaspoon freshly ground nutmeg – optional

1. Roll out the pastry to fit a 10½ inch glass or metal pie plate (not removable bottom). Crimp the edges, poke

the bottom with a fork or the tip of a sharp knife, and place the pastry in the freezer for 30 minutes.

2. Preheat the oven to 425°F.

3. Line the pastry with aluminum foil and pastry weights and bake in the bottom third of the oven until the pastry is golden at the edges, about 15 minutes. Remove from the oven and remove the aluminum foil and pastry weights. Return the pastry to the oven to bake until the bottom is golden, an additional 5 minutes. Remove from the oven and reserve.

4. In a medium-sized bowl, whisk together the eggs, cream, and the milk until thoroughly blended. Season with the salt and pepper, then add the cheese and stir until it is blended. Turn the mixture into the pre-baked pastry, and spread out the cheese evenly over the bottom of the pastry. Sprinkle the top with nutmeg if you've used a Swiss-type cheese, and bake in the centre of the oven until the filling is golden and puffed, and is completely baked through. To test that it is done, shake the quiche – if it is solid without a pool of uncooked filling in the centre, it is done. You may also stick a sharp knife blade into the centre of the filling and if it comes out clean, the quiche is baked through.

5. Remove the quiche from the oven and serve immediately.

6 to 8 servings

ON RUE TATIN PASTRY

——————— ∽ ———————

This pastry is short, buttery, and wonderfully easy to put together. I make it in the food processor, for the less it is touched by warm hands, the shorter and flakier it will be.

Be sure to let the pastry rest at least one hour at room temperature, so it is easy to roll out, then chill it before baking.

For the pastry:
1½ cups (200g) all-purpose flour
Large pinch sea salt
8 tbs (125g) unsalted butter, chilled and cut in small pieces
5 to 6 tbs ((75–90ml) chilled water

1. Place the flour and the salt in the bowl of a food processor and process to mix. Cut the butter in chunks and add it to the flour. Process it, using pulses, until the butter is incorporated into the flour and the mixture looks like coarse cornmeal (semolina). With the food processor running, add the water and process briefly, using pulses, just until the pastry beings to hold together in large clumps. Turn the pastry out onto a floured work surface and gather it into a ball. Proceed with any recipe calling for an unbaked tart pastry.

Pastry for a 10½ inch tart pan

ROAST CHICKEN
Poulet Rôti

Nothing simpler!

1 roasting chicken, with giblets
Sea salt and freshly ground black pepper
12 imported bay leaves

1. Preheat the oven to 450°F (230°C).
2. Pat the chicken dry all over with paper towels. Remove the giblets from the cavity of the chicken, generously salt and pepper the cavity, and return the giblets. Stuff the bay leaves into the cavity.
3. Truss the chicken and place it breast side up, on a rack if you like in a large baking pan. Roast in the centre of the oven until the bird is golden on the outside and the leg joint moves easily when you rotate it, about 1 hour.
4. Remove the chicken from the oven, and salt and pepper it generously all over. Flip the bird onto the breast side and let it rest, uncovered, for at least 15 minutes and as long as 30.
5. Carve the chicken and arrange it on a warmed serving platter. Cut the giblets into thin slices and arrange them on the platter. If a substantial amount of cooking juices remain in the baking pan, place it over medium heat and bring to a boil. Scrape up any browned juices, add ½ cup (125 ml) water, reduce by about one-third and pour over the chicken.

4 to 6 servings

The Florists

About three years ago our neighbours, the florists, sold their shop. Viewed through the eyes of the twin sisters whose family had owned the business for just short of one hundred years, it was an agonizing process. Viewed through the eyes of the husband of one of these diminutive, silvery haired women, it was pure and simple liberation, from a lifetime of hard labour and flower petals strewn in every square inch of his life.

When we had first taken possession of our house on rue Tatin, all three of the florists had greeted us with an icy welcome. To be sure, we had asserted our ownership by asking them to remove their dog – which used the front garden as a playground – and the multitude of carts, trees and plants that crowded the backyard of our house. They had no reason to be happy about that, never mind that we were simply doing what was necessary.

After those early years, however, the temperature of our relationship had warmed, thanks to the ice-breaker of warm rolls made from my grandmother's recipe. They helped our neighbours see that we were simply a family who had moved in next door, not some evil interlopers. Once this realization dawned they opened their hearts. We learned that their son had passed away after a serious illness and their daughter had moved, with her husband and two young children, across the world to the Île de la Réunion in the Indian Ocean. Their son's sons lived close by but visited rarely, and they had no one on whom to lavish their grandmotherly affection. Joe, just by being a little boy, afforded them someone to bestow *bon-bons* on at Easter, Christmas, and just about every other holiday in between. Gifts came in other forms, too. We were the recipients of roses and tulips whose blooms were too faded to sell, but which brightened our home for days as they slowly faded into elegant decline. Every July, before they closed their shop for the month of August, they gave us plants they hadn't been able to sell, and we now have a panoply of beautiful old-fashioned rose bushes, hydrangeas, lilies of the valley and hyacinths that brighten our garden.

The sisters look like the negative space of each other. One is pink-cheeked and curvy with a quick, wry wit; the other is pale, concave and serious. The husband, attached to the pink-cheeked sister, is tall, silver-haired, ruddy-faced and brusque. They all worked in the shop together and we would see them there, busy from dawn to well after dusk, and be impressed by their stamina. Once in a while I'd see the husband wander off down the street, or I'd pass a café and see him sitting inside with his cronies. I never saw the sisters anywhere but in their shop – they didn't even close it at lunchtime. They would eat their meal – a pot au feu or *boeuf mode*, oven-baked fish or coq au vin, which the husband usually prepared – poised to descend into the shop when alerted by the loud bell that announced a customer. No matter how early we got up in the morning, they were already up, and the plants and flowers that they had brought in at 8 p.m. the night before were already carefully set out on the pavement.

On Thursdays they got up even earlier so that the *belle-soeur* and the *beau-frère* – the sister-in-law and brother-in-law – could go to the wholesale flower market at Rungis, just outside Paris. Sometimes I accompanied them, hoping they would let me drive, since their collective eyesight hardly measured up to my own. The *beau-frère* did the driving, often using all his strength to keep the van on the road, because their sense of thrift hadn't allowed them the luxury of power steering. Sometimes, as he hauled away on the steering wheel, I worried an artery might pop. Another economic measure he took was to drive fifteen kilometres out of the way to get on the autoroute rather than get on near Louviers, and when I asked him why he said it was to avoid paying the ten-franc toll. He did not seem concerned that the petrol he used to get to the free exit probably cost twice that.

He never did let me take the wheel, and those middle-of-the-night adventures as we crawled along on the auto-route while cars and trucks roared past undoubtedly shaved some years off my life. I loved those times, though, from creeping out of our front door in the dark and cold morning to huddling three abreast in the front seat, a blanket over our knees because the heater didn't work very well. By 5 a.m. we would arrive at the market, a town-sized collection of huge hangars and the occasional brasserie which, at that early hour, would be warmly lit and crowded inside. We would make for the golden light of the *halles aux fleurs*, flower hangars, which were so bright and busy inside that I felt as if I was entering Times Square at noon. The *beau-frère* pushed a huge cart along as I followed the *belle-soeur*, who walked as though fighting a stiff wind –

bent forward and swiftly, her list in hand and wads of cash in her wallet. She was well into her seventies yet I could hardly keep up with her.

I stuck close because I didn't want to get lost in the labyrinthine maze of the halls, which were so identical-looking that there seemed no way to get geographical bearings. Flowers were segregated according to variety, and if ever I found myself alone in the tulip section, for instance, I might as well have been in Holland for all I could recognize amid row after row of tulips. Getting lost at the ripe old age of forty-six would have been embarrassing, so I stuck close. After a few visits there I came to recognize the vendors or their signs high above the small glassed-walled sales booths, the only heated spots in the place. But I still tagged along because I could learn so much from the *beau-frère* and *belle-soeur* about flower varieties: which kept well and which didn't, which were popular and why, where they were from.

I also enjoyed going up with the sister-in-law to the booths where the money was exchanged, and waiting in a queue with all the other buyers. Somehow this wholesale shopping when it was dark outside always had something *louche* or shady about it. Everyone looked haggard and a little tough – except the *belle-soeur*, of course, who was the picture of decorum. There were lots of cigarettes hanging from lots of lips, cash changed hands with lightning speed, conversations were held in a sort of commercial short-hand, so that I wasn't always sure what was being said. It was murky and mysterious, edgy and fun.

The *beau-frère* harrumphed slowly along behind us, exchanging friendly insults with the vendors or muttering under his breath as he slandered the creaky cart, the colour of the roses or any number of other things which annoyed him. At first I was worried he would lose us or vice-versa, but I needn't have given it any thought, for he could have wandered around with his eyes closed and still found us. He would park the cart at about 6.30 a.m. and disappear, to return with a bag of croissants or brioche and coffee. This little tenderness and a wicked sparkle in his eye told me more about the old man than all his gruff words. I wouldn't call him warm or cosy – he was in fact ribald and mischievous – and I didn't really know anything about him, but I imagined he'd married into this family of florists without any real passion for the job. His heart seemed to be in another, more socially active place, where work was something that ended in the late afternoon so that the evenings could be spent in rousing company.

After our breakfast, which we took leaning on the cart, I hurried off after the *belle-soeur* while the *beau-frère* disposed of the coffee cups and disappeared for a while. We followed the same route each time, choosing flowers and leaving them for him to pick up and put on the cart. I felt like a kid in a sweetshop as we ordered bunch after bunch of tulips and daffodils, chrysanthemums and anemones, dusty rose peppercorn branches and fern fronds, Gerber daisies and mimosa. The flowers came from all corners of the world and I felt a frisson of nostalgia when I saw that the ferns came from the Pacific Northwest, our US home. I remembered all the hiking I had done in high school and college along trails lined with the same variety, never imagining then that they might wind up in a French bouquet.

My favourite part of the flower market was the rose alley, where the vendors looked different from others at the market, with their ruddy skin and weathered hair. This was because they were farmers and not wholesalers, who cultivated their flowers in myriad little villages just outside Paris. According to the *belle-soeur*, their roses had always been renowned for their quality. 'Now there are fewer growers outside Paris. The south of France provides many more,' she said, 'but some of the best still come from around here.' I was in awe at this little chunk of history still alive at the market, amazed to find growers and not just middlemen. I also loved the hues of the roses. There were mauve and pale yellow roses, ruffled pink and fragrant, tightly budded and almost black. There were velvety burgundy roses speckled with bright yellow, red-tipped orange ones that looked as if they were on fire, and the richest, creamiest ivory roses that looked more waxy than real. One woman sold rose petals and she offered me a bagful when I admired them. They were so fragrant I couldn't keep my nose out of them, and when I got home I emptied them into a basket, which I placed in the entry way.

The exotic plants and flowers took up one end of a hangar, and the ambience there was as warm as the countries that supplied them. No one had any more time to chat here than at any of the other stands as they all frantically took or filled orders, but there was a feeling of gaiety among the exotics that didn't exist elsewhere, and that encouraged people to buy. The *belle-soeur* and I succumbed once and bought tall banana stalks, their phallic flowers not quite in bloom, their diminutive green bananas stillborn.

One of my favourite visits to the market was in November, just after the new Beaujolais wine of the year had been released. It was a freezing cold morning with hail and sleet pounding down on the van as we drove slowly through the dark to Rungis. As we entered the first warehouse there was a decided aroma of wine and garlic mingling with the fragrance of the flowers. We spent some time buying roses and delphinium, then the *belle-soeur* and the *beau-frère* motioned for me to follow them. We went to a large, bright stand that sold flowers from Holland – from Gerber daisies and orchids to tiny rosebuds and bright yellow sunflowers – and in the corner was a lavish table set with plates of sliced garlicky dried sausage and *andouillette*, or tripe sausage, and a big bowl of rillettes. Alongside was a pot of Echiré butter, the best in France, and a basket mounded with slices of baguette. I watched as men and women slathered their baguette with butter, pasted a round of sausage or andouillette or a big slab of rillettes on top, and clinked glasses before crying, '*Beaujolais nouveau est arrivée.*' I closed my eyes and inhaled: we could have been at Les Halles in Paris, I imagined, instead of these sterile hangars which had been built to replace it in the 1960s, the aroma was so rich and ripe. We muscled up to the table and did as everyone else was doing. The sausage – studded with peppercorns, rich with garlic and that ineffable porky taste of French sausage – was so delicious I almost forgot about the Beaujolais. But then I remembered the point of the exercise so I clinked glasses with my neighbours and sipped. The wine was sweet and berry-like, not awful but . . . well, it was Beaujolais nouveau and meant to please immediately, not savoured. I drank it down.

We passed other stands decorated with grapes and vine leaves; some had fancy canapés and glass rather than plastic glasses, others offered cheese along with cured meats, and everywhere people were munching and sipping. The ambience at the flower market is always brisk and friendly. This morning it was positively festive.

The *belle-soeur* usually finished buying flowers by 9 a.m., and we would all convene at the van. This was the *beau-frère*'s moment of glory as he carefully packed everything in the van with the precision of an engineer. Our precious floral cargo carefully installed, we would head for the plant section to load up on pansies and primroses, chrysanthemums and lobelia, hyacinths and impatiens, which he painstakingly fitted in. Then we would drive to the accessories section of Rungis, hangars that were divided into boutiques of richly coloured ribbons and fancy labels, beautifully delicate floral paper and cards, candles, vases, shelves and all the other accoutrements of the trade. At Christmas time I would find decorations there I couldn't find anywhere else, and at Easter it was a goldmine of furry bunnies and fragile eggs, yellow ribbons and garden figurines.

Once we were finished we still had one more stop. The *beau-frère* drove us to the vegetable part of the *halles*, and left us there to wend our way through the myriad stalls of fresh produce from near and far.

The *belle-soeur* navigated her way to a stand overseen by a middle-aged Provençal woman, who greeted her familiarly. 'We buy most of our vegetables here,' the *belle-soeur* explained. 'It's so easy for us to load them into the van, and we pay half the price we would at any shop.'

I remembered coming here long years ago as a cooking apprentice, when I would accompany one of the chefs. Then, we left in the inky chill of early morning, around 1 a.m., to be sure to get the best fish and meat. It was much more crowded at that hour – and I'm sure still is – and we would have to elbow our way around other white-suited chefs who were dressed against the chill in their stylishly bulky leather jackets. Going with the florists was luxurious by comparison, since most of the crowds were long gone, back in their restaurants, chopping and sautéeing.

I wandered among the different stalls while the *belle-*

soeur chose her produce. There was the *Allium* vendor with strands of purple garlic, braids of russet or red onions and fat bunches of shallots; the best that France had to offer. I picked up one of each. The potato vendor had a dozen different varieties and I opted for a case of knobby '*rattes*', considered the best potato in France. I love *rattes*, and my favourite way to prepare them is the simplest – steamed and tossed with extra virgin olive oil, minutely minced garlic and fresh herbs. Because I was buying so many I would sauté some to a golden crispness in a mix of olive and grape seed oils, roast some on a bed of rosemary or in the ashes of the fireplace and make a vinegary potato salad with lots of onions and capers.

Back at the Provençal lady's stand I buried my nose in a crate of mangoes that smelled like honey and tried to decide if I should buy it, then opted for a box of fat, ripe purple figs instead. A friend of mine who owns a restaurant in southern France prepares pigeon with fresh figs, and with this crate I would have enough to experiment myself. The florist, who was buying sacks of potatoes, boxes of oranges and grapefruits, leeks and celery root, eyed me. 'What are you going to do with those?' she asked. I told her about the pigeon dish, promising I would bring some of it over so she could taste. She wondered about the potatoes, too, and I said I would share. I noticed that she routinely bought a big sack of BF15 potatoes, a variety which corresponds with our starchy russets. There is nothing wrong with them, but they don't compare in flavour or texture with the waxy, nutty, buttery *ratte.*

Finished, we wheeled our treasures out to the van where the *beau-frère* was slumped in his seat, snoring. He was good-natured enough when we woke him up, and he carefully stashed our goods in the back. We headed for home. I was so excited with my purchases, from the green bananas on their decorative stalk to the figs and potatoes, the shallots for braising, the onions and garlic to use in many a dish to come.

The drive back was easier since it was light outside. The florists liked to stop at a rest stop about halfway home, just long enough to buy a chocolate bar, a box of biscuits or an ice cream. They wouldn't consider taking the time for lunch, even though I offered to buy, for they had to get home, unload the van and get to work.

Michael happened to be home when we parked across from the house at about 1 p.m., and together he and I helped unload the truck. How we hadn't noticed them struggling before, and how they managed on their own I didn't know, for the flowers were unwieldy and heavy. From that first trip on we both tried to be aware of when they returned from the market so that we could help them unload.

These nocturnal adventures cemented our friendship with the florists. Once they even invited us to lunch at their comfortably overstuffed apartment above the shop and across from the front door of the church. There the television, the sofa and the dining-room table vied for space in the main room, along with many old pieces of furniture whose tops were littered with the paraphernalia of a lifetime: photographs of the grandchildren, drawings that one of the sisters had done, old photographs of Louviers.

In one hallway of the apartment hung pictures of the wholesale market at Les Halles in Paris as it was during their childhood and early adulthood. I loved looking at the pictures and hearing their stories of going to Les Halles at night with their parents, about the colourful hue and cry of the market, and about later visits when they went on their own.

The married sister and her husband occupied this apartment, which seemed to go on forever and in all directions, down short, narrow hallways. The other sister lived upstairs in an apartment of the same size that was as tasteful and spare as this was crowded and chaotic. Their views of the church differed from ours, as their apartments were twenty feet closer, so that carvings and statues seemed even more lifelike than they did from our house, as though at any moment they might turn and speak, or take a step across the space right through the window.

They had the corner apartments in a building that wrapped around the corner of rue Tatin and continued down the whole block on rue Pierre Mendès France. It had been hastily constructed after the Second World War to replace the beautiful old timbered houses and businesses that had been destroyed. Apparently, residents could pay extra then to have insulation and better quality building materials used in the construction, and their parents had done so. We were there for lunch, which was stolid, traditional, tasty. It began with a tuna salad tossed with tomatoes and lettuce, continued with roast pork and potatoes, went into cheese and ended with ice cream for Joe and a fruit tart from the patisserie down the street for the adults, all washed down with a Bordeaux wine that the family had been buying from the same chateau every year for at least fifty years.

When we first came we hadn't understood the florists' initial reactions and had imagined they were negative and unfriendly people. We now knew that they were anything but. Old-fashioned, yes; bound in certain traditions that caused them to be wary of change, certainly. But negative and unfriendly? Far from either.

So we watched them go through the process of selling the shop, and experienced some of their anguish when they discovered that the business to which they had devoted their lives and energy, as had their parents before them, was not a hot commodity. They advertised it and had no response for almost a year. After that they had a few enquiries, and even an offer or two, though for much lower than they were asking. They continued waking early, putting the flowers and plants on the pavement each morning, bringing them in each night, making wreaths and bouquets until the wee hours, becoming more and more discouraged. 'We don't want to work until we are dead,' said one of them. 'And my husband is fed up,' said the other. Still, the shop didn't sell.

They had one very good offer, but after weeks of negotiating, the deal didn't go through. Finally, one day, I ran into one of them and she said they'd found a buyer. She was ecstatic. 'Will you stay in the apartment?' I asked, fearing they would move away, for I'd grown very fond of them. '*Non, non, non,* we will never leave our home,' she said, as if I were crazy for asking. They were going to sell just the business, the *fond de commerce,* and not the *murs,* the walls of the shop. I wondered how it would be for them to stay upstairs from the shop, connected as their apartment was to the comings and goings of the business.

The deal dragged on, but finally it was concluded, and we found ourselves with new florists across the street. A couple about our age, with a son Joe's age and two much older sons from different marriages, they swept into Louviers bought up two other businesses, and moved into an apartment above one of them just a few blocks from us. The sisters had agreed to help them settle into the florist shop, and we would see them all over there working together, wondering how everyone was faring.

Once in a while one of the sisters would confide in me that she thought the new owners were going about it all wrong. 'They aren't *du métier* – in the business,' she said. 'They don't know what they're doing.'

It was obvious the new owners weren't florists as they awkwardly went about making bouquets and serving loyal customers who would flounce out and announce to the world that they were never coming back. It wasn't that the new owners were unpleasant: they were simply inept.

We worried, we fretted, for everyone. One day, one of the sisters and I were talking and she got tears in her eyes. 'We had such a good business here and they are just ruining it,' she said. 'Almost one hundred years in the family, and look what they are doing.'

How hard it must be, I thought, to live upstairs from all the change, in a business that had been your life. It must have been excruciating.I commiserated as much as I could, but I had to admit that the changes made by the new owners were lightening up the place. Before, the shop had been dark and cavernous, and its windows had been stuffed with all manner of old-fashioned and outmoded garden decorations. I loved it in a way because it rep-resented another era, a France I hadn't had the chance to know. Whenever I went inside to buy flowers I loved looking around at all the fusty, old-fashioned things that had taken on a dimension of value simply because they had been there so long. There was the little elf that swung over a mirrored pool, a tiny plaster doe with limpid eyes, miniature birch-bark benches, embossed cards and gilt vases. Though it was all faintly dusty and faded, it was charming, and it obviously appealed to a large clientele who didn't seem to notice that time was passing by.

With the younger owners came a younger feel, which I thought would ultimately help rather than hurt the business. And I admired the new owners, for they made changes gradually, as though they could sense how hard it was for the twins. They waited until the first August after they had bought the place to close it for a month and scrape, stain and paint the façade back to life. They slowly took down old metal display shelves and replaced them with new glass ones, and threw away bin after bin of junk that they hauled out from the back room.

The twin sisters were aghast. They had lived in the heart of occupied France for five years and suffered privations we could hardly imagine, so to them nothing must go to waste. I would see them rummaging through the rubbish bins, extracting things they'd purchased years before. Now and then one would come over with a box of something. 'We can't believe they threw this out,' she would say, handing me a box of dusty, straw-hat-like things that were probably used as '*cache-pots*', or flowerpot holders, in the 1950s, or a box of crinkled wrapping paper. 'Surely you must have a use for them,' she said. I took what she gave me and promised that if I couldn't use it myself I would donate it to the school jumble sale in their name.

They watched as Michael rebuilt the house and garden and became convinced he could fix anything. They offered us a small stream of broken tables, chairs, and benches with the catch-phrase, 'Your husband will be able to fix it.' Able and willing were two different things, I wanted to explain, but never did. Michael would return home and see whatever it was sitting by the front door, glance across the street to be sure no one was looking, then stealthily load it into his work van where it would sit until he went to the dump.

One of the new owners confided that they were trying to be sensitive about cleaning out the back room of the florist shop. 'I know it's hard for them, but you wouldn't believe the junk pile it is,' she said. 'I don't think they threw anything away for fifty years.'

As time went on I heard less grumbling from the twins as they became accustomed to their new leisure time, and to the new owners. I also think they recognized that many of the changes were beneficial to the business. The new owners became more confident, and customers noticed. The shop was gradually taking on a new life. And surely life had become less stressful for the twins and the husband. They could now rise when they wanted to and go about their day as they liked. They took their dog for long walks in the woods, went to visit friends, kept abreast of all local events and went to most of them. The husband was left to his own devices, which meant he strolled around town a lot, and rested in cafés a lot. I knew that he had put a lot of pressure on his wife and sister-in-law to sell the business, and I had thought he would want to travel, or work on hobbies. But he refused to go anywhere, and he seemed lost and without direction. His wife confirmed it to me one day. 'He has nothing to do, so all he does is nothing,' she said, shaking her head. 'He doesn't want to go anywhere with us. I don't know what he'll do.' She looked longingly around our garden. 'If only we had a garden,' she said.

I offered it to them. 'Why doesn't he come over here and sit in the garden?' I said. 'Do you think he'd like to do some work over here? We can always use a helping hand.' She was interested in the offer, but he never did pursue the idea. I think he was perfectly happy wandering around town, talking with people, stopping for a drink when he wanted. It didn't seem like such a bad way to live!

The new owners are workers like their predecessors. Their learning curve has been steep, and while they may not be '*du métier*', they've learned quickly. They have obviously had plenty of experience owning a small business, and they understand the pressure it entails, along with that of simultaneously raising a young child. It is nice to have someone in the neighbourhood with whom to commiserate, and we laugh together from time to time at ourselves and our hectic schedules.

The *monsieur* bubbles over with entrepreneurial ideas. I can't count the number of times he's buttonholed me, his intense, deep-set eyes burning with excitement, to out-line a plan he's got for making a fortune, or a project he's thought about doing with Michael. Recently he bought his eleven-year-old son a professional cotton-candy machine to make '*barbe à papa*', or papa's beard, as the French call candy-floss. 'Every kid needs spending money,' he said. 'He'll be able to earn his by setting the machine up at local fairs.'

He's an inveterate real-estate junkie, too, and I suspect he's purchased other businesses and buildings in Louviers, for I see him everywhere all the time, chatting, wielding hammer and saw, always busy, ready with a *bonjour* and kisses on both cheeks. His wife rolls her eyes when she talks about him, and whenever she asks him to run an errand she concludes with, 'And please don't spend a half an hour talking with someone on the way.' She's obviously got his number.

He broke his back last winter in a skiing accident and returned to Louviers on a stretcher. He refused visitors (though he accepted homemade cookies), then suddenly there he was, walking. A bit stiffly, but walking nonethe-less. Six months later he was back to running, walking, lifting: Louviers' own man of steel.

Their son is a lonely figure who roams around town as though the entire place is his private playground, mostly on roller blades, often holding a hockey stick. He looks dreamy, and I have the impression he plays a lot of hockey in his head as he whips down streets and around corners. He's a sweet boy, and he and Joe sometimes career around together, play computer at our house or theirs or go off to the movies together. Once in a while he invites Joe for dinner, and Joe comes back ecstatic over pizza from the local pizzeria, something delicious from the charcutier, the butcher, or a kebab from the Turkish restaurant across the street.

Changes in this one corner of town over the past three years have been enormous, but everyone has settled nicely into their roles and we all have a lovely, comfortably neighbourly coexistence. We invite the twins and the husband for dinner occasionally, and the new florists stop by now and then for a drink in the garden. The twins babysit once in a while if we want to go to a movie or out to dinner. I put Fiona to bed because her night-time ritual of reading and songs is something only a parent would do, though the sisters are always sorry when she's not awake. They love it when Joe is up, for they are inveterate game players and always get him involved in cards or a board game. The daughter and two granddaughters come to visit from the Île de la Réunion once a year, and this is cause for great excitement, as the twins plan an activity for each and every day. The two girls love Joe, which makes him crazy. 'Oh mom,' he says when he hears they are coming, 'I hate to play with girls.' Once they are together, however, the laughter and giggles begin within a short while.

The daughter knows how much I love to cook and she always brings me many small bags of exotic spice mixtures from one of her local markets on the Île de la Réunion. I've become addicted to the curry mixtures, whose spicy freshness brings us a hint of life far away, where the sun shines daily and the winds blow warm. I particularly love the mixture for fish: a sweet mélange of turmeric and

117

paprika, cumin and cloves. Lately I've been dusting it on fat, tender little sea bream which I oven-roast on a bed of thinly sliced baby turnips, fresh onions and lemon zest. It's deliciously exotic.

We are fortunate to have both sets of florists as neighbours. The twin sisters and the *beau-frère* enrich our lives with their opinions and their perspectives, and through them we get a glimpse of the recent history of Louviers, and of France. The younger set adds zest to the neighbourhood. It is a fine and lively balance.

THE FISHMONGER'S FAVOURITE
La Préférée du Poissonnier

———————— ༄ ————————

I like to prepare this dish with the beautiful orange-spotted *carrelet*, or plaice, or with *lieu jaune*, pollack, that M. Onfroy from the market sells during winter. It is as good with these mild, white fish as it is with mackerel or tuna – consider it an all-purpose recipe for fresher than fresh fish!

Four fish steaks weighing about 8 oz (250g) each
Sea salt and freshly ground black pepper
7 dried, imported bay leaves
8 oz (250g) shallots, thinly sliced
3 tbs (45ml) extra-virgin olive oil
1 small bunch fresh thyme, separated into branches
6 tbs (90ml) dry white wine, such as a Sauvignon Blanc
1 lb (500g) ripe tomatoes, cored, seeded, and diced
1 cup (10g) flat-leaf parsley leaves, loosely packed
1 small clove garlic, green germ removed

1. Preheat the oven to 425°F (220°C).
2. Trim the fish steaks if necessary, and rinse them well, scraping along the bone to make sure it is completely clean. If using any cod-like fish, trim out the bones from under the dorsal fin, and pull as many bones as possible from the belly area. Pat the steaks dry and refrigerate until ready to cook.
3. Sprinkle the shallots in an even layer on the bottom of a non-reactive, flame-resistant baking dish and drizzle them with 1 tablespoon of the olive oil. Season them

generously with salt and pepper, and arrange the thyme branches and three of the bay leaves over all.

4. Season the steaks on each side with salt and pepper, and lay them on top of the shallots. Drizzle them with 1 tablespoon of olive oil, and set a bay leaf on top of each. Pour ¼ cup (60ml) of the wine around the steaks, then strew the tomatoes around and on top of them. Drizzle with the remaining 1 tbs of olive oil, season generously with salt and pepper, and bake in the centre of the oven until the fish is almost but not quite opaque through, 18 to 20 minutes.

5. Remove from the oven and carefully transfer the steaks to a warmed dish. Loosely cover with aluminum foil and keep warm in a low oven, where it will cook until it is opaque through while you prepare the garnish.

6. Remove the thyme branches and the bay leaves from the tomatoes and the shallots, add the remaining 2 tbs (30ml) wine and stir, then place the pan over medium-low heat and cook, stirring often, until the vegetables soften and begin to turn golden, about 6 minutes, and the liquid evaporates.

7. While the vegetables are cooking, mince the garlic and the parsley. When they are nearly softened, add a heaped tablespoon of the parsley mixture. Season to taste and remove from the heat.

8. To serve, place equal amounts of the garnish in the centre of four warmed plates. Top with a steak, then sprinkle with equal amounts of the remaining parsley and garlic mixture. Serve immediately.

4 servings

ROSEMARY BAKED POTATOES
Pommes de Terre au Romarin Cuites au Four

———————— ∽ ————————

6 long branches (about 12 inches; 30 cm each)
fresh rosemary
2 lb (1 kg) medium-sized potatoes such as Yukon Gold,
Mona Lisa, Yellow Finns, scrubbed clean
3 tbs (45ml) olive oil
Coarse sea salt, to taste
Freshly ground black pepper

1. Preheat the oven to 450°F (230°C).
2. Arrange half the rosemary in a large baking dish. Set the potatoes on top of the rosemary, drizzle the oil over them, and turn each potato so it is coated in oil. Sprinkle the potatoes with salt and pepper, and lay the remaining rosemary over them. Bake in the centre of the oven until the potatoes are crisp and cooked through, 1 hour to 1 hour 10 minutes.
3. Remove the potatoes from the oven and transfer them to a warm serving platter or individual plates, discarding the rosemary. Serve immediately.

4 to 6 servings

SAVOURY BEEF STEW FROM THE FLORIST
Pot au Feu

———————— ⚬⚬ ————————

André Taverne, the florist across the street from us, doesn't look like he loves to cook for he is tall and angular, yet it turns out that many of the delicious aromas issuing from the apartment above the florist shop come from his cooking. He is particularly proud of his pot au feu and this is his recipe, given to me on a cold winter morning as we stood amidst the flowering plants on the sidewalk. It is rich and delicious and I make it several times during winter for it keeps the Norman chill away. It is delicious heated up the next day.

4 lb (2kg) beef including top or bottom round, beef cheeks, pot roast and oxtail
1 heaped tbs coarse sea salt
1 lb (500g) small onions
6 whole cloves
1¾ pounds (875g) carrots, trimmed, peeled and cut in half, then in quarters lengthwise
1 medium (1 lb; 500g) rutabaga (swede), peeled and cut in eighths
1¾ lb (875g) small turnips, peeled and quartered
2 lb (1 kg) celery root, peeled and cut in 4×½-inch sticks
14 medium leeks, (about 2½ lb; 1.25kg) green part trimmed and tied in two bundles of six each
1 *bouquet garni* of parsley stems, dried, imported bay leaf, leek leaves, fresh thyme
4 cloves garlic, green germ removed
10 whole peppercorns, such as Tellicherry or Vietnamese
2 dried, imported bay leaves
1 marrow bone

For the croutons:
6 slices day-old bread that are roughly 4-inches (10cm) square
2 cloves garlic, peeled, green germ removed

For the condiments:
Coarse sea salt
Cornichons
Pickled onions
Horseradish
A variety of mustards

1. Tie the top or bottom round, the beef cheeks and the pot roast separately so they are compact bundles and don't fall apart during cooking. Place them, with the oxtails, in a large, deep stockpot. Add the salt, cover by at least 2-inches (5cm) with water and bring just to a boil, then reduce the heat so the liquid is simmering. When impurities in the form of an off-white foam begin to rise to the surface of the water skim them off, and continue skimming until you see no more impurities, which should take about 20 minutes.

2. Pierce the onions with the cloves then cut the onions in half.

3. Add one-half of the vegetables, the *bouquet garni*, and one of the garlic cloves to the meat in the pan, and make sure all is covered by at least 1-inch (2.5cm) with water. Add all peppercorns, cover, and bring just to a boil. Adjust the heat so the liquid is simmering – it shouldn't boil or the meat will be tough, partially cover and cook until the meat is tender and falling from the bone and the vegetables are completely soft through, at least three hours. Check the meat and vegetables to be sure that they are covered with water, adding water if necessary. It is fine if a bit of meat sticks above the

water; just be sure to turn the piece often so that the meat cooks evenly and doesn't dry out.

4. Remove the meat from the broth. Strain the broth and discard the vegetables and the *bouquet garni.* Return the broth to the pan and add the bay leaves. Bring it just to a boil. Add the remaining carrots and the rutabaga and cook until they are beginning to turn tender, about 10 minutes. Add the remaining turnips and the onions and cook until they are beginning to turn tender, about 10 minutes. Add the remaining celery root, leeks, and cloves of garlic. The vegetables shouldn't be floating in water but they should be just covered, so add additional water at this point if necessary, then cook until all the vegetables are tender. Remove the vegetables from the broth and place them in a shallow bowl. Moisten with some of the broth, cover, and keep them warm. Add the meat back to the broth along with the marrow bone and simmer for 25 minutes. Remove the meat from the broth, drizzle it with a ladle or two of broth, cover loosely and keep it warm in a low oven. Remove the additional bay leaves from the broth, and discard.

5. To make the croutons, rub each piece of bread with garlic and place one in the bottom of each of 6 to 8 shallow bowls. Pour equal amounts of broth over each and serve as a first course.

6. Remove the strings from the meat that is tied, and cut the pieces either into thick slices or into chunks. Arrange along with the pieces of oxtail on the warmed platter surrounded with the vegetables. Perch the marrow bones on top. Serve with the condiments alongside.

Serves 6 to 8

124

Be Careful of Me, I'm Dangerous

Fiona's first couple of months passed by in that wonderful hazy blur that I like to think of as 'the way life should be'. My parents had come to visit and help out, and those early days and weeks were a dream of my mother's delicious herb soups, stews and dense spice cakes, and a steady stream of well-wishers eager to see Fiona. They came in droves – friends, neighbours, parents of friends of Joe's, people we'd crossed paths with for the past seven years; all of them wanting to see the baby. Each visitor came with a gift: mostly fetching little outfits. My favourite made Fiona look like a little pumpkin – the body was orange velvet; the collar was vivid green velvet leaves. A classmate of Joe's brought a painting she'd done for Fiona, a turquoise fishbowl with a bright orange fish in it and the following words written in ornate script: '*Fiona, la plus belle des Américaines!*'

I had been teaching English in Joe's class right up until Fiona's birth, and the teacher had asked each child to make me a drawing, which she bound in a big scrapbook. I was deeply touched by all of the images and little messages such as, '*Bravo, Madame Loomis!*' or '*Vive les États-Unis!*' I had allowed myself two months' parental leave and, while I was keeping up with business (thanks to email), I succumbed to the luxury of a new baby. I woke and slept as Fiona dictated, played with Joe, spent time with my parents and my older sister who came to help. It was sublime.

Fiona was a very calm baby: we had to wiggle her toes once in a while to be sure she was still alive, she slept so much. Even when she was awake, she made little noise. During our annual Easter brunch that year, which was a feast of fresh asparagus, herb omelettes, sweetbreads and strawberries, one of our guests looked up halfway through the meal and asked, 'Isn't there supposed to be a baby here?'' Fiona was asleep in her lace-bedecked basket on the warm floor and she hadn't peeped.

Spring comes early in Normandy most years, and it is glorious. By the time Fiona was a month old we'd said farewell to the February '*grisaille*', or greyness, as everything woke up outside, fresh and new.

I treasure the memory of one day in particular, when I wrapped up Fiona, put her in the huge and highly sprung pushchair that neighbours had loaned us, and set out for our midweek market. The sun wasn't really in the sky, but its light refracted off everything in that spring way that makes everything look bright, washed and cheerful, and there was the hint of warmth in the air. I couldn't have been more content as I pushed Fiona through the heart of Louviers. I was 43 years old, I had a new and totally unexpected baby girl and I was going to market with no deadlines looming and nothing on my mind but Fiona, Michael and Joe, our next meal '*en famille*', and enjoying the soft, fresh air.

The Wednesday market in Louviers is small, occupying a fraction of the space that the Saturday market fills. It is held in the car park in front of Champion, our small-town supermarket, where the women at the checkouts greet customers by name, help the elderly or infirm fill their shopping bags or count out change, and generally take an interest in the comings and goings of the clientele.

The market itself consists of eight to ten stalls, many held by farmers who also come to the Louviers Saturday market. Baptiste is one of my favourite farmers at both markets. At twenty-five he is one of the youngest and, with his attractive, always-smiling round face and thick, corkscrew blonde hair he would stand out even if his gorgeous produce didn't beckon. Baptiste wears shorts when it's hot, baggy pants and sweatshirts when it's cool, and he looks as if he has just left school, but in fact he's been farming for five years on land he shares with his uncle. He has an obvious passion for his work, both farming and selling, and he chats and jokes with his customers, urges them to taste his produce, urges them to buy more. As he works he moves to a rhythm only he hears, slapping his hands against his legs, waving his head in controlled little shakes, doing occasional smooth little boogies as he bends to lift a crate or grab a handful of fruit, ending with a soft 'Yuh', and a fist thrust into the air. It turns out that another of Baptiste's passions is music, and in his spare time he plays bass guitar in a small band.

What makes Baptiste's produce stand out is, in part, the way he displays it. He mounds firm, russet-coloured onions, their rustling stems still on, in a graceful old wire basket. One of his specialties is Belgian endive cultivated in the traditional manner, in soil rather than in a hydroponic solution, which he artfully piles high in a wide, burnished wicker basket. His carrots are fetchingly

127

clumped with soil, his deep green Savoy cabbages as big as a manhole cover, his potatoes unusual varieties that range from starchy to firm, with names like Amandine and Mona Lisa.

Chemical farming is not Baptiste's forte. 'I use what chemicals I have to and nothing more,' he says, his jovial face taking on a serious expression. 'I'd lie to you if I said my potatoes are raised organically – frankly, anyone here who says that is lying to you because organically produced potatoes won't keep longer than a couple of weeks. But I do a fraction of the treatments most farmers do, the bare minimum.' Each time I ask Baptiste a question about his vegetables – why his cabbage has black holes in the outer leaves, why his radishes are never hot, what makes his strawberries better than anyone else's at the market – he tells me the whole story, not just part of it, so I leave him having had a lesson in agronomy, from soil composition to lunar planting cycles. Finally, though, aside from his adorable personality and his willingness to explain, what keeps me returning is his exceptionally flavoured produce. That he greets me with '*Salut, ma belle*,' only encourages my fidelity!

As I walked up pushing Fiona, Baptiste came around to peek at her. Her luminous blue eyes were wide open, her blonde wisps of hair moving in the slight breeze. '*Ah, qu'elle est belle, c'est son frère tout craché*,' he said. 'She's beautiful, she's the spitting image of her brother.'

I am addicted to Baptiste's Belgian endive, which he says is sweet because it matures in the soil and isn't fed too many chemicals, and I buy a kilo, which I will slice and serve raw dressed in a lemon and garlic vinaigrette and sprinkled with *fleur de sel*. I load up on potatoes: my Irish background dictates that my level of security rises with the quantity of potatoes in my larder. Unbelievably, Baptiste is already offering radishes, and I mention how surprised I am to see them. 'The ground has been warmer than usual. It's good,' he said, with fist-in-the-air joy. 'It's the beginning of a whole new season. We're over the worst of the year now.'

I move next to the fishmonger, whose stand is perpendicular to Baptiste's. M. Onfroy is about my age, a burly, energetic man with tight curly hair that hugs his head and a voice raspy from the hawking he does. He moves in lionesque fashion back and forth behind the *étalage*, or display, of luminous pink, peeled skate wings, large, meaty squid, live langoustine, whose fragile pincers bat at the air. '*Prenez de la belle langoustine!*' he yells, or '*Voici des coques de Bretagne*,' then spies me and adds decorously, '*Bonjour, Madame!*'

He acknowledges Fiona with a roll of the eyes. '*J'en ai un aussi, un garçon . . . ça change la vie, ça,*' 'I've got one too, a boy. They change your life.' I couldn't tell if he meant that in the positive or negative. M. Onfroy has pristine seafood, though the variety is limited. Accustomed while living in Seattle to buying seafood at Mutual Fish, a fish market whose Japanese owners brought in gorgeous, weird and wonderful seafood from all over the United States and Hawaii, I find myself pining for wild Chinook salmon, elegant Pacific halibut, silken Black Cod, tiny squid. But I've learned to love the local species too, particularly the incredibly tender and delicate large-flaked cod; mackerel which, when tiny, is called '*lisette*'; darkly luminescent sardines; small-flaked sea bass and meaty monkfish; tuna and rockfish; and sweet, firm shellfish.

M. Onfroy fits the stereotype of the fishmonger who is too often more interested in 'moving fish' to an unsuspecting customer than in providing consistent quality, as I've learned from watching and from my initial experiences with him. One instance stands out, when I let him

129

sell me fillets from a fish I had never heard of called 'l'Empereur', which turned out to be an old friend, orange roughy. I unwrapped the fillets at home to realize they had seen better days. I should have been more careful. I had made a foolish assumption that, because the bulk of M. Onfroy's fish was beautiful, all of it would be. I'd been taken in by his clean stand, and had been too trusting, thinking that just because he sold fish in a small country market he had my interests at heart, even though I had yet to become a regular customer. Disappointed, I let him know the next week what I thought. He started to make excuses, then stopped when he saw that I didn't care about hearing them. I explained what I did for a living, how I had trusted him, and how I didn't appreciate what he had done, even though I admitted it was my responsibility to check everything closely. He seemed chagrined. In any case, we have a very good relationship now: I'm very careful, and so is he.

His father is a different story. Small and ruddy-skinned, he wears a navy blue mariner's hat low over his beady eyes, and he looks as if he would sell his own son if the price was right. Once, he tried to steer me toward some faded flounder fillets. When M. Onfroy the younger spied what his father was doing he dived in and elbowed him out of the way. 'Madame, I know you love flounder but they've just laid their eggs and their meat is skinny. Try this sea bass, or wait a few weeks and the flounder will be fat and good again,' he said. He never, ever lets his father serve me now.

On this particular morning M. Onfroy had whole 'lieu jaune', pollack, whose meat is white, mild and softly flaky, and next to it a loin of beautiful, blood-red tuna. At one end of the counter, mussels and cockles were piled high, and at the other he had finnan haddie, soft, silvery whiting, conger eel and tiny little white fish called simply '*frit-ure*', which are fried in hot oil and eaten like French fries. I allowed myself to be seduced by the cockles, which I would steam with shallots and parsley then serve showered with pepper. The thought of their sweet, tender little orange-tipped meats made my mouth water. M. Onfroy scooped two litres into a plastic sack, I paid him, settled them carefully on the rack under the pushchair and moved along.

My next stop was the handsome apple and pear man, Vincent. He's been at the market for about three years now, and when he first started coming he caused a stir that had nothing to do with the quality of his fruit. A queue with a decidedly female cast immediately formed in front of his neatly stacked crates. There is no doubt he is awfully nice to look at, with his permanently tanned, peachy skin, solid dark eyebrows above large, appraising eyes, burnished blond hair and slow smile. While I stand waiting to be served I become mesmerized watching his hands; his fingers are long, spidery and surprisingly unblemished and move as though performing a ballet. He lifts each piece of fruit from its crate with a caress, then cradles it while he brings it down to the scales.

I queue at Vincent's for no other reason than that I am crazy for his pears, from the bulbous Passe-Crassagne, which have slightly grainy flesh and a flavour like heaven, to the slender Comice, which are smooth textured and intensely floral and sweet. Both explode with juice at first bite, and I consider it a privilege to eat them. I buy kilos each week to eat fresh and to use in my ever-increasing repertoire of pear desserts, which includes a lusciously simple pear and cream tart that one of Vincent's customers told me how to make. Vincent's apples are fantastic, too, especially the tart and vivid yellow and red Cox's

Orange Pippins and the fat, rough-skinned and sweeter Boscop which, when combined, make the most flavourful compotes, tarts and cakes.

Recently, Vincent took time away from the market to be married, and he returned proudly showing off a glistening gold band on his finger. I'm sure he broke a few hearts, but it hasn't seemed to hurt his business.

Since Fiona was asleep in her pushchair I left her near Vincent and stepped next to the egg and poultry lady, Madame Breemeersch. She sells raw milk, eggs, butter, cream and poultry from a large, refrigerated truck, and seems sweet and kind. She used to set up a flimsy stand and awning each week and stand there bravely, in all weather, to sell her wares. The first week she arrived with her new truck she was apologetic about her comfort as we all, from clients to fellow merchants, oohed and aahed. She admitted to me, however, what a luxury it was, and no one, in my opinion, deserves it more. She cocked her head over at Fiona and smiled, then handed me two plastic bottles full of raw milk without me even asking, since I always buy the same amount. Occasionally I buy chicken from her and I don't need to ask if it is free range. The tendons that hold its joints together are tough as steel from all the running it has done, making it perfect for coq au vin.

I turn to the farmer across from Madame Breemeersch. Patrick Bisson is a lanky man in his mid-forties who grows a basic array of very tasty vegetables in large quantities. His frizzy hair sticks out on either side of his head, his attractive grin is lopsided and he moves awkwardly, like an adolescent who isn't used to the length of his limbs, ranging back and forth behind mounds of vibrant spinach, big bunches of leeks and beautiful Brussels sprouts. He also has long, thin dandelion greens, which were once a fall and spring green but this year have made intermittent appearances all winter. I buy a bit of everything for the rest of the week, to complement the vegetables I've already bought from Baptiste, intending to use the dandelions first, in a warm salad with bacon and a poached egg.

Even if I needed anything more I couldn't fit it in the pushchair, nor in the basket over my shoulder, so I slowly walk back through the market and down the main street of town towards home. What a luxury to stroll so insouciantly with no regard for time. Fiona might get hungry but, since I'm her food source, this poses no problem.

Nursing in France has been interesting. I nursed Joe for eleven months in the United States, with no comment from outsiders (except that I was accused of feeding him too much, since he was a pudgy baby: a comment I never understood). I planned to nurse Fiona for at least that long, too. Once past the first week of adjustment, nothing is easier or more practical.

I noticed in the clinic where Fiona was born that few of the other new mothers there nursed their babies. Most of my French friends hadn't nursed theirs either, and their comments were always the same. 'I had no milk,' they would say, blaming it on stress and fatigue. I was puzzled by this universal drought. It wasn't until I spoke to the husband of a woman who had just had a baby that the light dawned.

'Oh no, my wife doesn't nurse the baby. She wouldn't think of it. She doesn't want her body to sag,' he said. 'French women think nursing ruins their bodies.'

It is no secret that French women participate in the cult of gorgeousness. Each has a considered style no matter what her station, and each has her particular fetish. It might be impeccably coiffed hair that changes shades with the seasons (this winter, the number of bright orangey-red

133

heads that bob by my window is unbelievable, while last winter hair was maroon and very spiky), or supple, hairless skin, perfectly applied make-up, or just the right accessories. Fetishes aside, all French women share a studied manner of dressing. Even our cleaning lady arrives at the door dressed as though she were going out to dinner. It follows from this that if there is an ingrained belief among French women that nursing ruins the body, then obviously it isn't a high priority.

As Fiona approached two months and work deadlines niggled, I knew I needed to find someone to care for her. I began by calling the Service Petite Enfance in Louviers, a state-administered office that offers an array of day-care services. There is the crèche, where babies as young as Fiona spend the entire day, and the *halte-garderie* where parents can leave their children for the morning on an irregular basis. The Service Petite Enfance also manages the network of accredited day-care providers in Louviers, who are allowed by law to take up to three children at a time into their homes. I was, however, looking for something different from all of this. Michael and I wanted a *nou-nou*, or babysitter, to come to the house to take care of Fiona.

'Oh, Madame Loomis,' said the woman who runs the Service Petite Enfance, an acquaintance. 'We will have a very hard time finding anyone to come to your house. No one wants to do that. I will try but I don't think I'll find anyone.'

I was surprised. In the US it is very common to get someone to come to the house to take care of children. I knew very few people in France with babies, but I had assumed it was the same. I asked Edith and she told me that, indeed, either mothers stayed home with their own children and took in the children of others to supplement their income, or they sent their children off to the crèche or to a *nou-nou*'s home.

Despite discouraging words, the woman at the Service Petite Enfance called the next day to say she was sending me someone. Brigitte, a gorgeous young woman about twenty-five years old with long, curly blonde hair, huge eyes, and a sweet smile arrived the following morning. 'My dream is to work with babies,' she said, and pulled out a résumé that showed she had training in infant care, as well as apprenticeships in various crèches and *garderies*. Fiona was sleeping in her basket on the floor, and Brigitte kept stealing glances at her. I told her she could go and take a closer look, and she bent right in and nuzzled Fiona's cheek with her nose. I described what I wanted and she was eager, so we agreed she would come and try it out the following Monday.

From the minute she entered our house to the minute she left, her crooning filled the air and lulled us all. She was enchanted with Fiona, changed her clothes often, rocked her, took her for walks, brought her to me when it was time for her to nurse. When Fiona was sleeping, Brigitte ironed. After the first week, we all agreed it was going to work out.

By week three Michael and I were settling back into good, productive work routines. Then the Monday of the fourth week dawned, but with no Brigitte. Tuesday was the same. Wednesday she called to say she'd found a job on the assembly line at a local factory and she wouldn't be returning. 'The job lasts a month and they are paying me twice what I make with you,' she said, and that was the last we saw of her.

I'd learned from Joe's infancy never to trust a routine: the minute you do, it changes. Michael and I heaved a joint sigh and I began looking for another solution. I turned again to the best system I know, *de bouche à l'oreille*, word of mouth. I spoke with neighbours and friends, then went around the back of our house to the parish's administrative office to ask the director if she knew of anyone. She didn't off-hand, but said she would ask around.

The next morning she was at the door, early. 'I think I know someone,' she said, and gave me a name and phone number, with a little background. 'You try her,' she said. 'If she is available you'll find no one better.' I called the number immediately. The woman who answered sounded sweet and amenable, so I bundled Fiona up and went to see her. She had told me she was recuperating from a fall and, indeed, when I walked into her small, tidy house she was sitting on the couch with her foot up on a stool. Dark haired with gorgeous ivory skin, plump and cheerful looking, she welcomed me with a lilting '*Bonjour!*' We introduced ourselves. Her name was Dora, she had three children of her own and she needed a job. I unwrapped Fiona. Dora's eyes lit up and cooing issued from her mouth. It was more lyrical than Brigitte's crooning; more communicative. How do these French women learn to coo and croon, I wondered? It must be like eating baguette and cheese: it just comes naturally.

We talked, and this time I was enchanted. Dora was smart and lively, and she knew enough English from years as a secretary to feel comfortable around it. She'd run a crèche in her home for years when her first two children were small, and I could tell she didn't just like children, she loved them. She was perfectly agreeable to the hours I wanted her to work, and I was amenable to her leaving to pick her youngest daughter up from school for lunch and returning to us in the afternoon. She was very honest with me about needing to look for permanent work at some point, but she felt she could guarantee me a year if it worked out. We agreed she would start in three weeks, and I left with my spirits high.

Three weeks later, Dora limped into our lives and into Fiona's heart. Cooing was only the half of it. Dora enveloped Fiona, holding her, talking with her, singing softly to her, giggling and playing with her. A gentle, spirited soul, Dora enhanced all of our lives with her humour and outlook. I asked her whether she'd thought it odd that I wanted her to come to our house to care for Fiona. 'No, I think it's good, I think more people should do it this way,' she said. 'But the state won't support this kind of care, which makes it expensive, so no one will do it. Everyone wants state-supported child-care.' It was true that we were working outside the boundaries of what the Service Petite Enfance offered, though we had their sanction.

As we got to know Dora she told us her story, which was actually very sad. She was in the process of divorcing her husband of twenty-five years because he'd succumbed to his alcohol addiction, despite her love for him and her Catholicism. She was obviously sad about it, but she didn't bring her sadness to us. In fact, from watching her with Fiona, I would never have guessed that her life was anything but rosy.

Dora loved to laugh and giggle, gossip and chat. Our agreement was that when Fiona was sleeping she would do light housework and ironing, but Dora loved to be social, and more often than not she'd come into my office to see what I was up to, or go around back to the parish house and find friends there to talk with.

Dora's financial situation became increasingly perilous as her divorce dragged on. I increased her hours as much as I could, occasionally hired her eighteen-year-old daughter, and often sent recipe-testing leftovers home with her.

I told her I wanted comments, and she would report back the next day on how she and the children had enjoyed a veal stew, a bean salad or a pear tart.

Dora was supposed to be job-hunting but she had little interest in looking. She loved working for us, and why wouldn't she? She would arrive at 8.45 in the morning, when Fiona was usually sleeping, and settle in at the dining-room table like a chicken settles itself on her eggs, with a ruffle of feathers and a little shivery shake. Somehow we'd got into a ritual of serving her coffee as though she were a queen; she liked it so much, we just kept doing it. After all, there was precious little luxury in her life, so why not pamper her a bit?

If Fiona was awake, Dora would take her immediately and hold her on her lap while she sipped. If she was sleeping, Dora would linger as long as she could at the table before ironing. If anyone was within earshot she would begin talking to them, and could easily while away the morning without lifting a finger. Apart from her allergy to helping out, we loved having Dora in our lives, but she wasn't earning enough money with us. She finally realized it when the bills began piling up and she had to borrow money from her parents to pay them. She stepped up her job-hunting, and when she came one day to announce she'd found something, I cried.

I was mulling over ideas for a replacement when Michael came home from picking up Joe at school. 'Brigitte wants to come take care of Fiona,' he said.

'Brigitte? Why would she want to do that?' I asked, surprised. Brigitte was the mother of one of Joe's classmates, and we'd known her for years. She, her husband Paul and their son Jean lived on a farm about ten miles from Louviers, and they used to invite Joe up there when the two boys were younger. They were simple, generous people and we knew that Brigitte was an anxious, careful, almost smothering mother to Jean.

Brigitte had some personality quirks, most noticeable among them a very loud voice. She had the habit of not looking people in the eye when she spoke to them, and an antiquated manner of addressing people. She referred to her husband as 'Brionne', his last name, and he referred to her as 'Halard', her last name. When she spoke to anyone else she addressed them in the third person, so that instead of saying '*vous*' to me, she said '*elle*', which is like saying 'thou' in English. Both very independent, Brigitte and Paul operated under standards set up in a different century, relying on no one for anything, ready to help anyone who asked.

I have always enjoyed talking with Brigitte because her opinions are frank, unadorned, usually astute and always tolerant. With her loud voice and husky frame I couldn't quite imagine her with Fiona, but I called her anyway, holding the phone away from my ear as she bellowed her responses. She sounded excited about taking care of Fiona, was perfectly willing to adapt to our schedule, and could work from the minute she dropped Jean off at school in the morning until it was time to pick him up again. That meant four days a week from 8.30 a.m. to 4 p.m., which was ideal. We agreed to give it a try.

Brigitte arrived the first morning ten minutes early with a large bag of freshly picked carrots and potatoes from her garden. She plunked them on the kitchen counter, removed her heavy coat and her shoes, and proceeded to pad through our house and our lives with a storm of warm, generous energy.

Her loud voice took getting used to; it scared Fiona at first, as Brigitte would bellow, '*Oh, mon petit coeur*', 'Oh, my little heart', or '*Tu es la plus belle, mon coeur*', 'You are the most beautiful, my heart.' She would hunker right down on the floor with Fiona and sing nursery rhymes, miming the words with her fingers, crawl along with her, take her on piggyback rides through the downstairs, explain every little tiny thing to her in great detail. While Dora had crooned, Brigitte talked, constantly. She modulated her voice so as not to blow out Fiona's eardrums. Once Fiona had got used to her, she adored her, and their giggles would echo through the house. I was amazed. I'd had no idea that inside this brusque country woman was a gentle heart of gold, and a well of patience.

Brigitte, who was my age, remembered a surprising amount of English from her high-school days. She would repeat words and attempt to read books to Fiona, torturing the language to our ears. Fiona loved it: to her it was happy gibberish. As soon as Fiona could talk she called Brigitte '*paillette*', which means sequin, and we all took to calling her that. Brigitte was besotted with Fiona, literally inhaling the attention and the love she got from her. She carried Fiona around the house until she could walk, then she would closely follow her stumbling steps. Fiona was a '*casse-cou*', a reckless child who ran as soon as she could balance on her feet, which meant she fell often, right onto the concrete floor. Miraculously, she never hurt herself beyond a scrape or two, but Brigitte lived in a constant state of anxiety. I think if it had been up to her she would have carpeted our entire house, including the walls, to prevent Fiona from hurting herself.

Brigitte was the perfect babysitter. Exactly my age, she understood how absorbing my work was, and how important peace and quiet was to me, particularly when I was writing. I'd told her a bit about the cooking school we were planning, and she was fascinated by the idea of Americans coming to learn how to cook French food. I told her that when the classes began they would be intensely absorbing, and that I would like to call on her for more time. She was delighted, agreeing to come five days in a row from 8 a.m. to 8 p.m. if I needed her. I asked what she would do with her own son. 'Oh, he will go to my mother's house; it's not far from school. I would just need the time to go and pick him up and drop him off there. I could take Fiona with me,' she said. Brigitte, I was coming to understand, was worth more than gold.

She took Fiona for walks that lasted hours as they fed the ducks on one of Louviers' many canals, looked in shop windows along the way to examine all the tiny little things a baby notices, bought pastries at the patisserie. Brigitte's patience was endless, her capacity for love the same. From watching her we suspected she would have wished for a girl of her own, though she adored her son. But she must have felt isolated in her household, with a taciturn, brusque husband and a son who took after him. There, Brigitte was – with an endless flow of conversation and tenderness – left unshared. She unleashed it on us.

Brigitte always arrived early, kissed everyone twice on each cheek in good Norman fashion, then set down whatever her offering was that day – a half-dozen fresh eggs, more potatoes, berries and fruit in summer. Her generosity was almost embarrassing. I tried to pay for the produce, but she wouldn't hear of it.

Her coat hung up and her shoes removed, Brigitte would come into the kitchen to pursue a conversation, which usually began with her looking around and saying, '*Quest-ce qu'il travaille bien, il a les mains en or,* 'He works so well, he's got golden hands,' to Michael. To me she would say '*Qu'est-ce qu'elle fait de bon?* What are you making that's good?' She would then talk about the weather, which she consulted as soon as she got up in the morning

141

by calling the *météo*, or weather service. It was obvious she lived with a farmer, for her news was always dire. We would be ecstatic over a sunny day and she'd say: 'It won't last, they're giving us until Thursday, then it's rain.' If it was warm she'd say, 'It's going to be hot, hot, hot for days. *Quelle souffrance.*' If it was rainy she'd say it was going to be that way for the next two weeks. If it was cloudy she'd just look up, raise her shoulders and shake her head.

She was full of funny little sayings. One day she spied a plate of partially eaten cheeses on the counter. '*Ceux-la, ils ont vu la guerre,*' she said in passing. 'Those, they've seen the war.' On the subject of MacDonald's, which Jean convinced her to try, she was livid. 'The meat in those hamburgers is as thin as a cat's tongue,' she said. 'And it's disgusting. Is that really what you eat in America?' She couldn't get over it, convinced that the entire nation was feeding itself on such food. 'Suzanne,' she said, 'you know that's not good food at all. How can such a rich country eat such food?'

While Fiona slept, Brigitte didn't waste a second. She loved to polish the copper, clean the kitchen or do the windows. She was so zealous she would sometimes do housework while Fiona was awake and get so absorbed she wouldn't realize that Fiona was colouring on a wall somewhere, or trying to flush her own hair down the toilet.

Brigitte's sight was bad, which made her house-cleaning approximate, and while she ironed with the speed of light, reducing a huge pile of clean laundry to carefully folded clothes in minutes, occasionally I'd unfold whatever she'd ironed to find a network of crisp, ironed-in wrinkles on the inside. I'll never forget the day I walked downstairs from my office to make a cup of coffee and found Brigitte ironing in the entranceway while Steely Dan was belting out of the speakers. Talk about cultures colliding.

Brigitte's ninety-year-old, mostly deaf grandmother would spend two weeks a month at her house, often sleeping in a chair in the kitchen. Then the pitch of Brigitte's voice would increase. Michael would look at me and whisper, 'The grandmother is at their house.' He was always right.

'It's tiring to yell all the time,' Brigitte would say when she realized she was shouting, and she'd notch her voice down a decibel or two.

Brigitte brought presents for Fiona constantly, usually the kind of bulbous plastic toys we hated. I tried to get her to stop, but she simply didn't listen. Fiona's nascent desire to become a doctor bore fruit with a plastic trolley complete with pink plastic stethoscope, a handful of medical utensils and a miniature x-ray machine. When Fiona wanted to spend hours combing Brigitte's hair, the result was an extensive array of plastic '*coiffeur*' tools. The telephone was Fiona's first object of devotion, so Brigitte showed up one day with a hard plastic telephone complete with plastic coins and a ringing noise so loud that we removed the batteries. Eventually we confined the thing to the attic.

Brigitte really liked Joe and took great interest in his doings. She was funny about him, and children in general: at times it seemed as though she thought they were more like animals than humans, as if they would not be able to understand what she was saying. For instance, she would ask me all about Joe's grades, his habits, his friends, his problems, right in front of him, as though he wasn't there, and it could become embarrassing for me and for Joe. If she knew that we had a surprise for him or Fiona, she would invariably ask me about it right in front of them. I'll never forget the Christmas we were going to surprise Joe with an electric racing-car set. She knew all about it, just as we knew all about the metal-detector she was going to get for Jean. I was in the kitchen with Joe when Brigitte walked in, kissed us and, in the course of the conversation, asked me if I'd picked up the racing-car set yet. I could have killed her. Joe, all ears like he always is, perked right up and said, 'Race-car set, what race-car set?' It turned out that Brigitte didn't believe in surprises any more than she believed in spirits or Santa Claus. She had told Jean all about Santa Claus when he was five or so, and she already wanted to tell Fiona, but we wouldn't let her.

Only one thing about Brigitte ever caused a problem, and that was her insistence on referring to every single undesirable or forbidden item as *caca*, or poo. It came to the fore when Fiona developed an intense panic over her dirty diapers. We realized she was confused about why all that dirty stuff she and Brigitte were constantly coming across was also winding up in her diaper. We took pains to allay her fears. We also noticed that Brigitte, in her inimitable way, was urging Fiona to use the toilet, loudly and with gentle insistence. While we couldn't stop Brigitte from referring to everything and anything as *caca*, we did get her to stop pushing Fiona to go 'pee-pee' in the 'po-po'.

After a year, when Fiona was almost two, we took stock of our situation. Fiona was ready for the company of other children, and Brigitte was costing us a fortune. We decided that it would do Fiona good to be with other children at a child-care provider's house once in a while, if I could find the perfect person and situation. None of us wanted to live without Brigitte, so we decided that we would ask her to continue coming a day and a half a week. I had met an older woman at Joe's school who had already raised four big, lanky, friendly boys, and who cared for children in her home. She was outdoorsy and athletic, motherly and organized. She rode her bicycle everywhere, just like

I do. She had told me once, when Fiona was just a tiny baby, that she cared for children in her home and she'd be interested in having Fiona, so I called her to see if she had an opening. She did, and I took Fiona over for a trial hour, leaving her there while I did some grocery shopping. We never looked back. Tata, as she liked the children to call her, was wonderful. She took the three children she cared for outside every day, rain or shine, either working in the garden or taking long walks. Inside they sewed and played, listened to classical music and read books. She cooked good food for them, respected their individual schedules, embroidered towels with their names on them, and was generally like a busy, active, caring grandmother. When her sons were home they played with the children, and Fiona loved going there.

Fiona was an early talker, and the combination of spending time with Brigitte, going to a French home three days a week, and hearing English at home meant that she spoke baby 'franglais'. If her foot hurt she'd say, '*J'ai mal au foot.*' When it was time for her bath she said, '*Pas* bath.' From the start Fiona has wanted to do things herself and she would say, 'Me do eet', or '*Pas question!*' if she didn't want to do something. When she was tired she said, '*Babu dodo,*' which meant 'bottle and nap,' and she called herself 'Fofa Moomis.'

She was picking up many French mannerisms at Tata's. The minute she came home from Tata's she went to hang up her little coat and take off her little shoes. She was always organizing her belongings, picking up after herself, trying to colour within the lines. Like Joe, she even held herself in the erect French way. She was, in fact, becoming French. How odd, I thought, to have such a foreign little person in our family. She understood English perfectly – we tested her by asking her to do things – but she was growing up different from the rest of us. I wondered if she would always be more French than American? Would she always speak French more easily than English? Would she become hyper-American, like Joe had become? Would she speak English with a French accent?

After almost a year with Tata, potty-training again reared its head. Fiona was nearly *propre*, or clean, as the French put it, but she had lots of accidents. By French standards she was behind, but we didn't care, and when we had discussed it with Tata she had seemed as relaxed as we were.

One day, when I went to drop off Fiona at Tata's, she cried and clung to me, which was very odd. This went on in varying degrees for a month. When we asked Tata about it she couldn't figure out what had happened, and it obviously made her very sad. We asked Fiona what was the matter, and she didn't say anything, so we assumed it was a phase, since Tata assured us that once the crying fit was over, the day went fine. Summer was upon us, we made plans with Tata to leave Fiona with her again from September onwards, and we took our summer holiday.

Brigitte made us understand what had happened. I had told her about Fiona's reaction to being dropped off at Tata's. Brigitte took it upon herself to get to the bottom of it, and she point-blank asked Fiona why she didn't like Tata any more, tact not being one of her strong points. Apparently Fiona told her that Tata had given her a spanking because she wet her pants. This came as a real shock to us, but it made sense. Tata may have spanked Fiona, though if she did I doubt it was hard. But we don't spank, so it must have been a shock. Tata had never volunteered any information about a spanking, which she should have, and she had seemed reluctant on some level to take Fiona back in the fall, so we decided not to continue that relationship.

146

I found another very lovely woman to take Fiona for the fall, and we decided that we would put her in school in January, just before her third birthday. Fiona was mature for her age, she wasn't shy and she loved being around children. *La Maternelle*, French nursery school, and the part of Joe's schooling we'd loved the best, seemed a very good solution for her.

We were excited for Fiona because we were sure she would thrive in the balance of play and learning that makes up the *maternelle*. Her teacher would be a gentle soul who had taught Joe, a young woman who loved children, adored music, had a beautiful way about her and had told us often how excited she would be to get to know Fiona.

The one thing we didn't like was that she had thirty toddlers in her class, and just one helper. I asked the teacher about this and she admitted she would have been much happier with just twenty or twenty-five toddlers. 'But it all works out, and I manage to have time for the children, though not for each child every day,' she said. I think that, had we been able to find a smaller class in another school, I would have preferred it, but when we weighed everything it looked like the best option available.

Some days Fiona came home from school singing little songs or reciting poetry. Many days she came home, put her fingers to her lips, and 'Shhhd' us all, or said vehemently, '*Chacun son tour!*' 'Wait your turn!' We realized that school was, in many ways, simply crowd control.

By this time we had a young female au pair, who had come to live with us and help with the children. Her name was Brinn, she was from Olympia, Washington, and she'd contacted us because she'd read an article about us in the *Seattle Times* newspaper. She was so delicious with Fiona that we reduced Fiona's days at school in favour of her staying home with Brinn.

Brinn wasn't our first au pair. We've had a series of young American women live with us since we've been in France. They have all had their good points, but we have come to the conclusion that young American women are imbued with a sense of entitlement that I refer to as the 'I don't do windows' phenomenon. No matter how clear I think I've been, when they arrive they try to organize life on their terms.

We had just finished with six months of a young woman who was darling, sparkly and cheerful. Her very presence attracted the male of the species; I'd had no idea there were so many handsome young men who lived in our town until she arrived. She'd said she wanted to come to help with the children and work on her own projects, but she was really after a French boyfriend, and her naivety got her into scrapes she should have been able to avoid. Michael sat her down and gave her a fatherly talk, and after that all we could do was to cross our fingers and hope she wouldn't go home pregnant. Joe had his opinion, too. 'American girls are so boring,' he said, 'all they think about is boys.' We certainly didn't want another case like this on our hands, and when Brinn contacted me, I read her letter with a slightly jaundiced spirit.

But she sounded so interesting. She was a Quaker and a home-schooler, and her mother had always had foster children in their home, so Brinn was used to taking care of children. And we really did need help. She and I wrote back and forth for six months and I spelled out exactly what we expected, what life here was like, what we all were about. Each time she expressed what she hoped to do, I put it in a realistic context. I could see from my responses to her that I'd learned a great deal!

We were to be in the Pacific Northwest for a couple of weeks during the summer and we arranged to meet with

Brinn, who turned out to be a willowy, six-foot-tall beauty with a gorgeous smile and warm personality. She seemed just lovely, and when we dropped her off to catch her bus home, Joe turned to me and said, 'Mom it's OK, she can come live with us,' as if he was the decision-maker. Michael and I felt the same way, and four months later I picked her up at Charles de Gaulle airport. Brinn has proved herself a very willing worker, someone who actually does more than is asked of her. She pitches right in during the cooking classes, serving at the table, washing dishes, ironing tea towels and aprons. We include her whenever possible, too, because we consider it all part of her learning experience. Her mood is steady, she laughs and gets silly with us, and is very dedicated to keeping up her end of the bargain. Part of her goal while with us is to learn to speak French – not as easy as it sounds because we speak English at home. So once a week she goes to stay with acquaintances of ours who have two rambunctious boys, and there she gets a formal French lesson from their grandmother and an inside feel for the French culture. Brinn's father is a jazz pianist, and from him she inherited a deep and abiding knowledge and love of music. As luck would have it, she's become friends with Baptiste the musical farmer, and his circle of friends has adopted her.

Fiona now spends a lot of time with Brinn, and it works out beautifully. Brigitte is still with us, too, though on a very occasional basis. She takes care of another little girl who is friends with Fiona, so Brigitte takes them both out to play at the public garden at least once a week. Fiona's love for Brigitte hasn't dimmed, nor has Brigitte's for Fiona. She still always talks about her as though she isn't there. 'How beautiful she is,' Brigitte will say. She has a habit of comparing Fiona with other children, and she will point out to the other little girl how Fiona never cries, something that makes me cringe, since Fiona cries as much as any little girl.

Brigitte also helps us during the cooking classes, coming in three days a week to do dishes, which she loves. She eavesdrops on the classes, observes the students and revels in the smells and the conversation, though she can't really understand it. She also has a calming effect on Fiona during those weeks, which aren't always so easy on a three-and-a-half-year-old girl, au pair or no au pair. Fiona is fundamentally social, and she is very curious about all the 'peoples' who come, but she misses me and wonders at times why I'm so busy that I don't have time to play. Michael is busy too, teaching a bread class, being the sommelier, and generally adding his welcome presence, though he's more available to Fiona than I am. When Brigitte is there it doesn't matter whether or not either one of us is available, though, for she's got her *paillette*, and that's all that matters.

A year ago I wondered if Fiona would always be a little French girl, whether her English would have a French accent, whether she would identify as strongly with the US as Joe has done. Fiona now speaks fluent English and switches into French when she needs to. She doesn't hang up her coat every time she takes it off, nor take off her shoes the minute she walks in the door. Her drawings have taken on a vivid, free-form quality. She mostly speaks English, though she says things like 'le book' and 'le star'. It will all sort itself out as she grows up, and she will surely grow up with a personality in which there is a blend of the two cultures.

This year Fiona goes to a different school, about a ten-minute walk from our house. It is very small – just two classes of mixed ages, from two-and-a-half to five, and it has an excellent reputation. The classes are much smaller than at the other school, though they still seem big. Her teacher is also the director of the school, a woman dedicated to the theory of hearkening to the needs of children, a relatively unusual concept in France. The year is young and we're holding our judgement about it – Fiona hasn't yet opened up, so that her teacher tends to view her as a baby whose French is limited. 'If they only knew,' I think. This is the little girl who has a screaming fit and stops right in the middle and says, 'No talking while I'm screaming.' Or picks up a minuscule grape and says, 'I can't eat this because it isn't ripe.' Or asks me before she meets anyone new, 'Do they speak French or English?' Or says, 'You have to be really careful with me because I'm dangerous.'

If I were to go to Fiona's teacher and say that I think Fiona would be better with older children, that she really can be challenged more, that she's well beyond the tiny children in her class, I think the teacher might listen politely then, the minute my back was turned, pull her bottom eyelid down with her index finger in that most typical of French expressions that means, 'My eye.' So I haven't said much. All I can think is that when Fiona decides she's ready to show her true colours, it will be something to see, for she is startlingly adult in her reasoning, quick to learn and determined to do things correctly. And she understands every word of French spoken to her. For now, our sweet little daughter is just biding her time, sizing up the situation.

Meanwhile, we are happy with the school. Its size makes it warm and cosy, the lunch room looks like a big family dining room, and the playground has trees and even some grass for the children to play on. The two teachers seem very good, and the helpers there are all adult women with obvious warmth and experience. I had to go through some machinations to get Fiona into the school, as it isn't in our 'official' neighbourhood, but now she is there for at least two years. After that the school is scheduled to close, so we will see what transpires.

Our life, for the moment, has taken on a lovely, comfortable equilibrium. Experience tells me not to relax too much, but just enough to look around and think how lucky we all are!

OXTAILS WITH CINNAMON
Queue de Boeuf à la Cannelle

———————— ʊ ————————

An unusually delicious dish! A small note oxtail can render a great deal of fat. The fat is useful because it imparts a great deal of flavour to the finished dish, but you won't want to eat it all. To avoid it, simply follow the recipe and remove the meat with a slotted spoon.

1 tbs olive oil
4½ lb (2.250kg) oxtail, cut in 3-inch (1.25cm) chunks
Sea salt and freshly ground black pepper
3 medium (5 oz;150g) onions, cut in eighths
6 cups (1.5 litres) hearty red wine such as a Gaillac or a
Côtes du Rhône
3 sticks cinnamon
2 dried, imported bay leaves
10 high-quality peppercorns, either Tellicherry
or Vietnamese

For the garnish:
3 medium bell peppers
3 lb starchy potatoes such as Mona Lisa or russet
4 tbs (2 oz; 60g) unsalted butter
¼ to ½ cup (125ml–250ml) whole milk
Sea salt and freshly ground black pepper

1. Heat the oil in a large, heavy saucepan over medium heat and brown the oxtails on all sides over medium-high heat, which will take about 10 minutes. Season the meat lightly with salt and pepper, then add the onions

153

and cook them with the oxtails just until they begin to brown on all sides, about 4 minutes. Pour over the red wine and add the cinnamon sticks, bay leaves and the peppercorns, submerging them in the wine. Bring to a boil, covered. Reduce the heat to medium low, so the wine is simmering, and cook partially covered until the oxtails are tender and the meat is falling from the bone, about 3½ hours. Check the oxtails from time to time and stir them, so they don't stick. If the wine and cooking juices are evaporating too quickly and leaving the oxtails dry, reduce the heat further and completely cover the pan.

2. While the oxtails are cooking, roast the peppers. When they are cool enough to handle, remove the skins and seeds (don't rinse them – you want to retain all their sweet flavour) and cut them into ¼-inch thick lengthwise slices. Reserve.

3. Bring 3 cups of water to a boil in the bottom of a steamer, and steam the potatoes until they are tender through, about 20 minutes. Transfer the potatoes to a bowl and, using a whisk, a fork, or a ricer, mash the potatoes. Whisk in the butter and the milk, season to taste with salt and pepper, and keep warm.

4. When the oxtails are cooked and the meat is falling from the bone, remove them from the heat. When they are cool enough to handle (but still hot), remove the meat from bones, discarding the bones. Return the meat to the pan, heat it over medium heat just until the liquid begins to boil and the meat is hot through. Season to taste.

5. To serve the dish, evenly divide the potatoes among six warmed dinner plates, spreading it out in a thick, flat round. Top with equal amounts of pepper strips, then top with equal amounts of meat, removing the meat

from the pan with a slotted spoon so as not to bring the fat with it. Garnish with the parsley leaves and serve immediately.

6 servings.

GINGER MADELEINES
Madeleines au Gingembre

───────────── ✺ ─────────────

Fresh ginger lightly permeates these elegant little cakes, while tiny pieces of candied ginger sprinkled throughout burst with flavour. I like to serve these either with coffee, as an after-school snack or as a dessert – try them alongside rhubarb in red wine.

12 tbs (6 oz; 185g) unsalted butter
One 'coin' of ginger, grated (to give 1 teaspoon finely grated)
1¾ cup (230g) all-purpose flour
Pinch fine sea salt
1 scant oz (20g) candied ginger, minced
(to give 2 tbs minced)
4 large eggs
1 cup (200g) vanilla sugar
Butter for buttering the madeleine tins

1. Melt the butter with the fresh, grated ginger over low heat. Remove from the heat and cool to room temperature.
2. Sift together the flour and the salt. Add the dice of ginger and gently rub it into the flour so that each piece of ginger is coated with flour, to keep it separate.
3. Place the eggs and the sugar in a large bowl or the bowl

155

of an electric mixer and whisk until very thick and pale yellow. Fold in the flour and the candied ginger, then the melted butter with the fresh ginger so all the ingredients are thoroughly incorporated.

4. Butter 2 madeleine pans.
5. Spoon in a generous tablespoon of batter into each mould, so it is filled about ¾ full. Refrigerate the filled madeleine pans and the remaining batter for at least 30 minutes.
6. Heat the oven to 425°F (220°C).
7. Bake the madeleines just until they are firm and puffed, 7 to 8 minutes. Turn them immediately from the moulds, wipe out the moulds, let cool, brush the moulds with butter and fill them with the remaining batter. It isn't necessary to refrigerate the batter in the pans at this point, as it is already chilled. The madeleines are best when eaten slightly warm or at room temperature the same day they are made. The batter will keep well, refrigerated in an airtight container, for up to 3 days.

About 36 madeleines

Notes: A 'coin' sized piece of ginger means a slice about the size and thickness of a 1 euro piece. For successful madeleines, those that expand during baking and make a small bulb on top, the batter AND the pan must be cold. My solution is to fill the madeleine tins with batter and refrigerate for 30 minutes to 1 hour before baking.

ALLSPICE ICE CREAM
Glace aux Épices de Jamaique

We all love ice cream and I make it often, flavouring it with whatever spice happens to be uppermost in my repertoire at the moment. This goes particularly well with a chocolate tart, but it is also delicious all on its own!

4 cups (1 litre) semi-skimmed milk
1 tbs allspice berries
10 large egg yolks
1½ cup (300g) vanilla sugar
1 small pinch fine salt

1. Scald the milk with the allspice berries in a large, heavy-bottomed saucepan over medium heat. Remove from the heat and infuse for 20 minutes.
2. In a large bowl, whisk together the egg yolks with the sugar and the salt until they are pale yellow and light. Slowly whisk in the warm infused milk with the allspice berries, then return the mixture to the pan that held the milk and allspice berries.
3. Prepare a bowl with a sieve resting in it.
4. Cook the custard mixture over medium heat, stirring constantly in a figure-eight motion, until it is thickened and coats the back of the spoon, and a line run through the custard on the back of the spoon stays clear. Strain the custard mixture into the waiting bowl.
5. Let the custard cool to room temperature, then re-frigerate it until it is chilled through. Make the ice cream according to the manufacturer's instructions.

Makes 1 litre (1 quart) ice cream

The Place for a Party

Our house attracts parties, and when I step outside our life and look back into it, I understand why. With our American ways and our ancient house that's always changing, going from one fantastical evolution to another, we have become a bit of a local attraction. In addition we have the illuminated Gothic church in the background, the larger-than-life and beautifully designed kitchen, the unusual concrete floors. Decorating inside and out with hundreds of candles helps, and the clincher may well be the contents of our wine cellar.

Because we're not from Normandy where everyone drinks Bordeaux and forgets there is any other wine but Bordeaux, we have no limits on what we'll try, and what we are open to enjoying. I am always looking for wines to serve during cooking classes, and a friend of ours, Hervé Lestage, is a *caviste*, cellarman, who constantly introduces us to the kinds of wines we adore too – edgy, vibrant, quirky, rich; often from the southwest or the Côtes du Rhône – which means our *cave* is filled with a glorious and eclectic selection that I take enormous enjoyment in sharing with our French friends.

The fact that we celebrate many *fêtes* at our house doesn't mean our friends don't have beautiful, interesting houses, too. Take Edith's: she and Bernard bought their *maison bourgeoise*, family house, twenty years ago, and have worked on it slowly and insistently to modernize it and make it comfortable. Its crowning glory, aside from a majestic staircase wide enough to drive a car up, is a veranda designed by Edith's architect brother, Christian. It extends off from the kitchen and has two glass walls, one with gorgeous, antique stained-glass bay windows that Edith found at a flea market in Paris.

During the summer the veranda is her studio, her easel taking prime place among the baroque pots of flowers, the old blond oak buffet filled with dishes and silver, a piano that no one plays but which makes for a nice prop. I love to come upon her painting there. She wears a sun visor to keep the glare out of her eyes and hold back her voluminous burgundy-coloured hair and a long antique white nightshirt, splotched with paint, to protect her clothes. Her round, wire-rimmed glasses often have tiny paint spots on them, and she sometimes holds her paintbrush in her teeth as she surveys her work. When she's painting, she does so with swift, sure strokes, recreating warm, light-infused still-lifes and evocative portraits on her canvases.

The veranda smells strongly and pleasantly of her oil paints, which is fine for a painting studio, but not the best backdrop to a dining room, yet it has been the scene of many big and pleasant dinner parties associated with Bernard's roles in politics and Edith's annual painting exhibitions. It is perfect for those kinds of get-togethers, and Bernard and Edith are excellent hosts. Bernard is particularly proud of his wine cellar, and if he can't be there to choose the wine himself, he calls Edith to ensure she brings up the bottles he has chosen for the evening from their *cave*, so that the reds can be opened well before serving. Edith's active imagination extends to the kitchen, and her meals are colourful and vibrant. She gets into phases, so that for a certain period she'll repeatedly make moussaka, which she flavours with curry, or lamb shoulder seasoned with fresh garden herbs then cooked in the embers, Croatian-style. She always serves a huge green salad and several perfectly aged cheeses, and her desserts are simple and fun. I love it when she emerges from the kitchen with hot madeleines still in their moulds, or choc-olate-chip cookies that she's just pulled from the oven. Lately, her dessert of choice has been tender and juicy apple crumble.

Christian and his wife, Nadine, have a great house, too: a long old farmhouse with low ceilings and beamed walls that they renovated when their children were small. Like them, it is warm, cosy, and just slightly eccentric. For years Christian let his wild, grey hair grow so that it came to the middle of his back. He wore it in a ponytail and atop it wore a handsome leather hat, so that when he entered a room or strode down the street he made a very imposing figure. He favours corduroy trousers, collarless linen shirts and brocade vests, while Nadine lets her blithe spirit and artistic tendencies dictate flowing skirts, designer shoes that make her slightly taller than her five feet four inches, and low-cut, body-hugging tops. She wears her brown hair shaggily cut, and it offsets her delicate features and spark-ling eyes, which give her face an eternal, mirthful look. Together, they make a stylishly bohemian pair.

Nadine is enamoured of the British style, a taste she picked up when she and Christian lived in London at the beginning of their marriage, and she keeps the interior dark and cosy, has many precious objects on every surface. Her own charmingly naive paintings cover the walls, while enough chandeliers hang from the ceiling to make one think of a lamp shop. Her design sense harks back to Algeria, where they lived for many years when their boys were small, and there are North African accents around the house in the form of fabrics, rugs and other *objets d'art*. She is an excellent cook and her food leans toward the North African, too, with lots of herbs and spices, preserved lemons, which Christian makes, couscous and nut-filled desserts. Christian and Nadine do not do mid-size parties, however. When they entertain it is either an intimate dinner for six or a celebration for 200 – nothing in between.

Chantal and Michel recently bought an old farmhouse with a big and well-maintained garden, and proceeded to turn it from something simple to something elegant by painting the low-ceilinged rooms deep burgundy, the hall-way pea-green, the kitchen a smooth and buttery yellow. Their furnishings are like ours or Edith's: finds picked up from *brocantes*, second-hand markets,which Michel has carefully reupholstered or rewired, much as Michael does. Chantal and Michel are wonderful but shy hosts who live according to the impossibly rigorous schedule of a baker, so they keep their entertaining to a minimum. I love it when they do entertain, for they are extremely thoughtful hosts. Michel, who is small and wiry with a very narrow face and curly brown hair, is softly spoken and accommodating and completely focused on making sure his guests are comfortable.

Michel was diagnosed several years ago with a serious illness that is under control, but which means that he and Chantal eat only organic food and have eliminated all red meat from their diet. Once Chantal experimented with an aubergine casserole recipe that she found in a health magazine and served to us. We all tried to eat it, but it was pure and simply awful. Finally Chantal burst into laughter and said, 'Let's just throw this thing away, it's inedible.' The story has gone into the annals of our collective history, to be pulled out at appropriate moments when we laugh ourselves sick at the memory. That meal, and every other one at their house, was made wonderful by one of Michel's sumptuous desserts. He tailors each to either the occasion or the person being honoured, and he outdoes himself each time. He once made a multi-layered mango confection for Bernard, who loves mangoes, and for me once a dense, delicious chocolate cake with a layer of crisp praline running through it.'I know you like your cakes chocolate, and with lots of texture,' he said when I thanked him, 'so I specially ordered Cuban chocolate and adjusted the cake recipe so it would be the right density, just for you.' I almost cried at his thoughtfulness.

Chantal is very flirty and seductive and wears body-hugging designer clothing that she picks up for a song during the twice-yearly sales that occur, so that she always looks as if she has just stepped off the cover of a magazine. Her hair varies in colour from orange to burgundy and is cut just below the ears, and she wears small, expensive earrings and bracelets. She is the style and fitness guru of the group, and has no compunction about advising her female friends to take care of their bodies, their skin, their hair. 'You need to do it for yourself, and you need to do it for them,' she'll say, referring to our husbands. It's such an un-American, anti-liberated-female way of thinking, and I love it. Chantal is a reliable, wonderful friend, and very private. She never complains about anything, and she refuses to reveal her age. Edith and I think it hovers around ours.

Anne-Marie and Patrick are the only friends we have who opted for the contemporary rather than the old and to-be-renovated. They are the most conventional members of our group of friends, too. Patrick earns his living as a general practitioner, but his passion is sculling and sailing, and he looks the part. He walks with the swagger of an athlete, has weathered skin and a froth of frizzy hair that is gradually departing from his head, leaving a freckled pate. Sun and frequent laughter have crinkled his eyes. Patrick is very reserved and it took years for him to relax around us because, I think, we are so different from his other friends. But nowadays, finally, he does. Anne-Marie, on the other hand, has always been warm, funny, and the life of the party, though she can be reserved around people she doesn't know. Gorgeous, with sparkling, khaki-coloured eyes and a heart-shaped face, she has a shock of pure white, very wavy hair that probably drives her crazy but makes her striking. She tends to plumpness, which suits her perfectly, and she dresses in long skirts and loose tops and jackets. She is a trained dietician, but rather than opt for paid employment she volunteers at her parish church, devoting endless hours to decorating, organizing ceremonies, helping youngsters learn to read, and any other task that comes her way. She is our spiritual adviser and the shoulder everyone cries on, as well as the one who remembers jokes, can imitate just about any French comedian, and keeps us in stitches as evenings wear on.

Anne-Marie and Patrick's modern house has a prow of tall, glass windows that makes their two-storey living room a welcome pool of light, even in winter. My favourite dinners at their house are the ones that celebrate the beginning and the end of the oyster season, because they bring the oysters right from the dock of Patrick's native village of La Trinité in Brittany, and they are exquisitely crisp, tasty and bounteous.

Other friends have other interesting houses but, despite the possibilities, ours has become the unofficial gathering spot, whether it be for going-away parties, anniversaries or, lately, fiftieth birthday parties. It's easy for me, too, as I'm well-equipped to set a table for a large group, since I have collected chairs, tablecloths, napkins and sets of silverware over the years, with the lunches and the cooking school in mind. Actually, we debuted with one of Edith's birthdays, her forty-fifth, I think. The dining room still had its gravel floor then, its non-working fireplace and its many large chinks in the walls. I put candles in wall sconces, and set them on every available surface, hoping their collective warmth would take the chill off the room. I knew once everyone was assembled that it would be warm enough, but for the first hour or so I wasn't sure. Michael used the event as impetus to install more electricity in the room, so he spent most of his preparation time fiddling with tiny little wires.

The fireplace was a mess, so he cleaned it up as I began to make pasta, which I was perfecting for the *Italian Farmhouse Cookbook*. It was a grey and steely November and I had decided to make a Tuscan dish with showers of pine nuts and lemon zest, flat-leaf parsley and olive oil, because I wanted sunshine on our plates. I would follow it with roasted swordfish topped with a spicy tomato sauce, and would serve a Chianti from a wonderful winery north of Florence called Selvapianna. Edith tasted my birthday cake one year, which is always a multi-tiered chocolate cake with rich chocolate frosting, and she begged me to make her one – so I did.

When I returned to the dining room to light candles I saw that Michael had installed a drop light in the fireplace and hidden it with red and orange cellophane, so that it looked like the embers of a fire, a theatrical gesture to warmth. It was so realistic that I almost warmed my hands over it.

Everyone arrived and we congregated in the small, warm and somewhat funky kitchen for champagne, then adjourned to the dining room for dinner. There was a big heater burbling away in a corner, and the candles helped; no one complained and it seemed positively cosy to me and Michael. The plates were warmed and the food was blisteringly hot, the champagne had sent its own warmth coursing through us all, and the Chianti would help, too. I went to get the swordfish and returned to find Chantal and Anne-Marie standing deep in conversation in front of the fireplace, 'warming' their hands. I didn't say anything, just served the swordfish. After dinner we pushed the table aside so we could dance, and throughout the evening others sidled up to the 'fire'. Michael and I never said a word, to each other or to our guests, until everyone was gone. 'Did you see how people gravitated towards the fire?' Michael asked me, almost incredulous. I admitted that I had almost done the same thing before everyone arrived. 'I know, I wanted to go over there, too!' he said.

It wasn't that the room was so cold – it had been quite comfortable. It was the fatal attraction of fire that drew people. 'Well, maybe you don't have to fix the fireplace – maybe the drop light and cellophane is enough,' I said.

The party trend continued when my brother, Jeff, and his wife, Gayle, were visiting us, which coincided with Jeff's fiftieth birthday. We couldn't let such a momentous birthday pass without something remarkable, so we reserved our friends for a party. Jeff didn't know any of them, but they didn't care.

Jeff resembles my father, Joe. Both are terminally

sociable, able to make friends in any situation, to charm others with a sideways glance, to insinuate themselves into people's hearts with very little effort. Jeff studied Spanish in high school, but, although many people claim that the training in one language leads to understanding another, he doesn't understand a thing any French person says to him. He has a finely honed sense of the absurd, however, that crosses cultural barriers.

Michael and I looked forward to Jeff and Gayle's visit with pleasure, because they are a cheerful couple. Jeff, particularly, is a walking amusement centre, a never-ending source of side-splitting observations, jokes, commentary and witticisms. His humour appeals to everyone, though I have occasionally heard my mother, in mid-chuckle, wonder if he'll ever grow up.

Juvenile it may be, but his humour has always worked for me. While growing up I thought it was normal to have an older brother who sat at the dinner table and waited until one of his younger siblings had a big mouthful of milk before pulling a face so silly it would cause them to spit out the milk while laughing. It struck me as funny but not odd when Jeff would take one remaining item of food from the serving plate, something we all loved, lick it all over, then replace it and ask if anyone wanted it. Two nights a week our family would watch television together – we all loved a show called 'Adam Adamant', and 'Top of the Pops' kept us riveted – and I learned quickly to check my shoelaces on those evenings before setting off to bed, because Jeff, who generally sprawled on the floor, loved to tie together the shoelaces of whomever was sitting in the chair beside him, causing the unsuspecting sibling to fall flat on their face when they took a step. He was clever enough not to do this every time, so we would forget and get caught unawares!

I figured it was pretty normal for a sixteen-year-old boy to turn white with fear and jump up onto his chair whenever he saw a spider, and I loved – along with my other brother and sisters – putting cherry-tomato stems on his pillow at night to scare the pants off him when he went to bed because we knew that, in the dark, they looked like spiders. Children are cruel, and we were too.

I haven't seen Jeff cause anyone to spit out their milk in forty years, but overall his humour hasn't really changed that much. I couldn't wait until he and Gayle arrived.

The apogee of their first week with us would be the party, as his birthday fell on the Saturday midway through their two-week visit. We spent the week sightseeing in the region, strolling down the boardwalk at the coastal village of Houlgate, visiting the beautiful little village of Lyons-la-Fôret, sampling beer and French fries – satisfying food for all ages – at various village cafés, and being invited over to friends' homes for drinks and meals. Even to our friends who have travelled a great deal, a visitor from America is a novelty, and by Saturday night everyone had already met Jeff and Gayle, which would make the birthday party that much more fun.

Jeff, who is passionate about barbecue and grilling, really wanted to grill dinner, and I thought that sounded like a great idea. We had just a tiny Weber grill that Michael's sister had brought from the United States, so Jeff and Michael went out to look for something a bit more capacious.

They returned hours later with a small hibachi-styled grill, the only one they could find, since it wasn't grilling season, and two huge bags of lightweight, all-wood charcoal. Jeff assured us that if he started early enough, the two grills would be just fine for grilling enough meat and vegetables for twenty people.

168

The briquets stumped him, and us. I'd never used them before, because when I grill – which is rare – I do it in the fireplace over oak embers. The large chunks of shiny, black, burnt-out wood that fell from the sacks they'd bought were beautiful, homemade looking. I could just imagine the *bûcherons*, woodcutters, who might have made them, carefully lighting piles of logs then smothering them so that they smouldered slowly until they were left with these gorgeous lightweight chunks of charcoal, then carrying them out in huge wagons, their faces smudged like miners'. We had a friend whose father had been a *bûcheron* and she had once described his odd forest society, where only the tough survived. This was a generation ago, but I assumed *bûcherons* were still at work in some forest somewhere in France. In any case, this stuff was wonderful – I couldn't believe you could just go to the store and buy it by the bagful.

Jeff was excited. He built fires, put on an apron, got out tongs and spatulas, and made sure the beer he and Michael had bought was chilling in the refrigerator. Gayle and I blanched small onions, shallots and potatoes, then slid them onto skewers with green peppers, courgettes and aubergines. I rubbed thick little hand-cut lamb chops with a blend of garlic and rosemary so they could macerate until it was time to grill them, just before we sat down. I had planned *panzanella*, a tomato and bread salad, for the first course. Once the vegetables were grilled I would marinate them in balsamic vinegar, garlic and olive oil and serve them at room temperature, and we would eat them alongside the lamb chops.

The party was planned for suppertime. Because this was France, that meant it wouldn't begin until 9.30 p.m. at the earliest, so Jeff had lots of time.

The day had begun cool and overcast but, as so often

169

happens in Normandy, had burst into hot, brilliant sun-shine at about 4 p.m., just as Jeff lit his fires. Gayle and I were cool and happy in the kitchen as we cooked – we got rhubarb tarts in the oven, then moved onto making tapenade, prunes stuffed with Roquefort and toasted and salted Spanish almonds to serve as appetizers.

I walked out behind the house at about 5.30 p.m. to see how Jeff was doing. To my surprise my unflappable brother was red-faced and flustered, a small pile of grilled vegetables on one side of the grill, a huge mound of raw vegetables on the other. 'How's it going?' I asked. 'Uh, well, this French charcoal is really, really, really . . .' he tried to shift glowing embers around in his tiny little grills. '. . . It's really, really . . . French. It takes an hour for it to burn hot enough to grill something, then in five minutes it's already too cold. How do people grill here, anyway?' he asked.

I'd once read somewhere that, at best, charcoal contains fifty-five percent of the energy of wood, and at worst about twenty percent. It looked like we'd got the latter variety. Like so many things commercial, it was pretty to look at but ridiculous to use.

I realized that if my easy-going brother was flustered by grilling and had only got this far in an hour and a half, we were going to have to rethink dinner. I didn't want him struggling out here for the next three hours, so I suggested we roast the vegetables in the oven.

'No, no, I think I've just about got it figured out,' Jeff said gamely. 'I'm going to keep at it for a while.' I left just as Michael was running to the rescue with two cold Belgian beers. 'The charcoal is lousy here,' Jeff said as he took a long swig. 'But the beer's pretty darn good.'

Several hours and beers later, all of the vegetables were grilled, and Jeff raced up to take a shower as the first guests began to arrive. It had taken him the better part of four hours. I had made an executive decision to oven-roast the chops. They wouldn't have the same smoky taste as the vegetables, but they would be tender and delicious, and so easy.

Our friends arrived and we opened a wonderful white Châteauneuf du Pape to drink with the tapenade, to which I had added fresh basil and braised tuna, and the prunes and the salted almonds. We stood at the back of the house enjoying the by-now cool evening and clear blue sky. Michael and Jeff were regaling guests with the story of the vegetable grilling, which, in the retelling, had become hilarious. One of our friends, Patrick Madroux, looked at the grills, then looked at the sack of charcoal. 'This isn't what real *manly* barbecuers use,' Jeff was saying.

'No, real barbecuers cook over fresh coals,' Patrick said bluntly. He looked around for wood, which we didn't have.

'Michael,' he barked, 'why don't you have wood? I can't believe you let your brother-in-law suffer with this charcoal.'

Michael shrugged, Jeff demanded a translation, every-one was listening. Patrick went on about wood versus char-coal, and ended by saying, 'Suzanne and Michael, any time you need some wood, you just let me know. I know exactly where to tell Michael to go to cut it, or he can come with me if he wants,' Patrick said. 'You can't expect to do good grilling without real wood.'

I've never known Patrick to do anything in the kitchen more complex than shucking oysters, which he does very well, but I wasn't surprised to hear him expound on grilling. I've noticed that French men, or the French men we know, feel very free to critique cooking, even though they may never do any themselves. Sometimes they have a point, as Patrick did here. Sometimes they are simply sounding the French call to arms, defending La Patrie, the homeland, teaching the American infidel what's what.

We moved into the front courtyard to take advantage of the last rays of sun on the church and finish up the aperitifs, then went into the house for our sit-down dinner of oh-so-carefully grilled vegetables, which were exquisite and delighted our friends, who do not ever grill vegetables. The only thing I've ever seen on a French grill has been meat – merguez, which is spicy North African sausage, huge beef chops large enough to feed six, or an entire pig – never vegetables.

The lamb chops were succulent and aromatic, and no one – not even Jeff – complained that they hadn't been grilled. Salad and cheese came next, then the rhubarb tarts. Jeff sat between two English speakers, Bernard and Nadine, and most of the table's attention was on them, for they were pealing with laughter. My sister had sent some birthday props, among them the black balloons that covered the floor, and paper spectacles with moony, half-lidded eyes on them. Everyone had a pair next to their plate and, following Jeff's lead, we put them on. It was impossible to keep a straight face and soon we were all holding our sides. Then Chantal and Michel got up and began to swing dance with their foolish glasses on. Jeff doesn't dance, claiming to have 'spinach feet', so he started doing somersaults on the rug. Pretty soon he had at least four or five others doing them, and everyone else was dancing, laughing, communicating in a language that had no relation to either French or English.

Michael got out his Cuban cigars, and so did Bernard. Edith, who cannot stand smoke of any kind, had drunk enough red wine that she decided to light up, and she smoked the biggest cigar of the collection right down to the bitter end.

The next day we did a post-mortem on the party, our own eyes at about the same half-lidded state of those on the glasses. My conclusions were that: 1. My brother is great in any language; 2. We have a fantastic group of friends; 3. It is possible to spend four hours grilling vegetables over stupid French charcoal and still be the life and soul of the party.

The next fiftieth birthday party to roll around was Bernard's. Our house was perfect for this one, since Edith wanted it to be a surprise. She invited a big group of people and we planned the menu. 'Oh, Suzanne, let's make it really easy,' she said. We decided to do a French-style pot-luck. Edith wanted oysters as a first course, so she asked Patrick to order them off the boat in La Trinité. I offered to do the main course, thinking I would do something unusual like a simple steamed fillet of fish dressed with sake, garlic chives and *fleur de sel.* Bernard travels a lot in Asia and he loves Asian food, so I would do something that would relate to his travels and be a bit of a surprise. Edith wanted a gratin, too, but I dissuaded her. Everyone in France eats gratins all the time, and since I would do an Asian main course, I thought an Asian vegetable would be good, too. I decided on wilted spinach dressed in sesame oil and rice-wine vinegar, and Edith thought it sounded perfect as long as it was simple.

We decided not to do a cheese course, because we wanted the meal to stay light. Then Edith reconsidered. After all, in France a meal without cheese isn't really a meal, so we decided that goat's cheese would be acceptable. Edith said she would bring champagne and wine from Bernard's sacred collection. Our friend Anne-Marie offered to bring her signature chocolate mousse, the one she brings to every gathering, and Michel the pâtissier would make a glistening chocolate cake flavoured with passion fruit.

I got to thinking about a performance we could do at the party, and I hit on the idea of writing a song for Bernard. Edith was enthusiastic, and called three other women friends to help out. We got together two weeks before the party, at Edith's. Bernard was in China or Turkey or somewhere – Edith couldn't quite remember – and their children were all out, so we had the house to ourselves. Edith had opened a bottle of Graves, and Chantal had brought a sweet bread that Michel had made.

We all had pencil and paper and we began our collective effort. Pretty soon I set down my pencil and picked up my wine glass. I realized, as my four French friends began singing the tune of a French song from the 1950s, that I wasn't going to be of much help. The tune was one of those atonal French melodies that meant nothing to me from a cultural standpoint, and that was almost impossible to follow. I had imagined writing a lively, silly little ditty to the music of something popular from the Beatles or the Beach Boys rather than this slow, modulated melody. In my scenario I would have whipped out the verses quickly. In the real scenario I felt lost.

My throat closed a bit and my eyes welled up as I realized my position as a foreigner with this group of close friends. I hadn't had this feeling for years, not since I rode through a French forest with French friends and realized that what was so gorgeous to them hardly seemed like a forest to me at all; I could never understand their reference to beauty and nature any more than they could understand mine.

Lost in my cultural reverie, I didn't hear Anne-Marie saying 'Suzanne, we need a word here.' I just stared for a moment, wondering if I should try and explain what was going on inside my brain. Then I looked at these people with whom I've shared friendship over the past fifteen years and thought, why bother? I looked at the lyrics, threw out some ideas and vowed I would learn this tuneless song. They were having a ball, so why couldn't I? By evening's end we had finished the song, minus a few words which Anne-Marie and I would supply, and made good headway through two bottles of wine. Our next and last meeting would be in ten days, when we would rehearse it to perfection.

I thought a lot about that evening over the next week or two. I so rarely feel cultural barriers, whether because I don't see the ones that are there or because there are so few, I don't know. But every now and then one appears to make me realize that I am, still and for ever, a visitor in this beautiful country. It is not that I feel French, for I don't. I feel like me, and me is American through and through. But just as we sometimes assume that the people we love are going to love the same things we do, it's a come-uppance, a destabilizing realization, to see how different we really are. I don't have a clue about the culture that spawned the melody we were singing – what was happening in France when it was popular, what my friends were going through, where they were living – any more than they would have a reference to 'California Girls', and the surfing mania of my youth that accompanied it. Part of the edginess of living in France, being an expatriate, are moments like that, when the wall of culture, rather than the window, emerges. I tried to explain it to Edith but all she would say is, 'Suzanne you're one of us. Who cares if you didn't know the tune?'

As for Bernard's gift, we all chipped in to buy him the world's most expensive fountain pen, shaped like a torpedo and designed by Laguiole, an artisanal knifemaker in the Auvergne region of France. It was the perfect gift for this poor farm boy turned multinational executive. I could imagine the way he would roll it around in his fingers, just the way he might have, as a little boy, rolled around a beautiful marble or other treasure that came his way.

We'd already done the morbid black decor for Jeff's birthday. Bernard's birthday called for something else. I remembered buying some colourful Tibetan prayer flags then putting them away for future use, and this was it. I strung them from the beams in the ceiling and wrapped them around Bernard's chair, then put the legend that explains their significance by his plate. The flags, it said, signify the aspiration to achieve a goal. This couldn't have fitted Bernard better, for he sets his goals high and achieves them time after time.

Bernard and Edith are the most frenetic couple I know for, in setting and achieving his goals, Bernard is constantly on the road – one week in Hong Kong, the next in China, another in Turkey, then in New Jersey. He is always skidding into a dinner party or a family affair right off the runway, dressed in one of his elegant grey or khaki silk suits, a tasteful tie chosen by Edith at his neck. Sometimes he hasn't even had time to wash his hands, but you'd never really know it, as he has an uncanny ability to 'be here now'. I've seen him at dinners among friends here, and among strangers halfway across the world, and he is always right there with the appropriate question or response, the ease it takes to be international.

Edith is a reluctant traveller; she is frenetic right here at home. A very talented painter, she is a bit tortured by her work and does her best to avoid it, finding it as hard to stay put and paint as it is for Bernard to say no to an invitation or a meeting. She is constantly on the move:

ferrying something to one of her children at school; making a weekend trip to their home in Provence, which involves eight hours in the car one way; going into Paris to visit galleries; or running off to Brittany to visit a friend there. When it comes to enjoyable ways to pass the time, Edith is a past master. Because of their schedules, Edith and Bernard rarely arrive anywhere together, which is why I was sure Bernard knew something was afoot, because Edith had made it a point to arrive with him. Not only that, but she arrived empty-handed. Usually she comes laden with hand-me-downs from her youngest son for Joe, bottles of wine, something she's returning. She also usually comes dressed a bit like her painting palate. She is built in such a way that she can wear anything and look good, but her favourite type of outfit leans towards bright and baggy silk pants, long droopy sweaters on which she's sown some beautiful braid or buttons, and clunky, open-toed shoes. Her long, thick burgundy-coloured hair is usually piled haphazardly on her head, witness to the fact that she rarely brushes it, just shoves it out of the way. She's a delightful eccentric through and through, though her look is studied and she spends oodles of money cultivating it: her baggy pants and sweaters have designer labels on them, and her shoes cost the same as a one-way ticket between Paris and New York.

Tonight was different, however. She had on a beautiful ivory silk skirt and low-necked tunic, and her favourite red Stephan Kelian sandals. Her hair was down, and she'd put on makeup. I was sure Bernard suspected something.

Our house looked normal when they arrived, I think. We'd lit the fifty candles in the dining room, but since I always have candles burning it wasn't noticeably different through the wavy panes of glass. All was calm and quiet when we greeted them at 9 p.m. Our children were in bed and delicious aromas were coming from the kitchen. Edith had told Bernard it was to be an intimate dinner for four, and we played the part.

Bernard visibly relaxed as he kissed me and shook Michael's hand, then loosened his tie. 'I can't tell you how nice it is that we're going to be just the four of us tonight,' he said. 'It's a perfect way to celebrate my birthday.'

'Uh-oh,' I thought. 'Have we done a good thing?'

Bernard pulled two cigars out of his breast pocket to show Michael. 'For later,' he said with a wink, and Michael went into the kitchen to get some champagne from the refrigerator. I knew from experience that Bernard would follow him and go to the stove to lift a lid and see what was cooking. It was then that the group – hidden around the corner from the kitchen fireplace – would declare itself. I could hear muffled giggles but Bernard was oblivious, intent on relaxing with a glass of champagne in his hand. On cue he walked to the stove. '*Bon Anniversaire!*' rang out.

Fortunately Bernard has a healthy heart and quick reflexes. He smiled ruefully, looked at Edith and at me, then laughed and embroiled himself in the group. Bernard is more affectionate than most French people – he actually gives hugs to men and women both, whereas most French give sterile little pecks on the cheek and call it good. In this instance, surrounded with such good will and warmth, everyone was kissing and hugging in a very un-French display. '*Je n'ai rien soupçonné,*' he said, shaking his head and looking at Edith, who was laughing. 'I didn't suspect a thing!' He got his champagne and we toasted him, '*Bernard le Vieux*', 'Bernard the Elder.'

We sat down to our dinner, which was a lively success, with Bernard the centre of attention, loving this evening, this group, the meal. Despite his cosmopolitan life, Bernard is never far from his childhood: he grew up on a small farm near Louviers. Excess of any kind touches him. This was clearly a night of excess, and Bernard was clearly touched.

Just before dessert the chorus excused itself and we returned to the dining room in formation, to stand across the table from Bernard. As we sang it was as I had expected – Bernard had tears in his eyes he was laughing so hard. Each phrase referred to something in his life – the accident when he fell from a bridge and broke his legs and back, his love of flying, his command of English, his desire to travel . . . we hadn't missed a thing. None of the other guests had heard the song and everyone was, as the French say, *plié*: doubled over with laughter. The torpedo-shaped fountain pen Edith presented to him afterwards just about did him in. He admired it, fondled it, passed it around, then put in his shirt pocket with a satisfied pat. Ah, the pleasures of achieving one's goal, of turning fifty!

The most recent fiftieth birthday party was Michael's, and we decided to invite friends from near and far. Several came from the States, and when I included them with our local friends, the number of guests topped forty – too many for a formal dinner, since our dining room holds just twenty comfortably. Michael had requested something simple, but everyone still needed a place to sit, so I went into our dining room to try and figure out how I could get it to expand to fit the number of guests.

I had initially hoped to serve dinner outside using several round metal tables we keep out there. The weather was inclement, which precluded the al fresco idea, but I could easily move the tables inside. That was it: I would turn our dining room into a French café. It would be nice and crowded like a real café, perfect for the event!

The French love to give group gifts, and everyone asked

what Michael would like. This stumped me for a while, since Michael either likes huge, useful objects which cost the earth, or nothing. He does love music, though, so I asked everyone to bring him their favourite. Then I went a step further and asked each person if they could think about giving some of their time to Michael to help him finish the renovation on his studio, a malingering project. He was dreading replacing the roof, I knew, and I envisioned a sort of Amish-style barn-raising where everyone would work together, and eat together afterwards. I wasn't sure whether this notion would fly with our French friends, but I should have had more faith in them for, down to the last person, they were enthusiastic about the idea.

The day dawned and our American friends presented themselves early, ready to help. Michael was away at a baseball game with Joe and wouldn't return until much later, which made it easy to prepare for the party. We moved in the tables and I covered them with bright cloths, then we positioned chairs around them and Voila! Café On Rue Tatin! I set two bottles of wine and a stack of pretty little cloth napkins on each, and was going to add a bouquet when one of our friends said, 'No, what you have to do is put something in the centre of each table that relates to Michael.'

I ran up to the top floor of the house, the one we haven't touched since we bought the house, and whose two rooms serve as dusty *débarras*, or storerooms. I gathered up some beautiful old light fixtures and pieces of carved wood, along with a box of bright yellow electrical boxes. I'd brought a box of deep purple pansies home from the market and I planted one in each electric box. I put several of these on each table, then set the old lamp fixtures and moulds in strategic places.

Michael had asked for pizza, so I sliced pounds of

onions for his favourite, which combines them with crème fraîche and slivers of bacon, and I made a slow-cooked, tart/sweet Sicilian tomato sauce. I had freshly ground pork, too, and thinly sliced dried sausage, since I've noticed that most children don't feel as if they've eaten if their teeth haven't come in contact with meat of some kind. I had tapenade and leek purée – delicious for spreading on toasts – herbed olives and my special Sardinian sheep's milk crackers for the aperitif.

I set dishes of everything everywhere but, as usual, once people began to arrive they congregated in the kitchen, where Fiona – covered in flour from head to toe – was helping me roll out the pizza dough. Our kitchen is so perfect for moments like this because I can be working away on my side of the island while everyone else is sipping and partying on the other. Such was the case this evening.

I'd printed up certificates that people could sign with their 'time donation', and I asked a friend if she would circulate them, and simultaneously lead people out of the kitchen so that I could get the pizzas in the oven. Michael and Joe arrived in full baseball gear; the party had begun.

I loved listening to the blend of English and French that was being spoken. All French have studied English in school, and tonight everyone was making a huge effort to talk with our American friends who, in turn, were pulling out all the French they had studied. As people settled down at the tables there was one small one, tucked in a corner, which was surrounded by French friends who were too intimidated to try and speak English.

Nadine noticed the table and went over to it to shake them up. 'Come on, go try to speak English: you can see each other any time you want,' she said. Michael joined her. 'Come on, be international,' he said. They laughed, and stayed right where they were.

181

A silence fell and Edith said, 'Michael, open your gifts.' Everyone took up the cry and Michael could do nothing but go to the centre of the room, where a big basket held gifts, and another held the rolled-up 'time certificates'. Usually Michael is quiet around French people, but tonight was different. I guess when you've reconciled your-self to being fifty, anything that comes afterwards is a piece of cake.

He began opening his gifts, and at about the tenth CD he broke into vivid laughter. 'There is a theme to this party after all,' he said. The choices of music were broad-ranging and wonderful, from two different versions of Carmen to Guetsch Patti, Benabar, Eric Satie and tra-ditional songs from Quebec. Michael turned to the rolled-up certificates, mystified. He opened one, read it and looked up with a rueful expression on his face. He tapped a glass with a knife, for silence. 'I just want everyone here to know how much it means to me that you're here, how much I appreciate all the effort you've gone to, and how much I cannot wait to call you all to come help me finish *The Studio*!' he said, in perfect, lyrical French.

Our French friends were dumbstruck. Michael is the silent partner at every dinner party, almost every gather-ing. He looks, he listens, he rarely talks. Our French friends wish he would talk more, but they accord him room because of what they think is his difficulty with the language. It's true, he has had a difficult time learning French. But after this speech, his ship was sunk. No one would let him get away with being silent again. 'You've blown your cover,' said Anne-Marie. 'Now we know how good your French is, we're going to demand that you speak.'

Joe carried in Michael's poppy-seed cake, Michael's favourite, which I make every year. I followed with big bowls of homemade vanilla and chocolate ice cream, and a friend brought in a big basket of lusciously fragrant strawberries. The cake and ice cream was served, the berries passed around, the conversation and laughter in the room high and loud. I put the remaining ice cream in the freezer and settled into the party. Pretty soon Edith came up to me, a full bowl of ice cream in her hand, and bent down. 'I found the rest of the ice cream,' she whispered. 'You didn't think you would have any leftover, did you?'

I circulated among the tables, visiting. I got to the cowardly French table, which was raucous and lively, and sat down to tease them about not trying out their English, and to find out how they were doing. Michel the baker leaned over to me. 'Suzanne, I hope you don't mind my saying so, but the pizza dough had too much yeast in it,' he said. His comment stopped me, cold. Michel is the most self-effacing, sweet, humble, darling, considerate man I've ever met, and I have never heard him venture even close to commenting on what someone else cooks. What's more, he was correct. Normally I add the tiniest possible amount of yeast to dough, for that is all it needs. This time I was making so much I added an extra teaspoonful. I couldn't believe he'd noticed. We were pouring Côtes de Blaye and it must be going down easily and well for him to have worked up the nerve to say something. The ensuing conversation was interesting as we compared amounts of yeast. Patrick, sitting nearby, overheard.

'Suzanne,' he piped up. 'You won't live long if you keep using so much salt in your food. You really should pay attention – salt isn't good for you.'

It was a double call to arms tonight. I realized they had been sitting there, critiquing the food. I excused myself and went out to the kitchen to taste. 'Lord,' I thought, 'did I miss something?'

I took a large bite of the Sicilian Tomato pizza – it was scrumptious, salty and sweet, tender and crisp like a good pizza should be. Yes, there was a hint of yeast, a delicious hint. I smiled. I knew the party was a success, for all the elements were present: happy friends, happy husband, happy children, and the defence of La Patrie. Vive la France! And bring on the next fiftieth. I believe it will be Edith's. I'm already thinking about the menu and the decor.

WOOD FIRE GRILLED LAMB CHOPS
Côtes d'Agneau Grilles au Feu de Bois

━━━━━━━━━━ ❧ ━━━━━━━━━━

At our home, when the weather is chilly and a big fire has burned to hot coals, I love to grill these lamb chops. I ask the butcher to cut them extra-thick, then I rub them with olive oil, sprinkle them with herbs and lay them on the grill over the coals. They slowly crisp on the outside while they stay moist and juicy inside, and they make a fine and satisfying meal.

12 thick (about 1½ inches; 4 cm) small lamb chops
2 tbs extra virgin olive oil
Freshly ground black pepper
2 tbs *herbes de provence* (dried marjoram, rosemary, thyme)
Coarse sea salt

1. Rub the lamb chops all over with the olive oil. Sprinkle them on both sides with black pepper to taste and equal amounts of *herbes de provence*, and let sit at room temperature for one hour, or overnight in the refrigerator.
2. Light a medium-sized fire in a grill or a fireplace. (Preheat the oven to 450°F; 220°C). When the coals are red and dusted with ash, place the grill about 3½ inches (about 9 cm) above them and when it is hot but not smoking, place the chops on the grill. Grill them until they are golden on the outside and still tender and lightly pink on the inside, turning them 2 to 3 times so they cook evenly, 12 to 14 minutes. Alternatively, place the lamb chops on a metal baking sheet and roast in the oven until they are golden on each side, about 9 minutes, turning them once halfway through cooking.

3. When the lamb chops are cooked to your liking, remove them from the grill and season with the coarse salt. Serve immediately.

6 servings

SALTED SPANISH ALMONDS
Les Amandes Espagnoles Salées
———————— ✑ ————————

I like broad, flat, delicately flavoured Spanish almonds prepared this way, because they have a dry sweetness to them that other almonds lack. Sometimes I add a herb or a spice to the salted water to give an extra touch of flavour, though these almonds are so tasty simply salted that they really don't need much at all.

2 cups (9.5 oz.; 285g) Spanish almonds, skins removed
2 cups (500ml) water
2 tbs coarse sea salt
Heaped ¼ teaspoon hot paprika

1. Preheat the oven to 250°F (about 120°C).
2. Bring the water, the salt and the paprika to a boil, stir and boil until the salt is dissolved. Add the almonds, stir, and boil until they begin to look translucent, about 8 minutes. Drain, and spread evenly on a baking sheet. Bake in the centre of the oven until the almonds are pale golden and crisp, 1 hour. Remove them from the oven and let them cool. The almonds will keep up to one week in an airtight container.

2 cups (9.5oz.; 285g) almonds

There's an '*A do*' in Our Midst

I'm not sure how it has happened, but overnight Joe has gone from being a round, rosy-cheeked, pliable boy to being an ever-lengthening almost young man with a predilection for practical jokes and a single-minded determination to discover the facts of life. In short, he is becoming an adolescent or, in French, an *ado*. That he is only eleven counts for nothing in this day and age; everything happens way too fast, even in a small town in the French countryside.

Being Joe's mother, I naturally want to smother him. I don't go to extremes – I allow him to go to school, and to have friends – but we don't have a television and his voyaging on the Internet is strictly limited to, well, almost nothing. We are able to watch videocassettes, but that too is pretty strictly controlled. We slip occasionally, renting moronic Jim Carrey movies or putting in an Austin Powers video sent by a friend, only to find out how mindless and full of unnecessary stupidity they are. There are limits to the amount of control parents have, a lesson I learn if not once a day, at least several times a week.

Joe seems to be more restricted than most of his friends. From what I observe and from what I know in my own friends' homes, children here grow up with fewer limits. If they want to see an X-rated movie, drown themselves in violent computer and video games, or use the occasional X-rated language, they seem to meet no parental resistance. They also have a sense of sex and their bodies well before American children seem to, and in a much more natural and sophisticated way. In a country where nudity, mostly female but also male, is plastered in lifesize advertisements everywhere, it becomes part of life. Joe used to giggle at the lingerie ads we walk by in Louviers, which were larger than him. Now I'm not sure he even sees them. Also, families here tend to be larger than those in the US, and if his friends' older sisters and brothers aren't married and having children, they might be living together, or getting pregnant even if they aren't married, in an atmosphere where that is quite acceptable.

French children grow up with more of a sense of decorum than most American children I know as well. They learn from infancy how to greet others, so that even the tiniest French child willingly holds his cheek up for a kiss to an adult he doesn't know, or plants a kiss on a stranger's face. For boys, kissing translates quite early into shaking hands, so that now, Joe and his friends walk up to adults new to them, look them right in the eye and shake their hands. Adults who are familiar to them still get kissed, but not strangers. French children also learn how to sit at table and endure long meals without too much wiggling or complaint. I believe this is in the genes, because my children haven't entirely mastered it, despite the frequency of long meals in our home.

These are small differences that I've noticed. Joe feels there is no difference between his French friends and

American boys his age, but as he says to me, 'Mom, how would I really know? I've never even lived in the States.'

Recently, Joe and one of his racier schoolfriends – a wiry pistol named César who is already charming in that suave, French way which means he plays up to his single mother's female friends by being very polite and holding adult conversations with them – were sitting in the room off our kitchen giggling and snorting over a book. I was making *papillotes* filled with mackerel fillets, a fussy job I adore, and not really paying attention. I like this boy very much – he's smart, funny, mouthy and, while very disrespectful to his mother, who lets him do everything he wants, is very polite with us and fun for Joe. When it was time for him to leave I accompanied him to meet his mother out front and returned to find Joe sprawled on the couch with the same book they'd been looking at, laughing as he avidly turned the pages. I peered over his shoulder and realized he was reading a book I wasn't in favour of, whose main character is a little boy named Titeuf. Titeuf learns everything he knows from his older siblings, and the language the books are written in is ripe. In fact, after hearing Joe and his friends quoting from Titeuf I was shocked. It figures that César would have been the one to bring it into our home. It also explained why Joe was loving it so much: there is nothing like forbidden fruit.

I returned to the kitchen and Joe strolled in behind me. 'Hey mom,' he said. 'Listen to this.' He read a passage from the book, where Titeuf was trying to figure out why a little girl would hide a ruler under her dress. I was tucking and folding my *papillotes*, and when he got to the punch line I realized I hadn't been listening.

'Joe, will you read that again?' I asked. Joe complied, and when he finished it this time we were both in stitches. The author of Titeuf had, with a few silly words and sketches, hit right at the heart of one of life's more mysterious subjects, to little boys at least. You see, in French the word for ruler is also the word for menstrual period, and poor Titeuf and a friend had just heard his older sister talking about her '*règles*'.

Joe read me more. The subject matter was quite serious – from homosexuality to tattoos, body-piercing to divorce. The way Zep, the Swiss author, dealt with them was artless, side-splitting, and right on the mark for a pre-adolescent boy, as though he was that age himself and understood completely how their smart, enquiring minds work.

I did a complete turn around about Titeuf that day. I still deplore the language the writer uses but, as Joe pointed out, 'Mom, this is what I hear every day in the playground, this is the way we talk. Don't worry about it.' The situations Titeuf gets into are banal and without complexity, but the subjects are all too relevant and very difficult to broach. Through Titeuf he gets conflictual subjects out in the open, gets kids laughing about them and talking with their parents about them. Thanks to Zep we – and undoubtedly many other parents in France – have had our job made easier by a shrimpy little blond boy with freckles and a perpetual wrinkle between his eyes from trying to puzzle out life.

I was at our local bookstore with Joe, who was leafing through Titeuf books to see which one he wanted to buy with his allowance, and I asked the owner, who is deeply knowledgeable about books and very literary, what he thought about Titeuf.

'Well,' he said thoughtfully, 'it is hardly Astérix or Tin-Tin. It doesn't offer much in terms of sophistication, but it gets families talking about subjects that need talking about.'

So, he felt the way I did. Titeuf may not be contributing to the intellectual or literary culture of children, but he and his band of *copains* – mates – are, in a sane and healthy way, opening up vast pits of information kids are going to get anyway, and allowing them – even pushing them – to talk with their parents about it. Bravo, Titeuf!

We started reading to Joe when he was very young, and we're still reading to him now. Even before we moved to France I read him books in French. Once he learned to read at age six, however, that ended. I'll never forget it. I was reading a book called *Le Motordu*, which is written in fractured French. At the end, Joe said, 'Mom, I don't want to hurt your feelings or anything, but your French accent is really horrible. Would you not read me French books any more?' Well, OK, I thought. My French is actually pretty good, and my accent fairly slight, but to Joe, who spends four-and-a-half long days each week at school completely immersed in the language, and who is a perfectionist, it must clang. So both Michael and I switched over to reading English books. We navigated through all kinds of books, mostly supplied by friends and family who sent us regular care packages calculated to give Joe a sense of American humour and life: Matt Christopher, the Hardy Boys, Mrs Piggle-Wiggle, and many stories about immigrant children and their lives and dreams, and, of course, Tin-Tin. Then came the year of Harry Potter.

We were in London and the first book had just come out, but it hadn't yet zinged off the popularity charts. A friend pointed it out saying he'd heard it was good, so we picked it up. Michael began reading it to Joe one afternoon after we returned, and two hours later he was still reading. I went into the room where he and Joe were sitting and listened. Pretty soon I was sitting too. It was compelling: a fantastic antidote to winter rains and long, dark evenings.

Michael was the Harry Potter reader, and he read them

to Joe for hours; when I could, I'd sit in and listen. Joe was completely enthralled. He imagined himself the characters, invented games that resembled Quidditch – the fantastical game the characters in Harry Potter play – and dreamed of being a professional Quidditch player. There was no Harry Potter in France yet, nor – thankfully – any Harry Potter paraphernalia, but Joe described the books in detail to his friends and got them all dreaming about Quidditch (pronounced queed-eetch in French).

When Michael had read all the books in English, Joe decided he wanted to read the fourth one in French, and he awaited its publication with great anticipation. It was advertised everywhere. Our local bookstore's promotion included a gift to the first twenty children who came to buy it, and Joe couldn't wait. The day dawned and he was up and ready to go. It was only 8 a.m. and the bookstore didn't open until 10 a.m., but this was of no concern. He was ready. We convinced him to wait until nine, though it was like trying to get water on high heat not to boil, for he was convinced that the queue would be long. Finally he, Michael, Fiona in her stroller and an American friend who was visiting were out the door. It was 9 a.m.

They returned at 10.30 a.m., and Joe's eyes were shining. 'Mom, mom,' he shouted, 'they're going to give me the life-size cardboard statue of Harry Potter this afternoon because we were first in line.' He waved the book in my face, then went into the living room to begin reading. Michael rolled his eyes. 'We were the only people in line until about 9.45,' he said. 'In fact we got there and then left to go get pastries to eat while we were waiting. At about nine-fifty a bunch of people came and, in perfect French style, literally shoved in before us to get their books. That's when the owner told Joe he'd give him the cardboard Harry Potter.'

A note here about the French and standing in queues. They hate it, and do it badly. As Americans we are trained to respectfully wait in line, and we look down on people who cut in. Not the French. They turn into animals when doors or gates open, trains or buses pull up, jostling, cutting, pushing, shoving, completely belying their couture and decorum. We have never quite understood this.

That afternoon Joe went to pick up the cardboard Harry, which was taller than he was. He carefully set it up in his bedroom, and that night when I went to check on him before going to bed I jumped. I thought Joe was out of bed and standing there, silently. But it was Harry Potter who has, in so many ways, become a member of the family.

After Joe had been reading the French Harry Potter for a while, he came into my office to see me. 'You know mom,' he said, 'I don't like Hagrid as well in French as in English – he's not as funny.'

Of course he wasn't. I'd listened enough to know how Michael brought Hagrid to life with a thick and vigorous Cockney accent. That was imprinted on Joe's brain, as much a part of the mystery and delight of the book as the character himself. To imagine that same character speaking French must seem the equivalent of hearing John Wayne say 'Stick 'em up' in French. It borders on the ridiculous. Joe was really perplexed. He wanted to continue reading the book, but he didn't know what accent to assign to Hagrid that would make him jump from the pages.

I wish I could have crawled inside Joe's mind then, to see what it felt like to be grappling with this issue. Somehow he worked it out and finished the book. He wasn't capable of (or interested in) articulating how he had come to terms with the problem. All he offered was, 'Mom, I didn't really like reading Harry Potter as much in French.'

Indeed, I thought. Growing up bilingual offers all manner of consternation to the young mind.

Joe was in the final year of primary school and he would be changing schools the next year to go to '*collège*', Middle School. He would enter *sixième*, or sixth grade, and every mother I'd ever spoken with had told me it was one of the hardest classes of the whole school career.

Most of Joe's classmates would go on to the Catholic middle school in Louviers run by the same order of nuns who ran his primary school. We'd been satisfied with Joe's primary school career. He'd had several good teachers, including one who was excellent, but it hadn't been inspiring and we weren't excited about him continuing in the same system. When I asked parents whose children went to the Catholic middle school in Louviers about it, the best thing they could say was that the discipline was good. No one mentioned the quality of teaching or the spirit of the school. I began researching options in the region.

We weren't entirely certain what we wanted for Joe, but we didn't want him to drown in mediocrity, and that was the feeling we got from all the schools in Louviers. Joe has a facility for languages beyond being bilingual, and a desire to learn, so we wanted a school where he could take something besides just English and French right away. Joe leans towards the arts, so we hoped for a school less rigid and dogmatic than the one he would be leaving, something a bit more flexible, creative and interesting.

An American-French couple we know sent their daughter to a private school they really liked in Vernon, thirty minutes east of us. They encouraged us to visit, and I made an appointment to meet the director. He was charming and very engaged in the running of his school, but when faced with our desires for Joe he responded in a very straightforward manner. 'This is a French school, and all of us here are French,' he said. 'I'm very familiar with the Canadian school system, which resembles the American system, so I think I know what you want, but you won't get it here. I don't want to disappoint you – we do a good job, but we are all very French.' We appreciated his frankness and left, knowing this school wouldn't be all that different from one in Louviers.

I'd heard a lot about a school in Elbeuf that had once been considered the best in the region, had fallen on hard times, and was in the process of rebirth. It was about twenty minutes southwest of us, so not too far away, and it went from Middle School right through High School. I made an appointment to meet the director.

The school was a blend of old and new, with the administrative offices tucked into an old-fashioned brick building with turrets and arched windows, and most of the classrooms in a contemporary cement block addition. There were big chestnut trees in the playground, and the place had an intriguing, old/new world feel to it. The director swept into the room where we were waiting, his hand outstretched, his bushy dark hair rumpled, his smile wide and genuine. 'Bonjour, bonjour, what can I do for you?' he boomed, then proceeded to describe the school and his dreams for its future.

He had moved to the Institut Fenelon from a school in Paris just three years ago, with a mandate to return the school to its former level of excellence. With great vigour and fun he described what the students were doing, focusing on art classes, a huge sculpture the entire student body was creating in the school's courtyard, his philosophy of integrated education. 'Here we want the children to understand why they are taking maths classes,' he said. 'They can't just come and take them and not realize how mathematics affects everything, so sometimes the French teacher and the maths teacher give joint classes, or the mathematics teacher and the art teacher, or the science teacher and the French teacher.'

This man was clearly a revolutionary, for never before had we heard someone discuss education in France in this manner. He continued, carried away by his own enthusiasm, to show us paintings the older students had done in art class – they were good, expressive – to talk about the '*veillée*' or evening gathering before Christmas when students gave a concert and parents were invited to stay afterwards for hot chocolate in the school courtyard, for his outreach to the community. He admitted being short-staffed and expressed his plans to try and enlist retirees to come work with the children. 'This makes perfect sense,' he said. 'People here retire in the middle of their lives; they still have so much to offer. I'd like to get them here to offer what they have. No one has done this that I know of.' His ideas were as big as his ego, and we loved them.

He swept us along as he described the way the classes were organized, how students were encouraged to speak with professors, how designated professors were available to counsel children, how his desire was to challenge and create a spirit of openness.

He talked a bit about parental involvement, keying into Michael's sculpture. 'Perhaps, at some time, you could come in and do a class or two with the students,' he said, enthused.

By the end of our meeting we were sure that, even if he only did half of what he claimed, this school would be a good place for Joe.

We would have to apply to get Joe into school, he said, as they were careful to admit a good balance of students – not just those with good grades, but those whose records indicated they were motivated and involved. He gave us the paperwork, and we went home, filled it out and sent it in. Within two weeks we had word that Joe was accepted. We were all happy. This school, definitely the best option open to us, was very different from the dullness of his primary school.

The fact that the director had actually brought up the notion of parental involvement was almost unheard of. Not to be unfair – some parents did get involved at Joe's primary school, but they weren't really encouraged, nor was there much of a volunteer spirit. As an example, I had offered to teach English to Joe's grade level the very first year he started at the school. His teacher was eager but the principal wouldn't allow it. She felt the children were already learning enough.

I volunteered again the following year and this time my offer was accepted. Though English wasn't mandatory for primary students, it soon would be. The state had already provided the curriculum, which the principal wanted me to follow closely. When I spoke with Joe's teacher about English, however, she could not have cared less about the state curriculum. 'You do what you want,' she said. 'If the children learn a few words, I'm delighted. And I'm particularly delighted that I don't have to teach them myself because my English is horrible.' I had carte blanche and an hour and a half a week with the children. My idea was to get them having fun because I knew that, realistically, they wouldn't learn a lot in such a limited amount of time. If they just got a good feeling about English, I thought, they'd approach it willingly when classes became serious. I taught them useful phrases and got them singing, dancing, jumping around and doing role-plays. We made a lot of noise as I taught verbs like 'jump', 'clap', 'yell', 'cry', etc. 'Heads, Shoulders, Knees and Toes' was a favourite with all of them, as was 'The

Hokey Cokey'. After sitting in their seats all week for eight hours a day, they couldn't wait for English class, where they could move from their seats and let their voices be heard. Joe was in the class and, while he'd thought he'd be bored, he joined right in, having as much fun as any of his classmates.

The first year was a resounding success. The teacher, a young woman named Murielle, stayed at the back of the class correcting papers while I taught, and often when I looked up she was smiling, or joining in the songs. At the end of the year we did a short programme for the parents, all of whom were amazed and delighted that their children were learning English. It was such fun to be involved with the children, and it gave me a chance to understand the French education system a bit better.

The second year was less successful simply because the teacher, who had been delighted to have me volunteer to teach, didn't seem to like my methods. The children were just as receptive, but when the teacher looked up from the work she did at the back of the class while I was there, her expression was pinched and pained. I realized I was disrupting her sense of order and decorum.

The third year the teacher and I agreed that she would leave the room while I taught, so that she could go to a quiet room to get some work done. She left me with twenty-eight children, many of whom I'd never met. I started right in with simple questions to evaluate their level: they were an exceptionally bright group of nine year olds, and by the end of the hour I'd just about lost control. When the teacher returned I told her that we needed a new plan – I didn't want to spend my precious time disciplining the children. We decided to divide the class in half: I would take half to the multimedia room (which at this struggling private school consisted of a room with a television and VCR, and a row of benches) for half the lesson while she looked after the other half of the group. I agreed to work for an hour and a half, which gave me forty-five minutes with each group. It worked beautifully, and we had more fun doing skits, gymnastics, playing air-guitar, lip-syncing. Towards the end of the year I got them all back together and taught them 'Yellow Submarine', which they performed for the parents. I'm not certain the song contributed a great deal to their overall command of the English language, but they loved it. It is a very popular karaoke song in France, so it may stand them in good stead one day in the future!

I noticed many things teaching in a French classroom, the most odd being the lack of oxygen therein. Each time I arrived for class, in every teacher's classroom, the atmosphere was so hot and stuffy, I didn't see how anyone could stay awake. I once asked a teacher if I could open a window and she looked horrified. '*Oh non, Madame Loomis*,' she said. '*Il y a des courants d'air*' – 'there are draughts.'

I should have known. The French have a horror of draughts. They bundle their children against air with layers, bonnets and scarves, gloves and coats, as if it were poison. Kids come to school looking like the Michelin man, the poor things. I was never able to get Joe to keep a hat on, and I would arrive with him at school and get withering looks from the other parents, their bundled progeny by their sides. I felt sure they whispered about us foreigners, and how irresponsible we were, for surely our child would catch all manner of illnesses caused by a '*courant d'air*', including colds, flu, stiff necks, fevers, stomach-aches. In fact, the *courant d'air* has replaced *le foie*, or the liver, as the biggest health culprit in France. If ever I suggested that a teacher open a window in a hot, stuffy classroom, it was as if I were suggesting we inject each child with the pneumonia virus. The rooms stayed stuffy as long as the teacher was there. The minute she left, I went ahead and flung open a window, simply so we could all breathe.

Joe's final year in primary school was his best. The teacher, Frédéric, was a young man with verve and imagination. Short, balding and rumpled, what hair he had stuck out in a fine, ziggy cloud around his head, and the children adored him. He encouraged their sense of fun and imagination, and his sense of humour fitted easily with theirs. He got them to build imaginary universes, learn fun poems, perform short plays. Devoutly Catholic, he gave them a humanist view of the religion by comparing it with other religions. His own passion was theatre, and he helped the class write, direct and perform a play at the end of the year. Because I was in the classroom once a week, I could see how the children were blossoming under his tutelage.

Frédéric was over the moon that I was going to teach English. My challenge was greater this year, for he was such an entertaining teacher that the antics I encouraged the kids to perform were mild and banal compared with their everyday fare. Frédéric also split the class in two and took half to do theatre while I had half for English. This created another problem for me, because all the kids loved theatre, and most of them, at the age of ten, didn't care whether or not they learned English. Consequently, with their newfound freedom of expression and behaviour, discipline was more of a problem than in previous years. I mentioned this to Frédéric, who told me his technique for control. 'You see this hallway?' he said, opening the classroom door. 'A disobedient child goes here, right in this corner. We're not supposed to use it but I do, and it works *à merveille*.'

I followed his suggestion. The minute an unruly child started trying to take control, I calmly opened the door and directed them into the hallway. They hated going there and I hated doing it, but it was enormously effective – one dose of the corner generally solved the problem for all time, and I was quite careful to get them back in the classroom well before the teacher returned.

Towards the end of the year, which was the end of the children's primary school career, attention spans flagged. I decided one day to have the class act out a visit to a restaurant, and divided the class into two groups. We worked together on vocabulary, I helped them divvy up tasks, and then I let them go. The only rule was that they had to speak English.

Within minutes desks were pushed together to make tables, and places were set. Pencils served as knives and forks, glue stick spoons were laid carefully above workbook plates. One of the 'waiters', who had a strip of plastic stuck in his shirt for a tie, filled a dish with tiny pieces of chalk and placed it on a small chalkboard tray with two 'glasses', yoghurt pots normally used in painting class.

'Your aperitifs,' he said as he grandly set them on the table where four of his fellow students sat, primping and rearranging the table setting. Other children were busy writing menus on chalkboards, in English. Pizza, frites and strawberries figured largely, as did salad and hamburgers. One group offered omelettes for the first course and salad for the second course, then became flustered when they realized there was no real main course.

'Oh, we'll make the pizza the main course,' one said.

'No,' shouted another. 'Pizza can't be a main course. It's a first course.'

Meanwhile, in the kitchen, several chefs were whisking eggs in an invisible bowl, chopping tomatoes with a ruler, frying bacon with a compass. One of the chefs, a band around his long hair to keep it out of his eyes, danced as he cooked.

Much of the conversation and orders took place in French. I interfered and cajoled where I could, and otherwise observed. I was astounded, delighted at the incredible imagination of these kids, and at their ease with the idea of cooking, serving, being in a restaurant. I dissolved in silent laughter as I watched a diner at one table sample the 'wine' and spit it out into a bucket, saw another gingerly cut into her pizza and say, 'Ve-ery good,' to the imperious waiter, and witnessed yet another who ordered 'whiskee' to sip with his chalky aperitifs. One of the girls was smoking a pretend cigarette and complaining that the service was too slow.

The class ended in laughter and a measure of chaos. I won't say it was a total success as an English lesson, but it was so much fun that no one wanted it to be over.

The year ended with an outdoor picnic for the class – Frédéric was the first of Joe's teachers ever to entertain the idea of an alternate classroom. Everyone – Frédéric included – laughed and sang and danced and played, then the year was over. Most of the children would be together the following year, so goodbyes were swift and without emotion.

Despite the fun finale, Joe left primary school without a backward glance. Even though he would leave all his companions behind to go to a school where he knew no one, in a town different from his own, he was ready for the change and the challenge. What excited him most was that he got to take German along with English and French.

As Joe started his new school, I set about planning cooking classes. I realized that to make it work best for everyone I had to plan sessions around school holidays, so that Joe would be gone during the days and I wouldn't need to be concerned about how he would amuse himself while I was busy with participants. I called Joe's school to get holiday dates for the following year, completely confounding the secretary who answered the phone. 'But Madame, we don't have those dates yet,' she said. It was nearly the end of the year, so I knew this couldn't be true. I pushed, gently. 'Madame, I understand, but I need to plan my business around them,' I said. This transformed me from a nosey mother to a business person, and within moments she was reading me the dates. I looked at them. There were ten days at the end of October for All Saints, two weeks for Christmas and New Year and two weeks in February for the ski vacation. Nearly every weekend in May is devoted to a *fête*; when a holiday falls on a Tuesday or Thursday, the French often take an extra day off before or after the weekend to '*faire le pont*', or create a long weekend. Finally there was the end of school in June.

There isn't much point in planning anything in April, as it is one of the rainiest, most meteorologically uncertain months of the year. May and June are much more certain, so I would simply have to plan right through the '*ponts*', and into the first week of June. I left summer free, then planned sessions for the end of September and the beginning of October, when the weather is almost always glorious and Joe had no holiday time. I planned five weeks in all. I wanted to start slowly.

I wasn't quite sure how we would manage the twenty-minute drive to Joe's school each way, particularly during the cooking class weeks, and I would miss walking through Louviers each morning with Joe, though that would have ended soon as he was getting old enough to go by himself. I was discussing our decision with Brigitte Tois, our neighbour who owns the gift shop down the street, and she was interested that we felt we had to send Joe so far away. When I mentioned that he could take a third language right away she understood immediately, and this is how I took to explaining why we didn't keep Joe in one of the schools in Louviers. Otherwise, people thought we were snobs.

The next time I went in to Brigitte's shop she told me about another family whose children would go to Fenelon in the autumn. 'The mother wants to meet you,' Brigitte said. 'She wants to talk about sharing the driving but she doesn't dare call you. Here is her phone number.' She handed me a piece of paper. 'She told me they tried their son in the Louviers schools and it didn't work out at all.'

I called the woman and she, her husband and their three children proved to be friendly and very cooperative. We agreed to split the driving in half. This would be a huge help.

Joe settled into his new school with remarkable ease. The car pool helped, as the daughter was in his class, and there was a boy in his class who was half English, so they immediately paired up. Within a couple of weeks it was as if he'd always gone there.

The school made it easy on the kids. Though it was large – there were six classes of Joe's age group with twenty-five students in each – one teacher was designated the *responsable du cycle*, or liaison, between the administration and the parents, so that if there were any problems above and beyond those encountered in a specific class, she would see to solving them. While in most colleges the students move from class to class, at Joe's school the teachers moved. Joe was disappointed at first because he'd imagined his school would be like the one in Harry Potter, with student lockers and moving from class to class.

He got over his disappointment quickly. He liked his

teachers, liked the classes and loved German. He hated English, however, and soon he hated his English teacher.

I received a call from the school about the English class. Apparently, Joe was causing problems. I went to meet the teacher, and she explained. 'Joe is making it hard for me, contradicting me, not helping out,' she said, in French. 'He is talking back and generally being a problem in the class.'

I didn't know what to say. I knew Joe didn't like her, and didn't like the class, which made sense to me since it was very basic and undoubtedly boring. We had tried to get him out of it and, while the administration agreed with us, the scheduling didn't work out to get him into a more advanced class.

Joe had never before acted up at school or bucked authority in any way, but he was getting older and more courageous. I explained to the teacher that Joe was quite advanced for his age in English, loved to read, had a wonderful vocabulary, and probably needed more challenge. I suggested she make him an ally, a helper, remembering all the times he'd helped me when I was teaching his class English in primary school. She said she had tried but he didn't cooperate. I asked how the half-English boy was doing. 'Oh, he is very helpful, he plays the game,' she said. This was not sounding good, and not at all like Joe.

We talked a bit more, then she said she thought Joe should come and join us. I didn't disagree, because I didn't really know what had been going on in class, and I wanted to see how he was with her. She repeated her charges once he was with us, and I looked at him. He nodded his head and said he would try harder. I was surprised to see he was holding back tears, and I realized this issue was much deeper for him than I'd realized. He shook hands with his teacher and we walked him back to his class. As the teacher and I returned to our meeting room she started to speak in English. Her accent was terrible, almost impossible to understand, and her syntax was awkward. I was shocked. She may well have had a PhD in English, as she claimed, but her spoken English was reprehensible. A light was beginning to dawn.

Joe came home and we talked about his English class some more. He burst into tears and said he didn't want to learn British English, didn't want to say 'half-past' instead of 'thirty'. He said he was afraid he would forget his American English, and that he wouldn't be American any more if he learned her stupid British English. We talked with him for a long time, trying to help him understand that his English would only improve, take on an added richness, by learning British English. We threw in that we thought that he would attract all kinds of positive attention once he was older if he used some of the British English he was learning. We also sympathized, and understood how dull it must have been for him to sit through all those hours each week of baby English.

Soon after the meeting came the terrorist attacks on the World Trade Center and the Pentagon. The English teacher asked Joe if he would sing the US national anthem for the class, which he did. We thought this a very thoughtful, sensitive thing to have done. Joe was a hero to his classmates, and prouder than ever to be an American.

Hero status didn't last long, nor did Joe's calm and assurance in his English class. I scheduled a meeting with the head of all the sixth grades and asked the English teacher to be there. Michael came this time. Joe didn't.

We had two subjects to discuss. One was English, and the other were some disquieting developments that had occurred following the terrorist attacks and subsequent war in Afghanistan.

The English teacher joined us and it was immediately obvious she was threatened by Joe's mastery of English and didn't know how to cope with it. Though she said she was trying to enlist his help, she was doing the opposite. As for the half-English boy, we'd heard his English and it was so minimal that he was really learning in the English class. Joe truly wasn't. He would come home and recite the latest phrase she had asked them to learn, his favourite being, 'I am a boy. I live on Planet Earth. I like chocolate.'

Go figure out that one. We couldn't.

Joe's English teacher seemed extremely knowledgeable in grammar and rules, but she wasn't comfortable or very up-to-date with the language, the pronunciation or the vocabulary. She would insist a word be pronounced a certain way, and if Joe contradicted her, she argued with him. His favourite example was the word 'chocolate'.

'Mama and Papa, you wouldn't believe how she says chocolate,' he said one day after school. 'She says "cho-co-layte". I told her that isn't right and she insisted it was. She is so dumb.'

While we supported him and knew he was right, at least in this instance, we had sympathy for her. As the director of the school pointed out to us, 'Monsieur and Madame Loomis, do you realize that Joe is the English teacher's worst nightmare?'

To her credit, she suggested during our meeting with the '*responsable du cycle*' that Joe be put in an English class for sixteen year olds. 'His English is that good,' she said. 'I think he could handle it.'

She left us to return to her teaching, and the head of the *responsable du cycle* looked at us.

'She is a good teacher, but she's not handling Joe very well,' she said. 'But I must tell you that we think Joe is being a bit aggressive with his American-ness.' We acknowledged this. It was, we thought, his response to feeling insecure in a big, new school.

'We all like Joseph,' the young woman continued. 'You talk to him about all this, and remind him that I'm here if he needs to talk with me. It will be just fine.'

The other subject we needed to bring up with this young woman was the racism. Joe had received an anti-American put-down from one of his teachers that we found unacceptable – she had told him to 'go and live in America if you feel that way', and some of the children had begun calling him a *sale Américain*, or dirty American. Another student became violent towards Joe, and towards some of his classmates when they tried to defend him.

The young woman was visibly shocked, as news of this hadn't reached her. She promised to speak with the offending teacher, and to bring it up at the next staff meeting. Meantime, we scheduled a meeting with the director, as we felt there was a gap between his notion of the school fostering tolerance and a sense of family, and what was actually going on.

He greeted us and was surprisingly current with the details of Joe's 'case'.

'I must tell you, Monsieur and Madame Loomis, about your son,' he said. 'We all like him here, very much, but you must realize that he isn't French, and he will never be French. You see, he asks questions in a very American way, and we're not used to that. It is certainly as a result of the way he is raised.'

Michael and I just sat there. Joe had never before elicited the slightest comment about being American – mostly, we assumed, because he fitted in so well that no one noticed it. But in a much larger school in a town that wasn't ours, he had become noticeable, and was taking refuge in his difference. The fact that he was asking questions amazed and thrilled us – our shy boy taking such an initiative? We thought it was fantastic.

The director continued. 'You mustn't be concerned. Joe is a bright, nice boy, but he isn't like the other children, and all of us on the staff consider it a richness for the school and the other students,' he said.

When I mentioned the violence that Joe and his classmate had been talking about, the director's face hardened. 'We screen the children to some degree before they are admitted to Fenelon,' he said, 'not because we want just the brightest students, but because we don't want the behavioural problems. Despite this, you cannot believe the problems we're having. Each year's entering class is worse, and this year I've had to take measures I never thought I would have to take – I've actually expelled two students.'

This launched a discussion of morals and values in French society, which covered television and movies, and electronic games. 'Children have never been more on their own, less supervised, and more in need of supervision,' he said. 'We do what we can with troubled children and behaviour problems. If we can't solve the problem then I decide whether or not to keep the child here. If it becomes too disruptive, I have to ask them to leave.'

We talked a bit more, then left him with a hearty handshake, our confidence restored. We never heard the results of the staff meeting, but Joe visibly relaxed. He didn't talk about English any more either, unless it was to mention an obvious gaffe, like the pronunciation of chocolate. One day Joe showed me his plastic ruler, which was covered with beautiful, intricately coloured designs. 'When did you do this?' I asked him. 'During English,' he said. So, he doodles and dreams, gets straight As and a little advantage over the other students. Life could be worse.

As for 'playing the game', the term the English teacher

had used, we realized that the director had been talking about this as well, without calling it that. In France, one learns to 'play the game' at school – that is, go along with the system without questioning it. We mentioned this to a French friend and he smiled. '*Oui, on joue le jeu,*' he said. It explains a lot about schooling in France, and living in the country as a whole. You may not like the system, whatever system, so you complain about it or you beat it in a quasi-legal way, but you don't stand up and question it. Our Joe is getting a French education in the truest sense of the term.

HOT CHOCOLATE THE WAY WE LIKE IT
Chocolat Chaud Comme on L'Aime

———————— ᑫᑲ ————————

This is the kind of hot chocolate we all like to sip in the afternoon after school or on a cold winter evening, made with only the best!

4 cups (1 litre) whole milk
4 oz (120g) dark chocolate, preferably Lindt, 70% cocoa, broken into small pieces
2 tbs vanilla sugar

1. Place the milk and the chocolate in a medium-sized saucepan and set it over low heat, shaking the pan and whisking occasionally until the chocolate melts and the milk is steaming. Be careful not to let the milk come to a boil. Add the sugar and whisk vigorously until it dissolves and the mixture is foamy. Remove from the heat and serve.

4 to 6 servings

ONION, BACON AND CREAM PIZZA
Tarte Flambée – Flammekeuche

———————— ᑫᑲ ————————

This pizza recipe originates in Alsace. Thin-crusted and meltingly rich and delicious, the Alsatian *Tarte Flambée* is always made in a wood-burning oven that is so hot it burns, or 'flambées' the tarte when it is put into bake. Thus, the edges of the crust are always blackened and bubbled. I've adapted the recipe to make at home, since it is one of our favourite dishes. Do as the Alsatians do, and as we often do, and gather a group for *Tarte Flambée* – it makes its own party!

For the dough:
1 cup (250ml) lukewarm water
1 tsp bread yeast
2 to 2½ cups (265g to 335g) all-purpose flour
½ tsp sea salt

For the topping:
¾ cup (185ml) crème fraîche
6 tbs (90ml) large curd cottage cheese
6 tbs (90ml) sour cream
2 small, white onions (about 5½ oz; 165g) total peeled and
sliced paper thin
4 oz (120g) slab bacon, rind removed, cut in
matchstick-sized pieces
Freshly ground black pepper

1. To make the dough, pour the water into a large bowl or the bowl of an electric mixer and mix with the yeast and 1 cup (135g) of the flour. Let the mixture temperature rise until it begins to bubble, about 30 minutes. Add the salt, stir, then add an additional cup of flour and mix well. The dough should be quite soft and sticky, though it should leave your fingers clean when you touch it. If it is very sticky, add a bit more flour, reserving the rest for rolling out the dough. Cover and let sit at room temperature until the dough has doubled in bulk, about 1½ hours.
2. Preheat the oven to 500°F.

3. Punch down the dough. Turn out half of it onto a floured work surface, and dust the top of the dough with flour, then roll it out as thin as you can get it, into a rectangle that measures about 10.5 × 16.5 inches (26.5 × 41.5cm). The dough should be paper thin. Transfer the dough to a floured baking sheet by rolling it around the rolling pin and unrolling it onto the baking sheet. It will shrink back slightly so, using your fingers or a short rolling pin, simply pull or roll it gently back into shape.

4. Place the crème fraîche, the cottage cheese and the sour cream in a food processor and purée until it is smooth. Season it lightly with salt and pepper and spread it evenly over the dough, going all the way out to the edges. Sprinkle the cream mixture as evenly as possible with the onions, then with the bacon, and bake in the centre of the oven until the tart is deep golden at the edges and the cream is golden on top, about 12 to 20 minutes – the time it takes to bake truly depends on the dryness of the heat in your oven, and the time can vary wildly. The shorter cooking time is optimal so that the cream stays smooth, but either way the tart tastes delicious! Remove from the oven and cut into serving pieces. Serve immediately.

6 to 8 first course servings

Note: in France, *fromage blanc* is blended with crème fraîche then placed on the dough. The blend of cottage cheese and sour cream used here is a worthy substitute.

Driving *À La Française*

I'm not a procrastinator by nature, but something about needing to get a French driver's licence turned me into one. I had to do it, but I didn't want to do it and I didn't honestly see why I should. I've always been a good and careful driver, and even when I don't understand the rules of the road or the myriad signs one finds on highways and byways throughout the world, I do very well. But in France, no matter who you are or where you come from in the United States (except for a handful of states that have reciprocal agreements with France, none of them places I've ever lived), in order to get a driver's licence you have to go through the same hoops and expense as any French eighteen-year-old. This includes twenty hours of driving lessons, hours and hours of watching slides, and a hefty amount of money that, scuttlebutt has it, goes right into the coffers of – well – who knows, exactly, but every French person I know thinks the whole driver's education and exam system is an *arnaque* – a swindle.

Michael felt about the licence issue the way I did. He's been driving since he was fourteen, when he first took the wheel of a tractor on his family's farm (occasionally making it do wheelies when his parents weren't looking) and since I've known him – upwards of twenty years – he's never done anything crazier on the road than a few wild slaloms when it was perfectly empty.

In France, the rules of the road are complicated, multi-tiered, and absolutely unrelated to anything coherent or practical, as far as I can see. Instead of taking a logical, organized approach to driving, the French rules seem to have evolved over time to accommodate not only ancient and narrow roads that were never meant to admit vehicles larger than a small horse-drawn buggy and the French penchant for immortality that pushes them to drive faster than the wind, tailgating all the while, but also the Gallic allergy to waiting one's turn dutifully.

Take the Etoile at the Arc de Triomphe in Paris as an example, perhaps the country's most famous roundabout. The first time I drove around it I was a twenty-five-year-old cooking school apprentice driving a large van filled with food and several people. I approached what can only be described as a rat's nest of cars, held my breath and jumped in the fray, which spat me out safely on the exact street I'd wanted. My system of melting in and bursting out worked so well that I've used it ever since, and am very comfortable driving anywhere in Paris, or any other French city. So, as long as Michael and I had valid US driver's licences, and kept our international driver's licences up to date, we figured we were all right. Neither were officially 'valid' but they worked like a bad odour whenever we were stopped by a gendarme who, with one look at the unfamiliar papers, would quickly wave us away. But then my driver's licence expired. Michael's had already expired, so there wasn't a legal driver in the family, and we were now certain that our car insurance wasn't valid either. We had begun transporting other people's children back and forth to school, and I would soon be ferrying cooking school participants to farms and markets. We needed our licences and we needed them now.

Like the good French person I have become, I looked around to see if there was a way of 'fixing' this situation, of finding a *tuyau*, a 'tip' to avoid the whole process of driver's school. I asked everyone I knew, beginning with the most influential people on down, stating the situation boldly. No one could help. This was a first. I have become so accustomed to having 'fixers' at all levels of French society, and occasionally being a fixer myself, that at first I didn't believe it. As a last resort I went to a friend who is the ultimate fixer of everything for everyone, but who sometimes goes over into slightly shady areas. This friend created a swimming pool company on paper so he could buy swimming pool equipment wholesale; he is also, on paper, a contractor, restaurateur, skin diver, and ship's captain, with business licences for each profession, allowing him all sorts of entrées and wholesale shopping possibilities. If he couldn't fix the driver's licence situation, no one could.

He couldn't, and it vexed him. His delight in life is cheating the French system but, according to him, there was no fix possible for this situation. 'What I can do,' he said, brightening a bit, 'is I send you to my uncle who owns *auto-écoles*, driving schools. You tell him you're my friend and he'll give you a deal.'

I went to his uncle's *auto-école* and he did offer us a slight reduction in the price – $800 instead of $1000 for the entire process, including all the slides we could handle watching – which I was ready to accept. But then he told me I would have to do the twenty hours of driver's training in the car, which would cost extra. This would never do.

There are driving schools on every street corner in Louviers, so I went to another one, and the woman there suggested we go out in a car so that she could evaluate my driving. As I settled behind the wheel of the tiny Renault I felt thrust right back into adolescence, complete with a slightly resentful attitude. I listened to the *monitrice*'s careful explanations regarding the car, looked at the many distracting mirrors that would help her see what I was doing, saw the outline of what she would be looking for. Finally, she pointed to the brake under her right foot, which she said she would step on if I got going too fast. I inserted the key in the ignition, painfully grinding the clutch as I started the car.

Once we were off, I grew back up. This was fine; I knew how to drive. I negotiated roundabouts, drove down tiny little one-way streets, got onto and off the autoroute and returned to where we'd begun. The instructor said nothing to me the whole time we were on the road. I parked the car, and turned off the ignition. She turned to me.

'Madame Loomis,' she said. 'Your worst habit is that your movements are too fast. You must be more relaxed in the car.' I looked at her.

'*Pardon?*' I said.

'Your gestures,' she said, 'they are too fast. You mustn't be so rapid.'

That seemed to me to be a character assessment rather than a driving fault.

'You see,' she continued, 'you must move slowly to show that you are thinking about what you are doing and not just reacting.'

'Sheesh,' was all I could think.

There were other criticisms. 'You don't shift fast enough, you don't stay in second gear enough, you are

218

clumsy on the roundabouts. You'll need at least five hours' instruction in the car.'

My adolescence returned. There was no way on earth I would do five hours. I thanked her, paid my fee, and returned home to stew.

Fortunately Brigitte, Fiona's babysitter at the time, saved the day. She was outraged that we had to take the test, shaking her head at the stupidity of the French rules. 'If you've got to do it, go to Philippe Rio,' she said. 'He's honest.' That was high praise for someone in the *auto-école* business, and I wasted no time in heading out. I walked from our house through the Place des Pompiers to his office, a matter of ten minutes. Madame Rio, proprietor with her husband, welcomed me graciously. I told her our situation, and she did a quick calculation. 'This is what I think you need, and this is what it will cost,' she said, handing me the piece of paper she'd been working on. I looked at it. Her total was about $300 for both of us. 'This is everything?' She enumerated exactly what that fee would cover.

'You will have unlimited time for viewing the driving slides, and the fee for the exam is included here, along with the fee for the licence itself,' she said. 'Once you bring me your paperwork we will handle all of the administrative work, and one or other of us will accompany you to both the written and the driving test. Any time in the car with either my husband or myself will be extra,' she said.

'OK,' I thought. 'They must make their money through hours in the car.'

'If you've been driving for as many years as you say you have, then you'll probably just need an hour or two in the car,' she said.

This seemed to good to be true. I asked her to repeat

her offer once more, in case I'd misunderstood. This time, she wrote it down.

I left with a fistful of papers to fill out, returned them promptly to her and we turned up for our first class on a Wednesday afternoon. The room was full of teenagers and we slunk in and sat at the back. Madame Rio gave each of us a clipboard and pencil to mark down answers to the questions posed on the forty slides she would show, then proceeded to run through them. I would say that between us Michael and I knew the answers to five or six.

When the slides were finished, Madame Rio went slowly back through them, explaining the answers and entertaining questions. Michael and I both wished we could have disappeared. Not only was this dull and a waste of time, but we didn't know anything.

We were filing out when Madame Rio came up to us. 'I imagine that you didn't do too well,' she said with an appraising look. 'Why don't you come for individual lessons? It won't cost you any more.'

Who was this angel from heaven, I wondered?

We began to go three times a week, and each time Madame Rio patiently went through the slides, then the answers, with us. Michael did very well on the tests. I did horribly. I just couldn't wrap my head around either the subject, or the fact that this was necessary. I didn't like taking time out of my schedule, and I didn't like to face the ugly truth – I was going to have to spend time memorizing this material. No amount of native intelligence would get me through this one. Michael, on the other hand, took the experience between his teeth and fought with it. He studied, he thought about it, he paid attention while he drove.

Three times a week we took tests, each one different from the other, and three times a week our scores hovered around eleven mistakes out of forty questions, which was unacceptable. We were only allowed five mistakes on the actual test. Madame Rio was the picture of patient tolerance. She didn't mind that we got confused, she didn't mind Michael making cracks about the convoluted questions, or the intellect that inspired them. He was constantly going on about how 'French' the reasoning of the rules was. 'It doesn't make sense, why don't they just redo the whole thing?' he said more than once. Most of the time she agreed with him, and she always laughed. To her, I believe, we provided an entertaining sideshow, a departure from the ordinary.

Like many people, Madame Rio fell under the spell of Michael's cynical humour. He would literally snort when a slide came up that showed a ridiculous situation – such as the one that portrays two cars parked half on the pavement in a very narrow street, forcing any car wanting to pass through the street to go up on the opposite pavement. The question? Where should the oncoming driver look to be sure he didn't hit the cars? To us, the situation begged an entirely different question: why were cars allowed to park in such a narrow street?

The rules of the road concerning cyclists made him snort, too. There is one set if a bicycle approaches an intersection from the right, and another set if it approaches from the left. And if it is Monday the rules change, whereas if it is Thursday, they don't apply at all. Well, that latter is a slight exaggeration, but it is definitely in the vein of how the rules of the road in France work.

Our favourite *casse-tête*, or brain-teaser, was the 1–15/16–30 round blue and red parking sign. It meant that parking was legal on one side of the street from the first to the fifteenth of the month, inclusive, and that it was legal on the other side of the street from the sixteenth to the thirtieth. The placement of the sign was the key to which side of the street was legal on which days. That was arcane enough, but it got worse. These signs – like all traffic signs – can be amended to account for specific situations. Say, for example, this round red and blue sign with the infinitesimally tiny numbers on it had a small, rectangular white sign under it with more numbers – this indicated which days the rules applied. There might be yet another sign under the first two with a graphic of children on it, which might mean the dates applied unless it was a school day. Or maybe there would be an elephant graphic on the sign that meant no parking for elephants any time. The more we learned the rules, the more convoluted they seemed. It shouldn't have been that surprising to either of us, since life in France is more complicated that life in the United States on just about every level. Every single thing we try to do in France is complicated, whether it be registering a child for school, filing taxes, or going to the supermarket. The French mentality just doesn't embrace the notion of efficiency. What it appreciates is form and system. Everything from filling out multiple papers to the enormously complicated rules of the road seems to provide a comfort on some level.

One day, as I was struggling with the meaning of double red stripes on posts at the right side of the road, the light dawned. I realized that learning the rules of the road was something like learning the language. You didn't have to understand, you just had to guess well. In fact, as in learning the language, it was a hindrance to try and understand. I remember well when this same light dawned for me during my apprenticeship with the language. Long ago, in my tiny *chambre de bonne* – garret room – in Paris I would spend hours reading French, translating every word, taking notes, going over and over vocabulary. No matter how much I read and studied, my spoken French didn't improve. Then, one day, I realized I just had to close my eyes and jump in, rather like going around the Arc de Triomphe. I began to listen to people talk, get the gist of what they were saying, then respond with the gist of what I thought I should say. It was miraculous. Who cared about understanding all those '*qui*' and '*ça*' words. The point was to have a vague notion of what the paragraph meant. The same seemed to be true for the rules of the road. I could memorize all I wanted, but when it came down to pressing that button on the electronic remote control answering device, a vague understanding stood me in better stead.

Christmas was approaching, and we'd been watching slides for more than two months. One morning Madame Rio announced the date for our exam. It was two weeks away. 'We're not ready,' we both said. 'You will be,' she countered. She had decided it was time.

Madame Rio became stricter, more impatient when our scores were low (which they still were – we didn't seem able to get fewer than eight mistakes). Michael had studied so much he could have recited the book of traffic rules out loud with no errors, but the slides stumped him. 'The questions are so bizarre that there is no possible way to get them right,' he would say. Madame Rio shook her head. 'It's true, you Americans are much more clear and direct than we are, in everything,' she said. 'But you still have to pass the test.'

The big day dawned. Madame Rio had suggested we take the exam geared to foreigners, and that we hire an interpreter. 'You will want any advantage you can get,' she said. We agreed, and went into the examiner's office to meet our destiny. Madame Rio was there, a sheaf of papers in her hand. I was surprised to see her. 'Of course I'm here,' she said. 'It wouldn't be right of me not to accompany you, just in case there is any problem.' She waited with us until it was time to hand over the papers and go into the examining room. Then, she shook our hands and left.

We were assigned seats in the cold, drab room. Michael was in the front row, I was two rows behind him, and our interpreter, a tiny, nervous woman, was seated on the other side of the room. The *moniteur*, an officious grey-haired gentleman with a stylish tweed jacket and impeccably tailored dark trousers, imperiously gave us directions as he handed out the remote controls we would use to register our answers.

'There is to be no talking whatsoever,' he growled. 'If anyone says anything, they will be disqualified immediately. Each question gets one answer. For those with an interpreter, if you have a question raise your hand and the interpreter will translate the question. Absolutely no talking.'

The first slide went up on the screen. It was scratched, smeared, blurry, hard to see. I thought it was a mistake, but it wasn't. Subsequent slides were just as tough to read. Here we were at the moment of reckoning, and these were the only slides they had to show us? Didn't they understand that each of us in this room wanted one thing, and one thing only – to pass the test so we'd never have to see another stupid traffic slide in our lives? How could they make it even more difficult than it needed to be? I could only imagine what Michael was thinking.

After twenty questions the *moniteur* stopped the slides, then stalked slowly up and down the rows, glancing at each remote control to see that we were keeping up, harrumphing. The tension in the room was palpably moist and sticky as everyone fidgeted, scratched and eyed the examiner.

He stopped near a woman in the back and started talking to her in a very loud voice. It became obvious that she hadn't been able to figure out how to use the electronic remote control, nor could she, I suspected, read French well enough to answer the questions. In any case, she was hopelessly lost. The *moniteur* derided her, cruelly. He made her continue the exam and didn't let up on her the whole time.

A slide came up with an obscure word in it. Michael raised his hand for an interpretation, and the interpreter started in. She mistranslated so badly that I said, 'Wait a minute,' before I even realized it. The examiner growled at me. 'Madame, you are risking disqualification.' 'B-but,' I stammered, 'she is incorrect.'

'Madame,' he growled some more. Finally the test was over. I was wrung out and so depressed I could hardly look up. I hated the *moniteur*, the interpreter, and everyone involved in this humiliating exercise. I'd failed, and all I could think of was more hours in that dark little room with Madame Rio and her slides. To crown an awful experience, the *moniteur* went to the front of the room, sat down at a table with a cash-register-like machine on it, and called the first person's name. This meant that each one of us had to stand in front of the room and wait to hear whether or not we'd passed, while the rest of the room looked on. I don't know why this surprised me – shame is a fundamental precept of all French education, and the driving test was not exempt.

A young man slouched up there and looked at the ceiling while the machine oh-so-slowly spat out tickets with his score. The monitor tore off the ticket, looked at it and barked, '*Bon.*' The young man signed the paper, sprouted wings and flew out through the door.

We all watched our fellow exam-takers as they stood in abject fear awaiting their results. An Asian woman failed by one point and she began to argue about the poor quality of the slides. The torturer, which is how I now thought of the examiner, simply looked at her and said, '*Au revoir, Madame.*'

He called Michael's name. I almost passed out with anxiety as Michael waited for his slip of paper. '*Tout bon,*' the *moniteur* said. Michael nearly collapsed with relief. I was so happy for him, but I was still depressed and I had a long while still to wait. I didn't even care. I knew I'd failed.

He called my name and I walked up there in a nervous daze. My ticket chugged out and he slowly tore it off, enjoying himself immensely. '*Madame,*' he said as I stood there trying not to cry, '*vous avez tout bon aussi. Félicitations,*' he said.

Michael grabbed me, which kept me from fainting. I'd passed. We whooped with delight, ignoring the solemn, awful atmosphere. I signed my paper and out we walked, giddy with relief as we did a post-mortem on the exam. 'Could you believe how awful the slide quality was?' 'What was the answer to number four?' 'I was sure I'd failed by number twelve.'

I had forgotten about the interpreter, who couldn't have interpreted her way out of a paper bag. There she was, stuck to us like glue, waiting to be paid. I paid her and off she went.

We were free from bondage, how fabulous! I called Madame Rio to share the good news – I knew she would be as relieved as we were, and indeed she was. 'Bravo,' she said. 'I knew you'd pass. I didn't want to tell you before you took it, but the test is actually much easier than the exercises we did together in class.

As we drove home, Michael looked at me. 'You know what I was thinking, all through the test?' he asked. 'I was thinking how humiliated I'd be if I had to tell Joe that I failed.'

I had been thinking the same thing. Joe had observed us studying, memorizing, asking each other questions, writing out little cheat notes (which Madame Rio encouraged us to take to the test.) There we were, his parents, encouraging him to study, telling him that hard work is the road to success. If we'd failed, our credibility would have evaporated.

Our travails weren't over. We still had to go through driving lessons and the driving test. Michael went for a lesson with Mr Rio the very next week. A strong, well-muscled, friendly man, Mr Rio has been instructing novice drivers for more than twenty years, and he has the same good-humoured patience, the same dedication, the same pride in his work as his wife. Their goal, it was obvious, was that each and every one of their students would become a good driver and get their licence the first time around. Michael returned. 'How was it?' I asked. 'Fine,' he said. Apparently Mr Rio just pointed out a few things to be careful of – it would be no problem. He did one more hour with Mr Rio, took the driving test, and passed.

'The examiner was a woman,' he told me when he came home from the driving test. 'When I got in the car I told her I was nervous and she looked at me and said, "Don't worry, you'll do fine." She chatted the whole time, had me do a few manoeuvres, then it was over.' The Michael Loomis charm at work, I thought. I should be so lucky.

I took a driving lesson with Mr Rio, who said nothing about my movements being too rapid, and scheduled me for one additional hour. I did that one with Madame Rio, who pronounced me ready to take the test.

The *moniteur* was tall, concave and pale, a look-alike for one of the aunts in *James and the Giant Peach*. He stood quietly talking with Mr Rio – no doubt about how he was planning on torturing me and another young woman who was waiting to take the test, too. He indicated we should get in the car. I volunteered to go first, and the young woman, who was by now nearly in tears, darted into the back seat next to Mr Rio.

After verifying my name, address, age and nationality, he indicated that I should start the car. We drove out into the traffic of Louviers, and he got me to wind around little streets, turn sharp corners, even back up a long road. Then we took to the country roads. Aside from cocking his head and saying, 'Now turn left, and now turn right,' he remained impassive. He finally signalled me to stop, and I traded places with the young woman, who tried to kill us many times before she jerkily stopped us where we'd begun. I looked at Mr Rio and all he did was raise his eyebrows. 'Oh lord,' I thought, 'what does *that* mean?'

Monsieur Moniteur continued making little notes on his pad, fussily crossing t's and dotting i's then signing with a flourish. '*Madame Loomis, c'est bon.*' Whew. '*Mlle,*' he turned to my fellow examinee, '*ce n'est pas bon.*' Oh dear, the poor young woman had just failed her third driving test. I pitied her the hours she had in front of her, watching those miserable slides and taking those hours of driving lessons.

When Joe came home from school that day and we told him, he high-fived us. 'Bravo Mom and Dad,' he said with feeling. We'd lived through this one together, and we were *all* glad it was over. Now I needn't worry about driving anyone's children, nor about driving during the cooking classes: we were not only well instructed, but we were legal.

We had realized very early on our good luck in encountering the Rios to help us through this experience. What could have been horribly grim and painful had been only moderately painful and not at all grim. We owed them much and decided to invite them to dinner as a thank-you. Madame Rio and I had talked enough about food for me to know that she and her husband were gourmands, yet it was risky inviting them over. Being chummy with someone at the workplace is one thing; getting them into your home is another. I prepared myself to hear Madame Rio make an excuse about not being able to come, but I was pleasantly surprised when she accepted. We settled on a date, and that was that. 'We won't stay late, Suzanne,' she said. 'We've got classes the next day.' I assured her that was fine.

The week of the dinner I received a call from a British friend I hadn't seen in many years, saying he was going to be in our neighbourhood and could he stop by? It turned out that it would fall on the same night the Rios were coming to dinner. I told him yes, then when I hung up the phone, I was suddenly struck with doubt. What if the Rios were standoffish in private, or didn't like English people? In our time in France, we've seen it all: the shy, the reserved, the anti-foreigners, the curious. We didn't think the Rios were any of these things, but we'd been surprised before.

The dinner was on a Saturday night, and my British friend David had said he would arrive around teatime. When I got to thinking about it, I couldn't remember when teatime was. I was ready at 4.30 p.m. with cookies and tea. Then I brought up a bottle of wine from the *cave*. Just in case. Then I put some olives in a bowl. I was ready for everything.

I was working in the office when David arrived with a beautiful young Turkish woman named Deedum, his children's au pair, at 5.30. It was an emotional reunion, as I hadn't seen David in almost thirty years, not since before his younger sister, my dearest childhood friend, had died in a car accident. David was as handsome, relaxed, funny and warm as I remembered. The Turkish au pair was gorgeous and sweet. I could see we were in for a fun time.

I offered tea or coffee but I could see that wine and olives were much more the mood of the crowd. Michael came home from working in his studio, dressed for dinner, and everyone settled into the kitchen while I cooked. The Rios were due at 8 p.m., and I doubted they would be late.

I was going to grill rabbit in the fireplace, but first I had to cut it into serving pieces, slather it with mustard, and wrap it with bacon. I began cutting it up on the butcher block across from where everyone was sitting to enjoy their aperitif, listening to the conversation and laughter. Suddenly, it became quiet. I looked up and they were all staring. 'Not used to seeing someone cut up a rabbit,' David said, raising his eyebrows. Both Deedum and our new au pair, Brinn, had horrified looks on their faces. They had all just discovered the downside of a comfortable kitchen with stools across from the work surface.

The rabbit was ready, macerating in the mustard and bacon so it would absorb flavour before I put it over the coals. I turned to making scallion bread, which I would cook in a skillet as the Algerians do, then serve with fresh goat's cheese seasoned with black pepper, some garlic and chives. I had made pastry earlier in the day for the apple, pear and brown sugar tart I was going to make. All I needed to do was cut up the fruit, assemble the tart and put it in the oven. Pretty soon, Deedum was standing beside me, asking me questions. I turned to get some cinnamon from the spice drawer, and she exclaimed when I opened it up. She asked if she could smell the spices and, when I said yes, she began to open each one and inhale, trying to guess at the ones she didn't know. 'When I get back to Turkey I will send you spices,' she said. 'And a Turkish cookbook. You must learn how to cook Turkish food.'

With her help I finished a potato and cauliflower gratin and put it in the Aga's oven. Then I rolled out and cut the sweet and savoury olive cookies that we would eat with champagne, and put them in the oven. Michael had baked bread that afternoon, so I cut thin slices, rubbed them with garlic and set them around a bowl of Sardinian olive oil. I thinly sliced kohlrabi, dressed it in lemon juice and white pepper and put a bowl of it next to the bread, and put out bowls of pistachio nuts, and hazelnuts from our tree.

Just then a knock on the glass of our front door announced the Rios. Everything was nearly ready but I hadn't yet dressed for the evening. Now it was too late. I hoped they weren't formally dressed, as many French people are when they come to dinner. I needn't have worried; they were nicely but casually dressed, and in they walked, smiling and delightfully at ease. I saw that I their attitude to the other guests was not going to be a problem, either. David plunged into conversation with his fractured French; Michael was in good form goading everyone along; Deedum and Brinn got along famously.

Madame Rio handed me a hostess gift – twelve gorgeous fat brown eggs from her chickens – and Michael handed her and Mr Rio glasses of champagne. Our evening had officially begun.

The scallion bread and cheese, the rabbit and the gratin, the salad and the fruit tart, which we ate in our timbered dining room with the backdrop of a big fire and candlelight, turned out beautifully, though the best part of the evening was the crowd. Here we all were – this wonderful French couple, our English friend and a Turkish au pair, a young American girl and our two children who ran in and out all evening – laughing, eating, drinking and having the time of our lives. And on top of it all, we had our driver's licences. Life was definitely good.

A funny thing has happened to my driving since I acquired my French licence. It has deteriorated. I was better off when I relied on instinct. Somehow, knowing the rules has meant that I pay too much attention to what should be done instead of seeing what is done. Take my last encounter with the Etoile in Paris. I had three friends in the car and did my usual jumping in. This time, though, instead of simply negotiating my way through the maze, I was conscious of priority on the right, hanging back on the left, signalling, turning my head, not turning my head . . . and all the other rules that have nothing to do with actually getting through it. I almost got us all killed. Michael has noticed a similar phenomenon with his driving. I wouldn't want the Rios to know this, though I'm not certain either one would be surprised, but we assume our skills will return to normal as we gradually forget everything they helped us learn.

GRILLED RABBIT WITH MUSTARD AND BACON
Lapin Grillé à la Moutarde et Lard Fumé

This is simple, and simply scrumptious!

One 3 lb (1.5kg) rabbit, cut in serving pieces, liver and
kidneys removed
¼ cup (60ml) Dijon-style mustard
8 oz (250g) thinly sliced slab bacon, rind removed

1. Slather the pieces of rabbit all over with mustard. Wrap
   each piece of rabbit with bacon to cover it – the large
   pieces of rabbit will need two pieces of bacon to wrap
   them. Hold the bacon onto the rabbit with small metal
   skewers.
2. Build a medium-size fire in the grill or the fireplace.
   When the coals are red and just slightly dusted with
   ash, place the grill about 5 inches from them. When
   the grill is hot, place the rabbit on the grill and cook
   it, turning frequently, until it is golden and cooked
   through, about 35 minutes. About half way through the
   cooking time, place the liver on top of one of the pieces
   of rabbit, and the kidneys directly on the grill, and cook
   them until they are cooked through (they will each take
   about 15 minutes). Watch them carefully so they don't
   over cook.
3. Season the rabbit with salt and pepper, remove from
   the grill and serve immediately.

4 to 6 servings.

SCALLION BREAD
Pain aux Cebettes

———— ᴄꙅᴏ ————

Cebettes are wild onions that resemble scallions – I use them in this bread, or fresh spring bulb onions, which have a sweeter flavour.

1 cup (250 ml) lukewarm water
1 envelope (2½ tsp) active dry yeast
2 cups (265 g) unbleached all-purpose flour
½ cup (70g) fine semolina
1½ tsp salt
1 cup (70g) thinly sliced spring onions
2 tsp Japanese sesame oil
2 tsp peanut oil
1 tsp dried red pepper flakes (optional)
1 tsp kosher (coarse) salt (optional)

1. To make the bread, place the water and the yeast in a large bowl, or in the bowl of an electric mixer, and mix well. Add 1 cup (135 g) of the flour, mix well, and then add the salt. Continue adding the flour, then the semolina, ½ cup (70 g) at a time, mixing well after each addition, until the dough becomes stiff. If you are using an electric mixer, change to the dough hook and knead the dough until it is elastic and no longer sticks to the sides of the bowl. Or knead it by hand on a lightly floured work surface until the dough is elastic and no longer sticks to your hands, 6 to 8 minutes. Cover the dough with a kitchen towel and let it rise at room temperature until it has doubled in bulk, about 1 hour.

2. Punch down the dough, and gradually knead the scallions into it. Keep working the dough until the scallions are thoroughly combined – they will have a tendency to pop out of the dough, but just gently work them back in. Divide the dough into 4 pieces, and let them rest for about 15 minutes.

3. Heat ½ tsp of each of the oils in a heavy 10-inch (25 cm) skillet (preferably cast-iron) over medium-high heat.

4. Roll out 1 piece of the dough on a lightly floured surface until it is about ⅛ inch (3 mm) thick and about the circumference of the skillet. Transfer it to the hot skillet, sprinkle the top lightly with ⅛ teaspoon of the dried red pepper flakes and ⅛ teaspoon of the kosher salt, if desired. Cover, and cook until the top puffs and begins to look baked, about 5 minutes. Flip the bread, repeat with ⅛ teaspoon each of the red pepper flakes and the salt, and continue cooking until it is baked through, 4 to 5 minutes. Remove the bread, cut it into quarters, and serve immediately. Repeat with the remaining dough and seasonings.

12 to 14 appetizer servings

Paris

Ahh, Paris. The city of *'manèges'*.

You thought it was the City of Light? It is that, too, but for our vivacious three-year-old daughter, it is the city of merry-go-rounds, or *manèges*.

Fiona was born loving Paris. I believe this predilection came to her through the umbilical cord that joined us, and it fits her well. Pert and feminine, a natural *coquette*, flirt, as well as a *coquine*, or rascal, she is right at home there, prancing down the busy pavements, looking up at the waiter through her eyelashes when she orders a *chocolat chaud*, racing down the alleyways of the Jardin des Tuileries to get to the ice-cream stand before anyone else. She loves all of these things, along with the métro, the man playing the barrel-organ with the cat sitting on top who stands near Printemps, not far from the train station at Gare Saint-Lazare; the old-fashioned tea shop, La Durée, near the church of the Madeleine; the Tour Eiffel – they are all as magic to her as they have always been to me.

At least three mornings a week, Fiona gets up, has her breakfast of baguette slathered with butter, then collects her little *sac* and says, 'Bye, I'm going to Pehwis.' We kiss her, and off she goes into the dining room and the Paris of her mind. What she finds there is any number of things, from 'Kehwee', my wonderful assistant who lives there and whom Fiona adores, to Madeline and her convent school.

Up until Fiona was a year old, I took her to Paris often. She would ride in a little carrier I wore on my front when she was tiny. I loved those trips, for I felt as fancy-free as ever, only I had the wonderful company of her golden curls just below my chin, her warmth on my chest. Not too many French parents carry their children that way, and I would get plenty of stares as I ran up and down métro steps, strolled along shady avenues in the sixth or the ninth arrondissements, two of my favourites, or stopped at a neighbourhood café for a *café crème*.

The first time I took her in, I had an appointment with the publicist of the French edition of one of my books, the *French Farmhouse Cookbook* which was being published by J. C. Lattès, a chic publisher on rue Jacob in the sixth arrondissement. Fiona was just a few months old, so there was no question that I would go anywhere without her, but I was a bit uneasy taking her with me since babies aren't the quintessence of chic. When I mentioned to the extremely young publicist that I would be bringing Fiona, she cooed and said, '*Pas de problème.*'

I was dressed in navy and white, carried Fiona in a little navy blue and white kangaroo pack, had a sober navy blue diaper bag over my shoulder and felt stylishly confident. I've lived in France long enough to know that if you're in navy blue you're *bon chic bon genre* (chic but conservative), and it is hard for people to fault your look. If no one can fault your look here, they don't tend to fault your behaviour either. I emerged from the train station at Gare Saint-Lazare, and walked briskly past the FNAC, France's huge and diverse bookshop, to Boulevard Haussman. It was spring and the trees there had just sprouted brilliant green leaves. Though it was long after Christmas, that year's decoration of fuchsia and purple spangles still hung in the trees, flashing and glinting in the breeze. I crossed the street and angled left towards Opéra, whose gilt statues were so bright in the sunlight they almost blinded me, then I turned right down the Avenue de l'Opéra to make my way to the Louvre. The Avenue de l'Opéra is one of the city's grand boulevards, lined on both sides with a mixture of duty-free shops, travel agencies, obscure banks from obscure little countries, a Boulangerie Paul, with its tempting-looking breads and tarts in the window, and a Monoprix. I love Monoprix: it is an inexpensive department store that offers everything from trendy and inexpensive clothes for adults and children, to popular beauty products, school supplies and some food. I rarely go in; I just like knowing that, in this world of Gaps and Zaras, it still exists.

I passed the Palais Royal and the métro stop there that looks as if it was designed by Ali Baba, because it is covered with baubles and jewels, then walked under the Louvre and out into the Cour Napoléon, where I. M. Pei's glass pyramids confound. Fiona was comfortably asleep, and if I hadn't felt her weight I might have forgotten she was with me as I hurried along, enjoying the sounds and the sights. I crossed the Seine, then headed down rue des Saints Pères, past antique stores and a magical florist who, this year, was featuring bouquets made with slightly wilted roses.

I turned left onto rue Jacob and dawdled at the windows of one of the antique stores there, with its gorgeous array of porcelain bowls and stacks of Limoges plates. I passed displays of ochre and green Provençal dishes, clothing with spare, sharp lines, a shop specializing in all manner of gardening and cookery books. Then I walked briskly into the publishing house and up the dingy stairs to the receptionist's office, where I asked for the publicist. She arrived: all tanned, blonde, and be-diamonded, with the news that her wealthy boyfriend had just proposed. She peeked in at the sleeping Fiona, then ushered me upstairs to her offices, which look like publishing offices everywhere – disorderly, dim, quiet, as everyone sits at their desks working miracles with words.

I was offered a straight-backed chair in a minuscule and very crowded office, where I sat down with the publicist and two other women who were going to work on the book's publicity campaign. Just as they got out all their papers and I reached down to get mine, Fiona woke up and began to cry. I'd planned the meeting for this hour because it was between her feedings and, theoretically, she should have slept the entire time. Life is not theory, however, and she was not asleep right now. I decided not to do anything, hoping that she might just go back to sleep, so we began to talk dates, books, events. Fiona continued to cry. In fact, she started screaming. I excused us, extracted Fiona from the kangaroo pack, picked her up and proceeded to nurse her. The women couldn't have been nicer. The young publicist was staring at me, then at Fiona, riveted. We needed her to continue the meeting, but her focus had entirely shifted and she began asking me a litany of questions – about babies, nursing, hospitals. Pretty soon all four of us were engaged in a lively exchange that had nothing at all to do with publicity for my book.

Fiona was still nursing when my editor poked his head round the door. I looked up and there he was, with a slightly horrified look on his face as he realized that we weren't working but *papoter*-ing, chatting, and that I was

240

– in addition – nursing my baby. He nodded, said hello, said he hoped all was well and he disappeared. Poor man. He had four children of his own, but his wife was probably not the nursing kind.

Once Fiona was finished and back to sleep we conducted our meeting, then I walked out of the office and made my way back to the train. This time I stopped for a while in the Tuileries to sit by the pond nearest the Place de la Concorde for some sun and relaxation. I found myself chuckling. My meeting at the publisher's was a first for me, and maybe for them. I'd gone to the meeting with some trepidation, knowing it was unusual to show up with my baby. I'd left realizing that not only had it not hurt my situation at all – we'd designed the bones of a very good publicity campaign – but I'd felt the establishment of a bond of warmth with these women who had been, until now, aloof. I laughed out loud, remembering the look on the editor's face when he stopped by. He and I have a very nice relationship and I was sure he'd come to offer his help yet, when he saw what was transpiring, he panicked. Seeing a woman nursing a baby isn't an everyday occurrence in any French milieu, and in the hallowed halls of this particular publishing house, for all I know it was a first.

Fiona's second trip to Paris was just a few weeks later, when I had an appointment with a dental surgeon in a very fashionable office in the seventeenth arrondissement in the northwest of Paris. He has a bevy of attractive dental assistants who dress in white, are very courteous and extremely formal. The offices are hushed, the floors parquet, the furniture Napoleon III.

This particular day I'd found out while en route to Paris that there was a transport strike in the offing. I had no further details, but I knew from experience that it could mean several things – the cancellation of all trains, métros and buses for the whole day, for a part of the day, or just at certain specific times during the day; or perhaps the cancellation of just certain trains, métros and buses. Whatever it meant, it wouldn't be convenient.

When we got off the train there was no métro service, and the bus service was limited. This didn't affect me, since I'd planned to walk to the dentist's office anyway. I set off with Fiona sleeping in the kangaroo pack, enjoying a beautiful spring day. I figured I would learn more about the strike as I walked, for usually the news kiosks on the street are mines of information. Not this day – apparently, this was a *méchante grève*, a nasty strike, that was evolving as the day wore on.

I loved this particular walk past the church of Saint-Augustin and around the edge of Parc Monceau, then down rue de Courcelles with its very fancy shops, bakeries, cheese shop and toy store. I stopped at the toy store because, in the window, was the very swing I'd been looking for, the kind that attaches to a door-jamb. The shop was closed, otherwise I would have dashed in to buy it. Instead I copied down the phone number and continued on to the 1920s building where, upstairs, I would find the dental surgeon.

By then I'd overheard that by noon there would be no more buses, and there was also talk of all train services being suspended. I entered the hushed dental offices and found – to my delight and surprise – a very warm greeting. This was thanks to Fiona. All the dental assistants, the secretary, and even the surgeon wanted a peek.

I'd made plans to meet my friend Martha Parker, an American screenwriter and director, at her apartment on the Left Bank after the appointment. I'd planned to take the métro, but I would have to walk instead. After a round of goodbye kisses and coos from the surgeon's office, I was off down the stairs with Fiona, outside and into a raging downpour. The timing couldn't have been worse. With no public transport the streets were choked with cars. There was no sense in walking anywhere now – Fiona and I would both have been soaked to the skin in seconds. I ran to a bus shelter where half a dozen people already waited. It was just past noon.

'*Est-ce qu'il y aura un bus?*' – 'Will there be a bus?' I asked a woman standing next to me, not really expecting her to have an answer. '*Qui sait?*' – 'Who knows?', she replied. I waited, the rain continued, no bus arrived. I began looking for a taxi, a hopeless endeavour – the combination of rain and lack of public transport meant that taxis were all taken.

I waited a half an hour along with everyone else under the bus shelter. An older man who was picking up his grandson at the primary school next to the bus shelter offered me a ride, but it turned out he was going in the wrong direction. When the rain let up, I started to walk – the air was fresh; I had time. I figured that if trains were running normally I could visit my friend and still make the 5.30 train home, which would get me there in time to make dinner.

By now the pavements were full of people, and there was tense drama in the air as everyone talked about the strike and how they were late for where they were going. As I approached Gare Saint-Lazare and looked at my watch, I realized I should take the next train if it was running, or else I'd likely have to stay in town overnight. It was a wise move. I just made it, and it turned out to be the last train for that day, and possibly the next, as the strike wasn't nearing resolution. No conductor came to punch tickets – he or she must have already been on strike. Fiona had slept through most of the day, waking up once we were on the train to look around and gurgle before dropping back to sleep and dreaming of her second warm, cosy trip to Paris.

As Fiona got older and heavier I wheeled her around in a big, comfortable *poussette* – pushchair – which folded up with the flick of a handle. I'd always wondered how parents with *poussettes* negotiated the métro stairs, and with Fiona I found out. They did it the same way parents in cities do worldwide: they rely on the good graces of others. Invariably, on arriving at the head of a long flight down into the métro, there seems to be someone who, without being asked, picks up the front of the *poussette* to shoulder it down to the bottom of the stairs. The turnstiles in the métro of two decades ago would have been just about impossible to negotiate. Now, they are manageable, though some still require the lifting of the *poussette* up and over. Again, someone is always there to help.

I like to walk in Paris so much that I don't use public transport unless I have to. While on the train from Normandy I study the *taride*, or city guide, to plan my route, then I set off from the train station fuelled by the thrill of being in the city. I have a pretty good idea of how long things will take, though this wasn't always the case. Michael teases me about when he first came to live with me in Paris and I'd say, 'Oh, let's walk, it's not that far,' and two hours later we'd still not be there. Today I am more realistic and I schedule appointments accordingly. The train I take most often arrives in Paris at 11.45 – I never plan to meet someone for lunch or schedule an appointment of any kind before 1 p.m.

Fiona loved riding around Paris in her *poussette*. She would twitter away happily as I pushed her down the streets and through the Tuileries, took her to Ladurée, my favorite tea salon on the rue Royale for a *bretzel,* a pretzel sort of pastry made with puff pastry and almonds, to Patisserie Millet on rue Saint-Dominique in the seventh arrondissement for their unforgettable croissants, or to Poujauran on nearby rue Jean Nicot for a crisp almond *financier.* I once dared take her to Dehilleran, the kitchen supply store on rue Coquillière near Les Halles. The sales force who work in this old-fashioned, crowded store where there is barely room to move down the narrow aisles between the knives and vegetable peelers, the copper pots and cast-iron baking dishes, the tart moulds and cooling racks, rolling pins and sieves, are notoriously unpleasant and aggressive. They already act annoyed to see customers, so imagine their reaction to a woman pushing a small child in a *poussette.* Suffice it to say that I didn't stay long enough to make the purchase I'd intended.

I remember one visit to Paris in particular when Fiona and I met my friend and colleague Patricia Wells for lunch in a wonderful old bistro across from the department store, Bon Marché. Fiona was dressed for the occasion in a beautiful Soleiado dress that Pat had given her, white tights, and shiny black Mary Jane shoes. She was only a year old but had been walking for a month or two and was surprisingly steady on her feet. We'd arrived at the restaurant early and the dining room was still quite empty, so Fiona could roam as Pat and I ordered our lunch. The chef came out to our table. 'Would you like me to make a simple little *filet* and *purée* for la petite?' he asked. I said yes and, after giving Fiona a little kiss on the head, he went happily back to the kitchen.

Meanwhile, Fiona made friends with the waitress, who picked her up and took her back into the kitchen, where they stayed for some time. She returned with Fiona when our first course was ready, and settled her comfortably in the chair next to me with a glass of water and a straw to keep her happy. Out came our first courses – mackerel braised in white wine for Pat, crisp lardons and a poached egg on curly endive for me, and the *filet* and *purée* for Fiona.

We talked and laughed as we ate our delicious dishes. Fiona took one taste of hers, chewed it up then looked at me with a doleful gaze. '*Pas bon,*' she said in her baby French. 'Oh dear,' I thought. I didn't want to insult the chef by telling him she didn't like it, and I'd decided that I'd have to eat some of her lunch myself, but out he came to see how Fiona was doing. '*Elle n'aime pas?*' he asked. '*Ce n'est pas grave,*' and he took the plate without rancour, to return later with some vegetables for her to chew on, a much more successful choice. As the restaurant filled up Fiona wandered from table to table, not too precocious but not too shy either, investigating what other diners were eating. We had a wonderful time and, when it came time to leave, the waitress – who was rushing about delivering plates of food – blew a goodbye kiss to Fiona.

As Fiona got older she developed the habit of running off after anything that moved, particularly cars, and an abhorrence of holding hands. I can't even count the number of times I walked down the street in Louviers trying to hang onto her wriggling little hand, which would compress into nothing as she worked it free. I took to holding her wrist so she wouldn't flare off into the street, but she hated that too. I realized it would be folly to take her to Paris while she was in this phase, imagining the nightmare of trying to hold onto her in the crowds. So I went alone.

Not long ago I was assigned a story to investigate a tea salon in the ninth arrondissement of Paris, and I thought this a perfect opportunity to reintroduce Fiona to the city. After all, she dreamed of going, talked about it all the time, made 'virtual' trips there constantly.

Our au pair, Brinn, came along, and we began our adventure on the train. Fiona was astonished from the start. First, she couldn't get over all those trees outside that were running so fast to keep up with us. Then we arrived at Gare Saint-Lazare and all she could do was look up at the foggy glass ceiling of the station as we walked through it to the métro. Once down underground she looked around. 'Where is Pehwis?' she asked.

I explained to her that this was all Paris. She looked troubled. 'But Mama, where is the *manège?*' she wanted to know. I'm not sure where she found out about the merry-go-rounds in Paris – perhaps I'd told her how I had taken Joe for rides on them – but it was lodged in her mind. I told her we would find it, but that first we had to have lunch.

We emerged from the métro on rue Notre-Dame de Lorette and began our walk to the *salon de thé*. 'Is *this* Pehwis, Mama?' she asked. I told her it was and she skipped along, looking down alleyways that ended in green gardens, jumping on short walls and walking along them holding my hand. I had to keep her from pulling napkins off café tables set on the street and prepared for lunch, and make sure she didn't run into shops. I was pleased to see that she stopped at the kerb when we approached a street – all those months of training had worked.

We arrived at our destination, a magical garden accessible by a green alleyway that was filled with old-fashioned fragrant roses, voluptuous hydrangeas and a magnificent maple tree. It was bordered on one side by an Italianate villa, the Musée de la Vie Romantique, on another by artists' studios, and on another by a high wall, which separated it from a school and the boisterous noise of children playing. Fiona stopped and looked around. 'Mama,' she said, indignantly. 'There is no *manège* here; this cannot be Pehwis.'

I reassured her that we were in Paris, and we were going to have lunch, then went to the counter of the little '*salon de thé*' called *Le Thé dans le Jardin*, which is tucked under an arched, filigreed, wrought-iron frame painted a gentle Mediterranean green, its slightly dimpled glass allowing light and sun to enter. I ordered a curried cauliflower quiche, a lentil salad and a fig, ham, and cheese bread, a wonderful apple and raspberry crumble, and glasses of *citronnade*, homemade lemonade, for all of us, and carried it to one of the tables where Fiona and Brinn were sitting. We settled ourselves in and I looked around, feeling as if we were in a French movie. To our left were a mother and daughter enjoying a light lunch of salad and dessert; at another table was a handsome middle-aged couple enjoying looking into each other's eyes. Across the garden was a single woman, obviously on her lunch break from the office, and at another table a threesome of elderly women sipping tea.

It was easy to imagine, sitting at one of the tables over-looking the garden alight with snapdragons and daisies, how this lush spot appealed to the writers, artists and composers who came here to visit Georges Sand, who lived in the villa for a time. They included Chopin, Delacroix, Liszt and Dickens. I had learned from reading the museum's brochure that they were all extremely pro-ductive at the villa and its adjacent studios, and they surely took time in the garden for tea or freshly made *citronnade*, just as we were.

When we finished our lunch we got on with the real reason of our visit to Paris, finding a *manège*. We got on the métro and didn't get off until the chaotic Place de la

Concorde. Fiona began to leap with joy and sing. 'We're goin' to the *manège*, we're goin' to the *manège*.' I pointed out the Eiffel Tower. 'Oooh, Pehwis is so beautiful,' she said. Then we turned the corner into the Tuileries and Fiona started running. 'Where is it, Mama, where is the *manège?*' she cried behind her. I caught up with her, grabbed her hand and slowed her down so we could look around. We walked past the pond, which was surrounded by tourists sunning themselves, and looked at all the sculptures. Then I spied the magic, old-fashioned ice-cream cart tucked under a tree. I whispered to Fiona. 'Look, over there, there's ice cream.' She stood stock-still then shot right over there. 'Ice cream, ice cream, I love Pehwis,' she said.

We got our ice cream, which is made with organic fruit and is incredibly fresh and delicious, and moseyed along, licking for all we were worth since it was warm outside. I steered us past the series of little trampolines, past the stylish little café that was added to the garden not too long ago, past the tired-looking ponies waiting to be ridden. Fiona was intent on them until she spied the object of her desire, the gilded, baroque *manège*. In mid-lick, chocolate ice cream obscuring the bottom third of her face, she looked up. *'Le manège, le manège,'* she screamed, and just about dropped the rest of her ice cream. 'Mama, mama let's go . . .'

I let her pull me over there, and I climbed up to the little window, where the man who runs the merry-go-round sits, hour after hour, day after day, handing out tickets as he teases the people who buy them. I passed over the money, thinking as I did so that it hadn't been so long ago since I had brought Joe to this same *manège* and bought him the same '*carnet*' of eight tickets. I counted the years and realized it was seven: time holds still for no one.

Merry-go-rounds are a dime a dozen in France, from the one near the Eiffel Tower, to the one at the entrance to the seaside town of Honfleur in Normandy, to the one at the Place Jean d'Arc in Rouen, to the one that goes up in front of our church in Louviers once a year, and they are all simply wonderful. Most are antiques built of wood and painted in slightly garish fashion, and they gently whir around to the strains of old French music, with the horses and – in the case of some of them – cows, chickens and elephants, going slowly, sometimes jerkily, up and down. Fiona is democratic in her love for merry-go-rounds, and this one was no exception. She had hopped on almost before it stopped, and began walking around trying to choose which animal she would ride.

She got on a horse. 'No, no, not this one,' she said and jumped off. She climbed on a sort of chariot and settled herself in. I attached her little safety belt and she sat there, beaming. Then suddenly she said 'I don't want this one,' undid the little safety belt and jumped down. Caught unprepared, I had to race to get her onto something before the *manège* started up. This time she chose – and stayed on – a goose, and I stood beside her in my role as protective mother. When this ride ended I got off and Brinn got on, Fiona sat in the chariot, and away they went. After about two rotations I noticed Brinn was looking a bit green. I caught her eye and she smiled, wanly. That was her last ride. I accompanied Fiona for all the others, but I didn't mind. I love the merry-go-rounds almost as much as Fiona does.

By the eighth trip, however, I had had my fill. Fiona wanted more, but when I pointed out the rubber-floored playground next door she jumped off and took off at full tilt. When we got there it was bubbling with children racing, screaming, shoving, rotating, bouncing, tilting, falling. Fiona was briefly intimidated, then she got right into the fray, spinning, jumping, climbing and pushing her way in with all the other children.

Eventually it was time for us to catch the train home. Fiona was dishevelled, red-faced and worn out. She'd already made about five friends and she waved goodbye before getting on my back so that I could give her a piggy-back to the station. We got to the train, punched our tickets, found our seats, and Fiona settled in.

'Where we goin' now, Mama?' she said, drowsily.

'We're going home, to Louviers,' I said.

'We're leaving Pehwis?' she asked, her little blonde head leaning hard against my arm.

'Yes, we're going home, but we'll come back to Paris again,' I said.

'OK, we have to, because I love Pehwis,' she slurred, and went to sleep.

I never imagined myself with a little girl, and certainly not one who would feel as besotted with Paris as I do. As our train rumbled home and her hot little form slumped further into mine, I thought of all the times in Paris we have ahead of us.

I can't wait!

CÈPES OMELETTE
Omelette aux Cèpes

လာ

This is inspired by the omelette I had in Paris as Fiona ran about the restaurant making friends with patrons and 'patron' alike! If you can't find cèpes (boletes/porcini) use the wild mushroom of your choice or, if all else fails, button mushrooms.

½ cup flat leaf parsley leaves
1 clove garlic, green germ removed
6 large eggs
Sea salt and freshly ground black pepper
1 tbs goose fat or clarified butter
12 oz (360g) cèpes or other wild mushrooms, trimmed,
cleaned, cut in thick slices

1. Mince together the parsley and the garlic.
2. Whisk the eggs in a medium-sized bowl just until they are broken up and blended. Season with salt and pepper.
3. Heat the fat in a large, heavy-bottomed omelette pan over medium heat. Add the mushrooms and sauté, shaking the pan and stirring gently with a wooden spatula, until the mushrooms begin to turn golden, about 5 minutes. Add the minced parsley and garlic and shake the pan so it mixes evenly into the mushrooms. Continue cooking until the mushrooms are tender through and the garlic is cooked, about 5 minutes. Season to taste with salt and pepper. Increase the heat under the pan to medium high and pour in the egg mixture,

stirring it into the mushrooms. Bring the cooked edges of the egg to the centre of the pan and tilt the pan so the uncooked egg runs to the edges. When the omelette is generally set but still quite liquid, let it cook without stirring until it is nearly set through but still somewhat liquid, 1 to 2 minutes. Turn the omelette out onto a warmed serving platter, sliding it out of the pan until half of it is on the platter, then folding the second half over the first half. Serve immediately.

Serves 4

CHOCOLATE ICE CREAM
Glace au Chocolat

———————— ເພ ————————

There isn't a better chocolate ice cream recipe than this!

3 oz (90g) dark chocolate, 52% cocoa
2½ ounces (75g) dark chocolate, 70% cocoa, or unsweetened
chocolate
3 cups (750ml) semi-skimmed milk, or a mixture of half
whole milk and half non ultra-pasteurized heavy
(whipping) cream
4 large egg yolks
1 cup (200g) vanilla sugar

1. Melt both chocolates with the heavy cream in a sauce-pan over how heat, stirring once the chocolate begins to melt until the mixture is smooth. Transfer to a large bowl and reserve.
2. Scald the milk in a medium-sized pan over medium heat. Reserve.

3. In a large bowl, whisk the egg yolks and the sugar until the mixture is pale yellow and falls from the whisk in a thick ribbon. Slowly whisk in the scalded milk about ¼ cup (60ml) at a time, to avoid cooking the yolks. When all of the milk is whisked into the egg yolks and sugar and the mixture is smooth, return it to the saucepan used for scalding the milk.
4. Set a fine mesh sieve over the bowl holding the chocolate and cream mixture.
5. Place the custard over medium heat and cook, stirring with a wooden spoon in a figure eight pattern so the custard moves constantly across the bottom of the pan and cooks evenly, until the custard is thick enough to coat the back of the spoon. Quickly strain the custard into the chocolate and cream mixture, then whisk the two mixtures together until thoroughly combined. Let cool to room temperature then chill for several hours, or overnight. Freeze according to the manufacturer's instructions.

1 quart (1 litre)

While Louviers Sleeps

Sometimes during what the French call *'la canicule'*, or the dog days of summer, when the air is thick and heavy, I wait until the children are in bed and night has almost fallen, and take to my bicycle. My intention is less to get exercise than to feel the air brush across my skin, for such nights are dead silent, without a breath stirring. Winding away on those pedals gives the illusion of coolness. It is also one of the few ways I can be alone to think, and the evening is my best thinking time.

It is possible that on a really hot day, like today, I haven't even been outside, for I wilt like a petunia in the heat. Oh, I may have run to the outdoor freezer for ice cubes, or taken Fiona to her little plastic pool in the front garden and splashed a bit, but mostly I'm happy to stay inside our thick-walled house. I love it inside when it's so hot out because, with the windows and curtains shut, the house harbours a cool, private stillness. But come late evening and I've got to move.

The easiest bicycle route from our house – and the one I take most often – leads me down rue Tatin, whose timbered houses survived the Second World War, as did ours. They have their shutters closed tight against the evening, though I'm certain their windows at the back are wide open onto what are surely lush gardens.

I swing left onto the newly restored rue Dupont de L'Eure, which is lined with more old timbered houses for one block before it melts into recent, postwar construction. I cross rue General de Gaulle, a main artery of downtown, which is empty of cars. Knots of people stroll down the pavements, most of them young, many with phones clamped to their ears. They are out, like I am, to get the illusion of coolness. I stop for the light at the Boulevard Georges Clemenceau, which rings Louviers like the périphérique rings Paris, and am immediately enveloped in heat again. The minute there are no cars in sight I cross, regardless of what the light says. It is way too hot to wait for it to turn green.

Streets in Louviers change names for no rhyme or reason, and though I haven't turned for blocks, the street I am on is now named rue François Le Camus, after the well-known renovator of Louvier's clothing and textile industry. It is lined once again with large old houses, whose shuttered façades give away nothing, whose inhabitants live their lives oriented to hidden gardens. I pass l'École Notre Dame where Joe went to school, and peek inside the gate to see a table set in the flower garden that sits across from the front door of the school. The sight pleases me, as I imagine the hard-working nuns who live there relaxing at the table in the warm evening air.

Despite the obvious desire the inhabitants of these houses have for privacy, I catch glimpses into their lives through small, high windows cut into their courtyard doors and gates. It is amazing how much I can see as I pedal past: families sitting at long tables, a swimming pool that is now still, someone watering their flowers. From one garden I hear – but can't see – laughter and the clinking of glasses. 'They're having a summer party,' I think as I roll by. The blue-white glow of television seeps out from around many shutters, and I wonder at those within, thinking how hot they must be. Hardy *rose tremières*, hollyhocks, grow tall against the hot walls of the houses, in the narrow chinks between wall and pavement where they somehow find enough soil to sustain them. They give soul to this otherwise blank street.

I pass our friend Joseph-Claude's house, on my right. His family was once one of the wealthiest in Louviers, owners of one of the town's largest textile mills until before the Second World War. They lived in a monumental villa which is just outside town on the River Eure, and which belonged to Joseph-Claude until just a few years ago. He took me in to see it once, and I wondered how it must have felt to him to leave such luxury: a vast kitchen in the *sous-sol*, the basement; a ballroom with gorgeous parquet; lodging for staff; curved walls; oodles of what is known as *patisserie* – ornate plaster work – on the ceilings and walls. It was truly the home of an other-worldly magnate. He is rumoured to have lived off the family fortune, and seems completely at ease in his newer and much scaled-down surroundings. I look into his small courtyard to see if he is there, but he isn't so I ride on.

I come to the corner and turn right. If I kept going straight I would be on the departmental road to Acquigny, which is too well travelled by cars to be welcoming to a bicycle. Michael and I rode it once when Joe was small enough to sit on the back of a bicycle, on our way to visit Christian and Nadine who live just beyond Acquigny. Drivers in our area aren't known for their patience with, or politeness towards, bicycles, and it was a hair-raising experience that I'm not eager to repeat. At this hour of the night, when everything is the same colour, it would be suicidal.

The street I am on now, rue Henri Dunant, is well lit. On one side are old-fashioned houses with lovely little front gardens and modest stone walls or fences. On the left is a big wooden hangar full of cars, with more cars spilling out on the street. I learned from our last neighbourhood meeting how much residents hate this garage because it is such an eyesore, and because the *garagiste* parks so many of the cars he is working on in a haphazard fashion outside. He has a legal right to work there and, according to the mayor, there is nothing to be done. I sympathize as I ride by.

Just beyond the garage is a two-storey apartment building constructed with public funds, which is surprisingly attractive. It blocks the view of the people on the other side of the street, who until it was built could look right out into farmland without end, but it could have been much worse. Seeing some of the other buildings being constructed in Louviers with public funds, this neighbourhood fared very well.

At the end of this street I can turn either right or left, for directly in front of me is the last remaining farm within the city limits of Louviers. I wish I could wave a magic wand and repair the crumbling walls and weak roof, and even out the small fields and bring back the kind of economy that would support such a place – but I can't, so I look at it with nostalgia and turn left. The old farm slides into several fields, then a patch of land that is owned by the city and given over to family gardens. Each patch is impeccably cared for, often divided by boundaries of dahlias or bachelor buttons, irises or daisies.

There are many North Africans who work these garden

plots, which overflow with fava beans and aubergines, tomatoes, onions and many varieties of peppers and herbs, all destined for sumptuous *tagines* or couscous, I am sure. Tonight it is almost dark and there is no one tilling the soil. When I ride by during the day there is a whole male society working away in the gardens. Each gardener has a small shed for tools, outside of which often stands a table, chairs and an umbrella. Now and then there are children, mothers and grandmothers sitting in the chairs enjoying the fresh air. I imagine most of the gardeners who tend these plots live in apartment buildings – how they must welcome this space.

Across from the gardens is more public housing, a handful of attached two-storey homes with patchwork front gardens. In another place and without any luck they might be stuck in a high-rise. Here, they may not have an excess of room inside, but their gardens abut fields and downtown is only twenty minutes away.

I leave the gardens and the houses behind as the street becomes a narrow road, which strikes out among the fields. It is nearly the end of July and, though closing in on 10.30 p.m., still light enough to see. It is never truly dark enough in and around Louviers for the sky to be black, and one of the things I love best here are the blues the sky achieves. They are unclassifiably beautiful and intense. Sometimes, like tonight, I ride along looking up in absolute awe at what is a deep royal blue, though that doesn't take into account the dark navy or the rich cerulean swaths. I wish I could pluck the blue from the sky and wear it, for it looks soft and rich and is unbelievably intense.

Further ahead I see a brilliantly lit combine harvester crawling down a field, looking like a miniature city with its many levels and illusion of inhabitants. In fact, there is just one man sitting in a tiny cab on high who pilots the machine, and by the time I reach it he's stopped and left the thing idling so he can jump down and check something in the back. I don't know anything about combines, but I see him reach his arm way up into it and I shudder – I've heard about so many farm accidents when someone does just this sort of thing. I feel as if I should wait to be sure he's all right, but then I feel silly – he knows what he's doing. He also must have information about the weather that I haven't heard, since a farmer only harvests at night if there is a risk of rain the next day. Maybe we'll see the last of '*la canicule*'.

The sight of the combine is comforting, though its hulking presence in this relatively small field is overkill, like cutting a tomato with a chainsaw. And I know that big farm machines like this one aren't good for the soil. Slowly but surely they pack it down into a layer beneath the surface that no one can see, so that some year, when the rain falls to nourish the soil and the aquifers, it won't be able to penetrate that hard layer. I wish I could stop and ask the farmer, who I see is young and strong, why he needs such a big machine, but I don't dare: he has his reasons and I couldn't be so presumptuous. I'm not a farmer; I just know what I've learned.

Seeing the combine makes me think of all the farms I've visited around the world as I worked on my cookbooks, and all I've learned in trying to understand and communicate the details of food production, the importance of supporting farmers like this young man. I don't know him, but I don't need to know him. Just seeing him in this one field tells me a lot – he either has a relatively small farm that he depends upon, or he's got a day job that pays the bills and allows him to keep farming, his true love and passion. I know plenty of farmers like him. They can't imagine not living on a farm, not getting into the tractor to sow and harvest, yet the world economy doesn't support them since its focus is increasingly on huge farms which produce huge quantities of corn, wheat, soybeans, rape seed and sugar beets. The more farmers concentrate on these crops, which are heavily subsidized, and the more they produce, the lower the prices they get for their hard work, so the more they must produce. At least there is a market for these crops, while for other crops, like buckwheat or millet, amaranth or rye or popcorn, there are no subsidies and no multinational markets either. So why would any farmer in his or her right mind try to raise such crops on any scale? Subsidies hog-tie farmers into producing limited variety and trap them in a cycle of production from which they are too fearful, or too dependent, to emerge. If I could, I would change the way agriculture is organized. I'm not sure I would stop subsidies, but I would arrange things so that farmers got the support they needed to produce a huge variety of foods instead of a few major crops. I would support farmers who saved seeds from year to year, who sought out antique varieties of vegetables and fruits and kept them valid and productive. I would support farmers who cultivated their crops with a minimum or no synthetic additives. I would rearrange the world economy so that farmers with small farms of, say, eighty acres, could not only survive but thrive. And I think I might go about trying to bust up some of the huge, multinational industrial farms in France, in the US, wherever they exist, to allow farming and food production to thrive on a human scale. If they were on a human scale, rural communities would develop, countries could produce their own foods instead of having to rely on imports, and there wouldn't be a need for such invented 'necessities' as genetically modified foods, one of the biggest scams in a long while.

I realize as I continue on, led by the light of the combine, that my ideas aren't realistic. I can't allow myself to pursue the kind of thoughts that my meditative bike rides stimulate, for I get too discouraged. Instead I shrink the issues down to a size that I can deal with. I think of the farmers' market I go to each week, and how fortunate I am to live in France where farmers have a very well-organized system for selling their produce direct to the consumer. I cannot affect global agriculture in a big way, but I like to think I have a small effect through my books, and through the cooking school. In my books I try to make farmers real, so that people reading about them can develop a connection with them, and thus a closer connection to the food they produce. As part of the cooking classes we go to a wonderfully vibrant market to buy our lunch, then come straight home and prepare it. There isn't a more direct producer-consumer link, and when people taste the unparalleled flavour of the food we've just purchased and prepared, I see their eyes light up, and I hear them talk about trying harder to buy at markets once they are home. I get so excited thinking about what I can realistically do that I begin to pedal faster.

The light is almost gone, the road dark. I have a bicycle light but it's '*en panne*', broken, and I don't bother to fix it because I don't like it. It works with the energy generated by pedalling, so the faster I pedal the brighter it gets, simultaneously slowing me down. I do wish I had it for the upcoming stretch of dark road, however, though it's empty now and if I stick to the side I'll be fine. I could get stopped by the police for riding without a light, but I've passed many bicycles this evening and not one has had a light on it. I doubt the small Louviers police force is out looking for us all.

I turn right, which leads me along a road bordered by

fields, then by nice new homes, each with its own large yard. Soon, housing may eat up all this farmland – I can't help this thought – but for now there are fields as far as I can see, up the hill to the black line of the forest and beyond. I turn right again and am once again on a lighted stretch of road, and in the hamlet of Le Haye le Comte, a little community forgotten in time. Many of the first houses are old and a bit decrepit, then they become more modern, larger, grander. On my immediate left is a beautiful and ancient private chapel that isn't used any more. Chapels like this dot the countryside and they are never torn down because they serve as family crypts, the graves being under the flagstone floors. This particular chapel is very well tended, and I hope someday to find the family who owns it, to see if they will let me in to take a look.

Beyond the chapel is a high stone wall; set into that is a big gate that stays open all the time, the entrance to a wonderfully quirky old hotel that was once a chateau. Half of it is the original stone building; the other half is modern. I've never stayed there, but friends of ours have and they loved it: it's a cosy, comfortable place with friendly owners, a decent restaurant and a huge garden filled with big old trees. Next to the hotel is a funny little old house with chickens pecking in the front yard and a vegetable garden that grows along one side. It always makes me do a double take, because it's so out of place here among the tidy homes, a living monument to what this 'suburb' of Louviers must have been. I have never seen anyone there, but it is very neat and tidy and I imagine an elderly couple who once farmed the land around it – now covered with houses – living out a quiet retirement there, an island of history in a sweet little village. When they are gone their testament to '*autrefois*', the past, will disappear along with them.

The road rises slightly, then becomes a residential street bordered on both sides by houses; these are of varying ages and sizes, with large front gardens. I love one of the smaller ones on the right, which I am certain is owned by a retired couple. It stands as a model of the perfect middle-class French residence, with geraniums at all the windows, a perfectly weed-free and tidy vegetable garden that is filled with cabbages and leeks in winter, green beans and tomatoes in summer. The tidy brick path up to the front door is lined with red and white dahlias, to match the whitewashed walls and bright red door, and the ger-aniums. Pots that are set around the house and carefully placed on the grass hold other flowers: petunias and impatiens, irises and hydrangeas. Not a blade or a petal is out of place. If ever I were invited to walk in, I do believe I'd hold my breath for fear of disturbing the perfection.

I coast down an incline and arrive at Louviers' ring road which, here, is called rue Beaulieu. I check for cars then glide onto it and ride on my way towards town. There is a low-income high rise on the left, which teems with children and adults during the day. It is quiet now. People rest at their windows, some leaning out to catch the air, which has cooled down considerably in the half-hour since I began my ride. I turn left at a small tree-lined street that curves around the large parking lot of Louviers' only supermarket, Champion. The temperature has risen again from the heat that radiates up from the tarmac, so I increase my speed to get beyond it. I pass a group of men working on a car with one single light to help them, and I see kids skateboarding languidly in the car park.

I turn onto a street that will lead me home, daring to ride down it the wrong way. Many of Louviers' streets have become one way, which may have looked good on a drawing board, but means that residents who live in the centre of the town must drive in circles to get where they are going, and cyclists must do the same. I often ride down this particular one-way street the wrong way because it is little used and wide enough to accommodate an errant cyclist and a car at the same time. Tonight, when I pass the new little park on the left, which centres around a smaller than regulation basketball court, a concrete ping-pong table, some picnic tables and a bit of grass, I notice a large family sprawled over the tables, enjoying the now-cool night air.

I ride past the corner barber shop, or *barbieri*, that belongs to our neighbour Giuliano. Originally from Naples, he speaks French with a gorgeous Italian accent, his voice booming down the street. He has daughters of his own and is obviously enamoured of little girls, so when he sees Fiona he kisses her on the head and says, '*Ciao poupée!*', 'Hello little doll!' His loud voice used to make her cry when she was a tiny baby; now she peeks up at him from behind me, not quite sure how to take his admiration.

His shop is locked up and the café across from it, which sets tables and chairs out on the narrow little pavement, is closed too. I ride up to our courtyard door and, as if on cue, the illumination of the church turns off and I'm plunged into darkness. It's 11.30 and Louviers, from the gargoyles on its Gothic church to the children in its homes, is going to sleep. *Bonne Nuit!*

MARVELLOUS BERRY DESSERT
Le Dessert Merveilleux

————— ⌘ —————

This recipe was inspired by a friend and colleague, David Lebovitz, who came to our house and charmed us with his sparkle and his wonderful desserts – this was just one of them, and now every time I see fresh berries I want to make it! I like to serve small slices of *pain d'épices*, the French version of gingerbread, along with this dessert.

1 cup (250 ml) fromage frais, or fresh cheese
Generous 2 cups (9 oz.; 270g) mixed fresh berries such as red-currant, raspberries and blackberries
1 tbs vanilla sugar, or to taste
4 tsp dark honey such as chestnut honey
Mint sprigs, for decoration

1. Place the berries in a small saucepan over medium heat. When the berries begin to heat through and give up their juices, add the sugar and cook just until it dissolves and the berries are hot through, 3 to 5 minutes depending on the ripeness of the berries. Remove from the heat and keep warm.
2. Using a small ice cream scoop or two medium-sized serving spoons, scoop equal amounts of the fresh cheese onto four dessert plates. Surround the cheese with the berry mixture, then spoon 1 teaspoon of honey over each scoop of cheese. Garnish each plate with a mint sprig and serve.

4 servings

Shopping and the Cart

Every time I go to a supermarket in France, I find myself engaged in a battle I can never win. Anyone who has ever shopped at a French supermarket will sympathize with me. The battle has to do with French shopping trolleys. I think they must have been designed by the same people who designed the French milk containers, which are so flimsy they collapse in your hand when you pour milk and – *voila!* – milk is over the counter-top or down your front, and nowhere near the cup, glass or bowl that was waiting for it.

The shopping trolley is well disguised. It looks harmless. In fact it resembles the American shopping cart with its metal construction and rubber-sheathed wheels. Most of them have a seat for a baby in the front, too. A quaint French addition is a small hook on the front of the cart, just under the handle, to hold a basket or a purse.

I come into contact with the shopping trolley at the supermarket where I go only when I absolutely must, about twice a month. Small local supermarkets, introduced to France in the 1960s, are bad enough, though they offer a certain quaint, small-town charm. But I don't like big supermarkets because I am convinced that, since their inception in France in the 1970s, they've sucked the life out of the small town centre, for a supermarket rarely stands alone. It forms, instead, the heart of a tacky mall that includes one or more restaurants, a handful of boutiques, a shoe store and a *tabac* or magazine and cigarette shop. In other words, it recreates the main facilities of a town centre in another location.

Part of the appeal of the supermarket in France is that its prices will be lower than one finds in the family-run shops in town and village centres. Certain things may be less expensive, it's true, but the quality and service can't compare, and by the time you've driven, negotiated your ridiculously large shopping trolley inside and begun to fill it with things that weren't on your shopping list but are such bargains you can't leave them behind, you've probably spent far more than you would have going from shop to shop on foot. And, as far as I'm concerned at least, you've had a lot less fun.

So I don't really look forward to my twice-monthly visits, but I go because I need to buy certain things in bulk, mostly for the cooking classes, like paper products, good olive oil for cooking, butter for baking, parchment paper, and so on.

What makes the French version of the shopping trolley so exasperating is that all four wheels swivel, which make it impossible, and I mean impossible, to steer. I can imagine its designer(s), who appear to have a stranglehold on the shopping trolley industry in France, fiendishly chuckling each time they go to the supermarket themselves and watch consumers fight their way down the aisle, driven or led by their trolleys.

The trolleys are tidily pushed together in covered shelters outside in car parks, connected by chains that are released when you stick a euro coin into a slot on the handle of the trolley. This system is perfect because it prevents the theft so prevalent in other places, and the spectacle of dead shopping trolleys littering the roads and countryside.

Once the trolley is released from its bondage it becomes giddy and swings drunkenly from side to side, and one must quickly take the upper hand by surging forward in a straight line, otherwise anything in its path will be mowed down. To make matters worse, the supermarket entrance is designed to further thwart the forward motion of the shopping trolley, because it slopes up gently so that the trolley tries to sidle down it as I try to push it up. Good biceps are necessary to get it up to and through the double set of automatic doors and onto the smooth, formica floor of the supermarket. The entry trials aren't over, for to get into the actual store you still have to pass through a barrier that opens automatically, and which seems to be timed to be just a bit slower than the speed necessary to keep the trolley going straight. You have to judiciously apply the brakes, which are the soles of your shoes, so you learn quickly *never* to wear slippery-soled shoes to the supermarket. With practice the choreography of this becomes automatic, with the bursts of speed timed to coincide perfectly with the motions of skid or acceleration.

I've analyzed the dysfunction of the French shopping trolley a great deal. At first I kept looking for the set of procedures that would result in perfect operation. 'Aha!' I thought. 'It malfunctions in the car park because the surface is bumpy, but it will work perfectly once inside on a smooth surface.' This is not the case. Once on that smooth floor a whole other set of driving skills have to come into play.

I've learned that it pays to go in as many straight lines as possible, so once through the barrier I have my itinerary carefully planned to make as few turns as possible. I swing wide to the right to turn left down the wine aisle, where I slow down so I can peruse the labels. Then I swing wide left to turn right into the water aisle to get Perrier, or Pierval or San Pellegrino. I take another wide swing to the left so that I can turn right down the soft drink aisle, a major artery which takes me to the sections where I will buy pasta, olive oil, flour, mustard, sea salt, cornichons, scrumptious canned albacore tuna, the occasional box of breakfast cereal or cookies, with Petit Beurre or Petit Lu covered with dark chocolate among our favourites. For these purchases I simply park the cart and run up and down the aisles getting what I need. When I've put the items into my cart I surge ahead, swing wide left and turn right down the nuts and flavourings aisle, another artery that will take me to the household goods section, where I might skid to a stop to buy aluminium foil or parchment paper, and then the dairy section beyond.

I park the trolley at the end of the dairy aisle and stay there a long time; I love this section of a French supermarket. It is excessive, like the breakfast cereal aisle of an American supermarket, its shelves stacked with every conceivable type of dairy product. There is *lait caillé* loosely curdled milk; fromage frais; *crème liquide* and crème fraîche, different thicknesses of cream; dozens of permutations of yoghurt – made with cow's milk or sheep's milk, or a combination of both, and flavoured with every combination of fruit imaginable; *lait ribou*, fermented milk from Brittany, or Yorik from North Africa; little creamy puddings or mousse-y desserts; dense little *petit Suisse* which are wrapped in paper then tucked in a plastic or cardboard cup and sitting in whey. Most of these dairy products are made from whole milk and are simply delicious. Even the low-fat versions aren't bad.

I opt most often for plain yoghurt because the fruit yoghurt is filled with things I don't necessarily want my kids to eat (I am not a fun mom), though I am sometimes tempted by the old-fashioned vanilla or berry-flavoured yoghurt that comes in the cute little glass containers and cause squeals of delight when I get them home. I buy organic fromage frais, which is lightly curdled and simply wonderful; *crème liquide,* which is like heavy or double cream; and if I happen to be planning to make a cheese-cake I'll buy boxes of individually wrapped Kiri cheese, which is like our cream cheese. Kids here eat Kiri as a snack, popping the flat little squares into their mouths the way Americans do a jawbreaker.

When I've satisfied my dairy needs I might go to the cheese department, which offers an impressive array. Recently the young woman working behind the counter began wearing plastic gloves to serve the cheese, and to cut and handle the pâtés and cured meats that make up part of her *rayon,* or section. She moves from one to the other without changing her gloves or washing her hands because, as far as she is concerned, they aren't dirty. I asked her why she wears the gloves, which, to me, are the worst health hazard in food service since industrially produced chickens. She rolled her eyes. 'It's EC regulation,' she said. 'I never have time to take them off.'

I ignore the probability of cross-contamination and order my Ossau Iraty (Basque sheep's milk cheese), my Comté and my aged Mimolette. Because I've asked her about the gloves, the young woman carefully removes the pair she is wearing and replaces them with a clean pair. I thank her.

Supermarkets aren't without interest because their

inventory reflects the region where they are located. In Provence, for instance, the cheese sections are rife with beautiful, locally made goat's cheeses, and one would be hard pressed to find a decent Camembert there, whereas in our supermarket there are dozens of varieties of Camembert, many of them excellent, and few goat's cheeses. In Alsace, the supermarket offers wonderful spice mixtures for *choucroute* and mulled wine, as well as some very soft vinegars that aren't to be found anywhere else. In the Basque country, fresh, vivid red *piments d'Espelette*, gently hot Basque peppers, sit in the produce section, and the crushed dried version is in the spice section. I can find neither in my supermarket. In Burgundy the biscuit section includes a huge array of *pain d'épices*, or spice cookies, and the sweet section offers large bags of *anis de Flavigny*, the sugar-coated anise seeds made outside of Dijon.

Produce sections at the supermarket are generally disappointing, but how could they be otherwise when they must compete with farmers' markets? I might buy imported fruit there like bananas or mangoes and the occasional avocado, but never anything else: its quality just doesn't measure up. All supermarkets have in-house bakeries which send toasty aromas throughout the store but whose breads are terribly disappointing. Our supermarket does have a crowning glory in the privately owned seafood concession. I always look to see what scrumptious species are available, for the choice is broader here than in our local fish market. I might buy a fat fillet of fresh tuna, which I love to gently brown and serve with a clove and pine nut sauce, or whole mackerel to grill over a rosemary fire, or skate wing to braise and serve as part of a zesty salad.

With my shopping finished I navigate my way to the

checkouts, hoping that I can stop the by now very heavy trolley before it dents someone in the back of the leg. The trolleys are very deep so that, in order to empty them onto the conveyor belt going to the cash register, you have to bend way over and, in the absolutely most uncomfortable possible position, pull things out that sometimes weigh as much as a small child. I don't know how the elderly or infirm manage.

Once the conveyor belt begins moving, at about the same fast speed as a driving apprentice is allowed to drive on French roads, it is necessary to slide the trolley quickly to the opposite end of the conveyor belt and position it to receive what you've just unloaded. There is no one to help pack up groceries. Nor are there any large sacks to pack them in, just flimsy plastic bags that seem to hold the equivalent of a bottle of milk and two packs of butter. Not only do you use thousands of them, they often break, sending groceries rolling all over. To avoid this, I try to remember to bring either collapsible plastic crates or a large basket, which I put in the trolley and pack right there. I still have to heave that into the car, but when all is said and done it's the most efficient way to manage.

I pack up everything and return it to the trolley, write a cheque or pay cash, then get myself, my goods, and my trolley out of the way before the next person's goods come sliding down the conveyor belt. The adrenalin rush is almost as good as that from successfully completing a ten-kilometre race. If I've ridden my bicycle to the store, which is the way I most typically get there, I park it between the two sets of doors at the entrance to the supermarket. I co-opted this spot almost ten years ago, rejecting the bicycle racks outside that are narrow and impractical, and thus far I've used it with impunity. I carefully transfer items from the trolley to the *paniers* on the back of the bike, and to the wicker basket in front. If I have overflow, I stack it on the rack between the *paniers* and attach it with elasticated cords: it's amazing how much you can fit on a bicycle.

Just beyond the doors is the death-defying tarmac slope. In order to negotiate it with a full trolley, I have to make sure that I have all four wheels perfectly aligned so that the trolley doesn't slide down broadside then swing out of control into the vehicle lane in front of the supermarket. Fortunately, vehicles using that lane are going slowly and can generally stop safely at a moment's notice.

If I've got a loaded bicycle my challenge is to get it and the shopping trolley simultaneously down the sloping entrance, across the vehicle lane, under the shelter and into a waiting row of baskets so that I can attach it and retrieve my one-euro piece. I've worked out a system that relies heavily on gravity, and the only thing that can confound me is if someone gets in my way.

As I stash the trolley and recover my euro, swing myself onto my faithful burgundy bicycle and take off out into the wilds of the car park, I am relieved to have, once more, defeated the wiles of the shopping trolley. I usually spend the first five minutes of the ride home doing the old 'is it me, or is it the trolley' routine, trying still, after all this time, to see the sense in the design. I just refuse to believe, in a country responsible for the perfectly engineered Paris métro and the TGV (*Train à Grande Vitesse*), that the supermarket shopping trolleys are so ridiculous.

TUNA WITH PINE NUT AND ANCHOVY SAUCE
Le Thon à la Sauce de Pignons de Pin et aux Anchois

This recipe is adapted from my first book, *Great American Seafood Cookbook* (Workman, 1988) and it is one I return to time and again. Everyone loves the sauce, and it is as delicious over salmon, mackerel, or even a delicate fish like ling cod as it is over the fresh tuna called for here.

4 tuna steaks (3½ to 4 oz each; 105 to 120 g), cut 1 inch; 2.5 cm thick
6 top-quality anchovy fillets, preferably those from Collioure, drained
¼ cup (60 ml) dry white wine
1 cup (200 g) pine nuts
⅛ teaspoon ground cinnamon, preferably from Vietnam
Small pinch of ground cloves
1 tbs balsamic vinegar
3 tbs salted capers, rinsed, soaked for 1 hour in warm water, drained
¾ cup plus 2 tbs (215 ml) extra-virgin olive oil
Sea salt and freshly ground black pepper
1 cup (10g) flat leaf parsley leaves – for garnish

1. Rinse the tuna steaks and pat dry. Refrigerate until ready to use.
2. If the anchovies are packed in salt, rinse them quickly, then soak them in the wine for 15 minutes, to rid them

of excess salt. Drain, discarding the wine. If they are packed in oil simply pat them dry.

3. In a food processor, combine the anchovies, pine nuts, cinnamon, cloves, vinegar, and capers. Purée, pulsing on and off. With the machine running, slowly add the ¾ cup of oil in a thin stream, and process until the mixture is quite thick, but pourable. Season with salt and pepper to taste; reserve.

4. Liberally season the tuna steaks on both sides with salt and pepper. Heat the remaining olive oil in a heavy-bottomed skillet over medium-high heat. When the oil is hot but not smoking, add the tuna steaks and cook until the tuna is cooked as you like it, about 4 minutes per side if you like it cooked until opaque. If you prefer the tuna slightly undercooked, reduce the cooking time accordingly.

5. While the tuna is cooking, mince the parsley.

6. To serve, pour half the sauce onto a warm serving platter. Top with the steaks, then pour the remaining sauce over the steaks. Sprinkle with the parsley and serve immediately.

4 servings

SKATE SALAD
Salade d'Ail de Raie

———————— ∾ ————————

The sweet, tender meat of skate is highly appreciated in France. Whether poached, as here, or cooked in a skillet until it is crisp on the outside and tender inside, it is always accompanied by something acidic, as its meat stands up well to bright, taut flavours.

To poach the skate:
1 generous lb (500g) skate wing, with bone
1 bottle (750ml) dry white wine, such as Sancerre or Vouvray
¼ cup (60ml) vinegar
1 quart (1 litre) water
1 small onion, cut in thin rings
10 whole Tellicherry or Vietnamese peppercorns
3 dried, imported bay leaves
Pinch sea salt
Three strips of lemon zest
10 sprigs flat leaf parsley

For the skate garnish:
1 tbs balsamic vinegar
2 tsp red wine vinegar
¼ cup (60ml) extra virgin olive oil
½ cup (5g) flat leaf parsley leaves, gently packed
8 cornichons, diced (to give 3 tbs)
1 tbs capers in salt, rinsed, soaked, and drained
1 tsp minced lemon zest (just the yellow part of the peel)

For the salad:
1 scant tbs balsamic vinegar
Sea salt and freshly ground black pepper
3 tbs (45ml) Lemon Oil
8 cups mixed salad greens

1. Rinse the skate, pat dry, and refrigerate until just before cooking.
2. Make a court bouillon: place all the ingredients except the skate into a large skillet with sides at least 3-inches high. Bring to a boil over medium-high heat, cover, reduce the heat so the liquid is simmering and simmer for 20 minutes. Return the liquid to a boil and slip the

277

skate into it. Reduce the heat to medium and simmer the skate until the skin begins to wrinkle, and the meat is opaque through, which will take very little time – about 5 minutes. Check the skate at the thickest part to be sure it is cooked through – if it is still translucent, let it cook for an additional 1 to 2 minutes, then remove it from the court bouillon, and transfer it to a work surface. Let it cool, then carefully scrape off the skin and any gristle (a clear, jelly-like substance) being careful not to disturb the pattern of the skate wing.

3. Cut the skate wing vertically into four pieces. Using a metal spatula or a wide-bladed knife, lift off the meat on both sides of the bone, being careful not to disturb the pattern of the meat. Arrange the skate in an even layer on a large plate or platter. About 10 minutes later, drain off any liquid from the plate.

4. To make the garnish, place the vinegars in a small bowl. Whisk in oil in a thin stream until the mixture is emulsified. Mince the parsley and whisk it into the oil and vinegar along with the cornichons, capers and lemon zest. Season with salt and freshly ground black pepper. Spoon half the sauce over the skate, turn it, and spoon the remaining sauce over the skate.

5. In a large bowl, whisk together the tablespoon of balsamic vinegar with the salt and pepper. Continue whisking while you add the lemon oil in a thin stream until the mixture is emulsified. Add the salad greens and toss thoroughly. Taste for seasoning.

6. To serve, evenly divide the salad among four large plates. Top each with an equal amount of skate, spooning up any sauce on the plate and drizzling it over the fish. Serve immediately.

4 servings

Michael's Studio and the
Gentrification of Louviers

All the while that Michael has been working on the house, taking care of the children when I'm away and restructuring the garden, he's also been sculpting. For years his workshop and studio were alongside the kitchen, an unfinished universe filled with half-modelled busts, hand tools and large machines, and the miscellaneous paraphernalia of our lives which would, as though on a predetermined course, find their way in there. Empty, his space was a large room. Crammed with the creative side of his life and the extraneous bits of ours, it was cramped. Michael declared he needed a separate place to work.

The city of Louviers offers a variety of classes for adults, and among them is a sculpture class. Michael struck up a friendship with the sculpture instructor, who convinced him to attend the class, and he began to go every Tuesday evening for three hours. The studio was in a beautiful, old and decrepit building in the heart of a small park, about five minutes' walk from our house. For the equivalent of fifty dollars a year, Michael had a place to work, all the materials he needed, and what he considered to be quality instruction. It became his stopgap studio, a place where he could work uninterrupted for three hours a week.

Once Joe and I stopped by to see what it was like, and we found Michael tucked away in a back corner of one of the two dusty rooms patiently working away, while others in the class chit-chatted and drank coffee as they worked on their projects. When he saw us it was as if he had awakened from a reverie. He'd been in his element.

Michael and I had owned a small house in Seattle, and our original idea had been to keep it as a pied-à-terre in the US. Circumstances suggested differently, and we sold it. We put part of the profit aside to purchase a studio for Michael somewhere in or near Louviers, and Michael began a search for the ideal place, sinking his teeth into the project. He talked to all the real-estate agents in town – there must be a dozen – and spent a lot of time pursuing leads. The first place he took me to see was a former *mairie*, or city hall. Situated on a tiny plot of grass out in the country along a narrow country road, it was an adorable little one-room brick building that had presumably once bustled with town business. It came with no land except what it sat upon, had electricity but no running water, and it cost next to nothing. Michael and I both loved it, but it was way too small, way too impractical, way too far away.

When Michael is intent on something, he leaves no stone unturned, and I couldn't believe the number of places he visited, nor the people he met along the way. He learned to run over and look at places the minute he heard about them, for property in Louviers was a hot commodity. He found one place, said he would buy it, then lost it. He found another and went to look at it before it came on the market, returned to the estate agent who was going to handle it and said he'd buy it. Someone had got there first. A gentleman who was buying up a lot of property in Louviers heard Michael was looking, and called him with an offer to rent him one of his buildings. Michael didn't want to rent but he went to look at the property anyway, which was a small brick hangar just five minutes from our house. He told the owner he wanted to buy it; the owner said it wasn't for sale. A decent sort, he told Michael that if he heard of anything that seemed suitable, he would let him know.

One day, the monsieur came to the house when Michael was away. He knocked on the door, introduced himself, and told me that he'd finished buying up property, but that someone had called him about a place for sale. It was reasonable; a good deal, he said. He gave me the address and the name of the owner, and said he'd told the owner about Michael.

I took down all the information and, as soon as Michael returned, gave it to him. He called the monsieur, spoke with him for a minute, then was out the door. Within a half an hour he was back. 'Susan, come with me, I think I've found what I need,' he said.

We literally ran down the street to the property, a sort of hangar behind one of Louviers' former hotels that was open at the bottom and crumbling at the top. 'Isn't it great?' Michael asked. It was a charming spot on a canal with a huge old tree at the back and brick buildings on either side so that, one day, it could be very private. Naturally, the hangar needed mountains of work to make it usable, but Michael had that familiar light in his eyes. 'I can see a patio and tables here,' he said. 'We can make a little *ginguette* – waterfront dining room, and have this as our summer house, our little vacation spot.' I loved the idea – a little dining room by the river, a place for summer soirées. 'But wait,' I said. 'This is going to be your studio.'

'Oh, right,' he said.

We wasted no time and bought it. In doing so we brushed up against the Louviers underground, the group of people angling and pushing to buy up all the prime properties in town and turn them hastily into rental units, since there was nothing to rent in Louviers. The owner of 'our' property, and his *notaire*, were two of them.

Signing the paperwork was interesting. Somehow we let ourselves be manipulated into using the same *notaire* as the buyer, which is never an advisable thing to do, because it creates a situation that is advantageous to the seller. In this particular situation, from the minute the negotiations began, the situation felt slippery. The *notaire* argued and prevaricated, trying mostly to keep the price high and to get us to sign away the owner's responsibility for cleaning up, while the owner sat there looking innocent and friendly. Fortunately Michael had done enough looking to know what the price should be. He held firm, and neither of us would budge on what we expected to be done before we took possession. We finally clinched the deal. The *notaire*, a plump, stuffy young fellow in a shiny suit, was miffed, and snootily held the papers for us while we signed them.

Acquiring this property was a big moment because, in truth, Michael has dreamed of having his own studio away from the house for years. He loves creating universes, and he has always wanted one all his own. This wood-slatted aerie would be it. He nearly skipped all the way home, even as he realized the work involved in fixing it up. He would do it slowly, gradually, bit by bit, as we could manage. He didn't emerge for weeks, it seemed, as he closed himself away to plan and figure, draw and design. When he was finished he showed me the result.

He'd thought of all the angles in this design, making it simple yet functional, creating a space that – should the need arise – could quickly be turned into a lodging, an income-producing property. The ground floor would be rustic and reserved for dirty work. Upstairs would be reserved for clean work; the walls mostly glass. He would try to keep the flavour of the old building, which the hotel had used for hanging laundry, hence the open slatted wood walls. He had blocked out space for a small kitchen where he would make coffee and heat up his lunch, and he would replace the crumbling roof with a metal one.

Between the overgrown ruin that existed and the spare, elegant studio he imagined was a lot of hard work. Michael was still working on our house, but he took time each week to go over to his studio. His first job was to secure it, so he built a big wooden gate at the front, and a fence on the property line. He organized his materials, moved a few of his tools over there, spent time looking and dreaming. He was fascinated by the canal, which rose and fell according to the height of the river, and he got right in it and created a small island, on which he planted a water garden.

Not long after we'd bought the property, the city published its intentions to fix up the *place*, or square, adjacent to it. Now a rundown spot, it was bordered on one side by the same canal that ran by Michael's property, and on the other by a much bigger and more powerful canal. We'd often walked by it, with its vestige of old-world charm, its cute little *halles*, or market place, complete with beautiful stone platform where fresh-off-the-boat seafood had once been displayed, and we thought what a shame it was that it had been left to decline. Even the old brick homes that defined it, the ones opposite the canals, could have been lovely if they'd been cleaned up. From the plans the city published we saw that they would get facelifts, the square would be paved with cobblestones, the charming market building would be entirely refurbished. Even the canal itself would get a new look, with gardens on either side that would run right up to our property. As I looked at the plans I could almost hear the hawking of past fish-mongers, the bustle of crowds.

Work began on the *place*, and Michael went over every day to check on its progress. The entrance to his property was a narrow alley owned by the city, and part of the refurbishing project included paving it. Before they paved it, Michael worked furiously to prepare channels for the utilities he would need, so that they could be laid up to his property before the city paved over it. If he hadn't jumped on that, the cost of having utilities brought in would have been prohibitive. As it was he got them for a *forfait*, a negligible fee.

As the city crew dug up the little *place* in preparation for paving it, they unearthed a collection of big, beautiful, ancient white stones. They were going to be thrown away, so Michael convinced the workmen to deposit the stones on his land, and he began to use them for terracing the bank. With the utilities available, Michael installed some electricity and began slowly fixing up the hangar, outlining where he would put windows, putting in a new floor upstairs, laying the structural groundwork for his plan. It was hard work and there were times when I could tell he was bone-tired from the effort, discouraged with all the work he had to do. One day he was perusing the little 'want' ad sheet that gets dropped through our courtyard door each week, and he saw a used *grue*, or crane, for sale. It was relatively small and very inexpensive, and Michael called about it. The person who answered was a friend of ours, a man who'd helped Michael buy a lot of materials for our house.

'I didn't know you had a crane,' Michael said, laughing. Our friend was laughing, too. 'Oh, this crane, it's been around. My friends and I have been selling it back and forth for years. None of us needs it any more, which is why it's in the paper,' he said. 'You should buy it: it will save you so much work you won't believe it.'

So Michael acquired the crane. Our friend delivered it and Michael was like a kid in a sweet shop. He rigged a sort of swing off the end of it and would swing Joe, and later Fiona and sometimes me, gently around on it. He would come home amazed at how much time and work it saved as he shifted heavy materials that he otherwise would have had to lift by hand.

The crane stood tall and yellow behind the hangar, and friends who passed the building noticed it. 'Where did that crane on your property come from?' Edith asked one day. When Michael told her he'd bought it, she couldn't believe it. 'You bought your own crane?' she said, shaking her head and laughing. 'You must be crazy. How many people have their own crane?'

Reinvigorated thanks to the crane, Michael made better progress on his studio, while continuing his work on our house. One day he came home from his studio, despondent. 'It is such a dump over there, I can hardly stand to go,' he said. He was glum for a few days, then he went over one morning and didn't return until late that evening. 'I'm working on the garden,' he said. 'I cannot work in such a messy place.'

For two or three weeks he spent all his time shifting the remaining big, white stones, levelling, building more terraces, sifting gravel, bringing in soil and new gravel. I went over to look and the place was transformed. Instead of the derelict property it had been, it was now landscaped, reflecting Michael's penchant for the wild yet orderly.

He'd planted roses and a lilac we'd had in a pot at the house for years. The composted soil he'd used was already sprouting a long, snaky squash plant. Along one wall he'd planted honeysuckle and clematis, and in front of those, snapdragons, hydrangeas and iris, all of them either dug from our garden at home or purchased from the Saturday market. Along one of the brick walls was a big stand of bamboo that he'd trimmed into submission, and another group of hydrangeas. It was beautiful, and pregnant with the promise of flowers.

That was in the spring. The months that followed were unusually warm and humid and his garden grew like Topsy. He would come home in the evening with huge bouquets of dahlias and a bright yellow flower that looks like Jerusalem artichoke. I began making picnics at noon and taking Joe, Fiona and Brinn down to the studio for lunch. It became our little summer getaway. One day we arrived and he'd made a dream come true for Fiona by building her a swing.

We would unwrap our picnic of fresh tomato and cucumber sandwiches, pâté and baguette, or pasta with tomatoes and goat's cheese, set it on an old wrought-iron table that Michael had painted oxblood red, and sit on the big stones that defined the garden. Michael and Joe built a throwing and pitching alley alongside the hangar on the new gravel. They were becoming baseball nuts together, and would spend hours at the studio practising.

The redone *place* was truly a jewel, with its washed and newly pointed brick houses, the lovely cobblestones, the little *halles*, with its grey slate roof and turquoise wrought-iron accents, a boardwalk and benches along the river. The minute it was completed people came to use it. Small children risked their lives dipping their hands in the canal, men fished, teenagers lounged or skate-boarded down the boardwalk. A kebab and pizza restaurant on the corner experienced a surge in business as people stopped by to get fat lamb sandwiches and eat them by the canal.

It wasn't the only part of Louviers to undergo a facelift. The mandate of the mayor who had been elected shortly after we'd arrived in Louviers was to bring the town alive, make it work for the people. Another interesting legislative change occurred in France a short time after that, which called for communities to group together in order to operate more efficiently, and to share the cost and performance of such things as road maintenance, garbage collection and physical improvements. The idea was the heavily funded darling of the socialist government, and it has allowed towns like Louviers to plunge into an astonishing array of impressive work projects. The *place* next to the studio had been one; the rue St Jean, one of the main routes into town from the autoroute was another. This latter was an enormous project that involved sprucing up the riverbanks, redoing the street, installing lighting, making a bicycle and pedestrian path that would connect the centre of Louviers with Intermarché, a large supermarket. Pavements were installed, a corner park was refurbished and fitted out with seating, paths and beautiful landscaping. It was a hugely ambitious project that went on for years and, finally, in the summer of 2002, was inaugurated.

The results are stunning, the bicycle and pedestrian path, which goes over a sweet little bridge spanning the River Eure, an instant success. What was a crumbling, rutted old street, lined by indistinct houses, is now a lively spot with lighting so bright and grand that residents refer to it as Louvier's Champs Élysées. We assume someone somewhere made an excellent deal on the lighting, for the wattage employed on this one street alone could light up the whole town.

As the very ambitious mayor waves his magic wand over Louviers, there are some casualties. A tragic one that still makes many people – us included – sad was the destruction of a small, brick schoolhouse on the street behind us. It had stood there solid, friendly and sweet, since the turn of the century, and was the neighbourhood school for children ages three to five. We loved having it nearby, hearing the children playing outside during their break times, seeing parents grouped around the gate at lunchtime and again in the afternoon, and we'd planned to send Fiona there when she was of school age. We'd heard that it was scheduled for the wrecking ball, but didn't believe it. Who could destroy such a signature characteristic of the area, such a lovely little building, such a monument to the charming past?

A petition went around the neighbourhood to save the school, and we had hopes that it, along with heartfelt pleas by the populace, would prevent its destruction. I asked the mayor one day when I ran into him if he truly planned to destroy the building. *'Bien sûr,'* he said with a look of incredulity that I would even ask the question. His justification was that the architect of historic monuments has deemed it of no interest. 'And we need the property,' he finished, with a big, hearty smile.

Sure enough, one day when I was returning home from walking Joe to his school, I turned the corner and saw the first hit of the wrecking ball. I burst into tears – of sadness, anger and frustration. Bricks began to fall, and with each successive blow the walls crumbled, the roof fell in, small atom-bomb clouds of dust rose into the sky. I was frozen, alone on the street to watch what I considered to be a crime against aesthetics, nostalgia and soul. I believe it is, in part, my American-ness that makes me think that way, that makes it so hard for me to understand why any intelligent human being wouldn't try to keep and work with what exists, when that thing is full of history, the laughter and tears of children, the sense of its time. Where I come from we have so little of that. To people who decide to destroy such things there must be a sense of history as nostalgic burden rather than strength. Nothing else could justify such destruction.

Everyone in the neighbourhood slumped around for days after the destruction. No one was happy about it, no one felt that what was planned would be an improvement. It was as though everyone had been hit with a *coup de blues.*

As though to wipe away a sin, all evidence of the building was gone within twenty-four hours. For months when I passed the site I could only think, 'What folly, what patent disregard for the past, for neighbourhood values.' In addition, I thought, what disrespect for the preponderance of elderly people in the area, all of whom lived through the bombing and destruction of the Second World War. I know from talking with many of them that it struck a personal blow.

Nothing could be built on the site of the school, whose pastel-painted back wall remained standing for years as a reminder, until a thorough archaeological exploration had been carried out. Even though my heart ached for the destroyed old school, I liked walking by the site and watching as the archaeologists dug and dusted, hunched over their work in the hot sun. They haunted the site for months, uncovering sarcophagi dating to the sixth century, according to the local newspaper. It was so exciting to see the ochre sarcophagi emerge, some of them tiny and certainly meant for children. At least one had remains in it still, and was moved to the city museum. I'm not certain what finally happened to the others – I saw many left out in the rain to crumble. So many ancient things are uncovered in and around Louviers that they almost cease to be of interest.

Not long after the destruction of the school and its surroundings, a large panel went up, showing what was to be built in its place. The idea is not a bad one: to connect city hall and its complex of administrative offices with the commercial centre of downtown Louviers by creating a thoroughfare that would run right through where the school stood. Louviers' *salle des fêtes*, a likeable monstrosity of postwar architecture that stood behind the old schoolhouse, was also razed. A large complex of apartments and some commercial space would go up in its place. In keeping with the city administration's socialist bent, a large percentage of the housing would be subsidized. In other words, the city administration had decided to welcome a project into its heart.

When the architects' rendering of the project went up, all we could do was roll our eyes. Everyone we talked with in the neighbourhood felt the same; so did friends who saw it. They weren't quite as horrified as we were, but almost, for the design was uninspired, generic and cheap, like so much contemporary, city-funded architecture throughout France. We might have hoped for something a bit more original, more suited to the perspectives of our particular town, but that would surely have cost too much. We can only hope for the best and believe in what our hungrily ambitious mayor says, that the new project will harmonize with the old part of town.

One thing that will surely make this project a bit extraordinary is the ancient timbered house on one side of the construction site that was preserved, since the architect of historic monuments found some value in it. The people who lived in it are long gone, the leaning building held together for dear life by thick metal bands that completely encircle it. It was impossible to tell from the renderings just how this fragile old home will be incorporated into the final structure.

Fearing for the future is senseless, so once the shock of losing two old buildings had worn off, I came to love the empty block they had stood on, which afforded a distant perspective of the church. I would imagine, as I walked through the Place des Pompiers towards the *herboristerie*, herbalist's shop, to get my organic vegetables, cereals and dried fruits, that when I turned to look at the church I was seeing it the way people in the Middle Ages had seen it, with nothing tall to obstruct the view. I could imagine the narrow, cobbled streets teeming with people, could almost hear their murmured conversations, their shuffling feet, the clopping of their horses.

After a several-year delay the construction project is underway, gradually filling up that empty skyline, hiding the church from that particular perspective once again. I can hear the muffled sounds of construction from my office where I write, and now, when I walk to the *herboristerie*, I pass concrete walls with rebar sticking out of them, watch a crane that dwarfs Michael's swing around with tons of concrete dangling from its hook, hear the yells and clangs of a crew at work.

Though the walls going up aren't promising, I figure it probably won't be as awful as most people fear, and it may turn out to be just fine. Meanwhile, Michael Loomis is certainly doing his best to add to the aesthetic wealth of Louviers – or at least he and I think so. Who knows, though, there may be passers by who find our ideas monstrous.

In any case, we hope it is all in the name of progress and not just change. We hope that the mayor's dreams are sound and will come true, that Louviers will live up to his ideals as a contemporary town with its bow pointed in the direction of the future. Like everyone else who lives here, we are along for the ride.

MICHAEL'S SOURDOUGH BREAD
Le Pain au Levain de Michael

———————— ⌾ ————————

Michael has been making our sourdough bread for 15 years, using a starter that he was first given by a farmer in the Dordogne region of southwest France. The bread is a living entity, as the dough changes each time he makes it, depending on the weather, the ingredients he adds, the temperature of the air. It is always, however, satisfyingly delicious!

For the starter:
1 cup (135g) unbleached flour
½ cup (125ml) water

For the bread:
2 cups (500ml) warm water
1 heaped tbs coarse sea salt
4 to 6 cups (about 540–800g) unbleached flour, or a mix
of flours

1. Make the starter and when it is bubbling and ready to use (after about 3 days), proceed with the bread.
2. Place the starter in a large mixing bowl or the bowl of an electric mixer and add the remaining water and the salt. Mix well, then add the flour gradually, mixing well after each addition, until the dough is soft (too soft to knead on a work surface), but no longer sticks to your hands. To test the consistency of the dough, touch it quickly with a clean finger. If some dough sticks to your finger, add flour in small amounts until the dough is the proper consistency.

3. Remove 1 cup of the dough to use for your next loaf. Now, add whatever seeds and flavourings you would like for your bread, such as:

1 to 1½ cups (90 to 130g) finely grated
Parmigiano Reggiano
Flax seeds
Sunflower seeds
Raisins
Walnuts
Apricots
Citrus zest

4. Line a basket or a strainer with a cotton or linen tea towel and heavily flour the towel. Shape the dough into the loaf size and shape you desire, turn it into the lined basket and let it rise until it doubles in volume, about 12 hours.
5. Preheat the oven to 500°F (260°C). Turn the bread out onto a heavily floured baking sheet or round baking pan. Slash it in several places, then place it in the bottom-third of the oven. Throw ¼ cup (60ml) warm water onto the oven floor, to create steam which will crisp the crust, then bake for 20 minutes. Throw in an additional ¼ cup (60ml) warm water onto the oven floor, reduce the oven temperature to about 450°F (230°C), and continue to bake the bread until it is golden and hollow sounding when you tap on it, about an additional hour. Remove the bread from the oven and turn it from the pan, or remove it from the baking sheet and let cool on a wire rack.

One 2 lb loaf

Bi-Culturalism and Play Ball!

When Joe was six he started judo at the judo club in Louviers, one of the best in the region. The head of the club is dynamic, the judo masters well trained, the competition results impressive. Joe loved it. He would dress carefully in his off-white kimono and Michael would drop him off once a week at the club, then pick him up a little over an hour later so that he could watch the last twenty minutes of practice. Twice a year we went to the club-wide competitions, which last three long hours in the sweltering gym, and watch little judoka's tossing each other around on mats, then proudly standing in formation to receive their medals. They all seemed to love all of it. We thought it was terrific both for the discipline, the reward and the way the big, burly judo masters bent and gently kissed the cheek of each child before carefully putting a medal around their neck. Afterwards parents, judokas and judo masters mingled during the *pot*, or aperi-tif, sipping warm soft drinks or hard cider and nibbling very sweet cakes.

Joe never liked soccer, what the French call *foot*, and

he has always been lukewarm about cycling. He tried out tennis for a year and liked it pretty well, though it didn't light any fires within him. He has been intermittently interested in basketball and ice skating, ice hockey and table tennis. Like most kids his age here, he's tried out just about every sport that is available.

I must backtrack and explain that extracurricular sports are very important for children in France, since sports are a minor part of the education system. Extracurricular sports are important for parents, too, since they keep children busy when school is not in session. I remember the first years we were here and friends would talk about their children and their various sports activities, and I would wonder how they found out about them, where they went to sign up. Joe was still too young then, but when his time came and I asked, the answer was always a quick, 'Read the paper, it's always announced in there.' I didn't want to press further and would buy local papers for a while and scour them for information, with no result. I scoured the yellow pages too, but found nothing there either. I didn't want to ask anyone again. There comes a time when, as a foreigner, you sense the moment to quit asking questions.

When Joe said he wanted to do judo, though, I was determined to crack the mystery of extracurricular sports. I called the *mairie* or city hall to see if I could get any help there. '*Bonjour Monsieur,*' I said politely to the operator who answered the phone. '*Je voudrais savoir si vous pouvez me renseigner sur le judo à Louviers.*'

I squinted my eyes, waiting for him to say, 'I don't have a clue.' Instead, he cheerfully gave me the number of the judo club, and the home number of the judo club's director. 'Call either one – they'll help you out,' he said. I hung up. This was all I had to do? I couldn't believe it.

I called the club right away. A recorded message told me the hours of the club, and I was at the front door when it was supposed to open. I waited, alone, for half an hour. Then someone walked out of the gym, and I asked them whether they knew the hours of the judo club. He told me there would be someone there tomorrow, at about that same time. 'The message said there would be some-one here tonight,' I said. He shrugged. '*Je ne sais pas, moi,*' he said. 'I don't know anything.'

I returned the following evening, and this time there was a little note taped to the door saying there wouldn't be anyone there for another week. I called the judo club director's house the next morning. A woman answered and said to call back at noon. I did. I talked with the director and he went into a long explanation of what was going on. I stopped him. 'Can you tell me when I can sign up my son?' I asked. He told me to call the office the following day and find out when someone would be there. He promised me that someone would answer the phone.

I called. "*Oui, Madame, c'est le club de judo. Tous les cours sont déjà pleins.*" 'Yes, this is the judo club, but all the classes are full already.' What? I thought. How can they be full already?

I asked them when registration for classes first opened. 'Oh, registration was last year at the end of the year,' was the response. I asked if they publicized the registration dates. 'No,' said the very friendly person I was speaking with. 'We don't advertise, everyone just knows.' Aha, I thought, this is one of those French things, like buying school supplies or registering a child for school. If you are born in France you've got the gene that knows how and when to do it. If you aren't, you lose out.

'I didn't know that registration was last year, and my

son who is six is counting on starting judo this year with all his friends. I'd really like to sign him up. Are you sure there isn't any more room?' I asked, determined.

She told me to wait a minute, spoke with someone, then came back to the telephone. 'What is your son's name?' I told her. She had some more muffled words with whoever was in her office, and returned.

'Oh, Joe-Joe Loomis,' she said, to my astonishment, Joe-Joe being a pet name we called Joe when he was very little. 'The judo teacher knows him, she had him in *maternelle*. Of course there is room for him. Come right now with his birth certificate, three photos, and a cheque for five hundred francs and we'll sign him up,' she said.

I felt very good about signing up Joe for judo, and not just because he was going to do something he really wanted to do. I felt good because I was in the possession of a bit of information that was more valuable to me than gold ingots. Never again would I be at a loss as to how to get by in France, for my *mairie* was there to help me. Since that fateful experience I have registered us for swimming lessons, dance classes, gymnastics and fencing, acting classes and sculpture, all by dialling the city hall number.

The summer of his ninth year, we decided it would be great for Joe to fly to the US so that he could visit our families for a few weeks, and when we mentioned the idea Joe was all for it. My older brother and his wife agreed to be his 'parents in situ', and they set about planning a good time for him. The closer it got, the more he couldn't wait to get to America, see his uncles, aunts, cousins and grandparents, and to be away from his little sister.

We knew he was mature enough for the trip, but it still wasn't easy to watch him ride up the escalator inside those clear tubes at Charles de Gaulle airport. Our house would feel awfully empty for a month, and we hoped he'd have a wonderful time.

We needn't have worried. Joe went boating and fishing, swimming and sailing, hiking and camping. He ate lots of pizzas and doughnuts, milkshakes and my mother's macaroni and cheese. He visited science centres and zoos, Niketowns and aquariums. He discovered the joy of Cosco, and with his allowance bought computer games and movies. But the most significant event of his month in America was his very first professional baseball game. He went to see the Tacoma Rainiers in Tacoma with my brother and his wife, my sister and her husband and son. 'You should have seen him,' my sister said, 'he was riveted. At one point in the game when we were all talking he asked us to be quiet.'

Whether it was brilliant playing by the Rainiers or the thrill of the game, we don't know, but something about baseball caught Joe's fancy and he returned in a whirl of passion for America's national sport. 'Mom, oh mom,' he said in the breathless way he can, 'all I want to do is play baseball.' Gone was his interest in judo.

Great, I thought. We live in France and he's fixated on the national sport of America, the only sport in the universe that it will be impossible for him to play here. This didn't really surprise me, as Joe has a penchant for finding the longest possible way out of a tunnel, but how would we resolve this?

I mulled it over. I had a vague memory of someone talking about playing baseball in Louviers. I thought and thought, then I snapped to it. 'Call the *mairie*,' I said to myself.

'Yes, Madame, there is a baseball club in Louviers. Here is the number, it's run by a Mr Casazza,' the friendly male operator said. I almost dropped the phone. A baseball club in Louviers? I'd remembered something, but not something this good!

I called Mr Casazza and he turned out to be a self-taught baseball fanatic, delighted to hear about Joe, enthusiastic about having him join the club and be on the team. 'Oh, I was bitten by the baseball bug when I lived in the States for a year,' he told me. 'That was twenty years ago. I've learned everything I know from watching the sport on TV.'

I wasn't sure this boded well for the quality of the club or team, but I could sense that what it might have lacked in finesse it made up for in enthusiasm. I signed up Joe for the bargain sum of four hundred francs for two years. When I told him, he was speechless with joy.

This began a new chapter in our lives, as we discovered that not only did Louviers have its own baseball team – named 'The Wallabies' for no good reason that anyone could explain to me – but that France has an Olympic baseball team and Rouen, a thirty-minute drive from us, has a sports high school where baseball is among the choices. Not only that, but five towns in our region have baseball teams. Play ball!!!

Joe was by far the youngest member of the Wallabies. There weren't enough children his age signed up to make a team, so Louviers combined its youth teams with those of the towns of Vernon and Les Andelys, and called the composite team Les Andelys. Joe didn't care where his teammates came from, or really even who they were, he just wanted to smack the ball. He practised Wednesdays and Saturdays and, once spring rolled around, he had games every weekend. We went to all of them and, ersatz as the training was, the kids were serious and energetic, and filled with team spirit. Les Andelys only won one game during the season, but it was a great year of discovery for all of us. Unfortunately Mr Casazza didn't coach the Les

Andelys team, but he would show up for some of the Wednesday practices, encouraging and cheering, an American teenager trapped in the body of a middle-aged French man.

Joe's coach was a young man with the face of an angel and the attention span of a flea. He was an *emploie jeune*, part of a governmental program destined to provide jobs for people in their early twenties. He was assured of work for five years, after which he would be spat back out on the job market. While he had an interest in baseball, he didn't know much about it and his style was soft and easy. He wanted the kids to love him, and he couldn't bear to make them stick to rules or baseball protocol. His heart was in the right place, but that a good team does not make. Joe was in heaven, however, wearing cleats, his great leather mitt, the red hat with its black LA on the front, of which he was so proud. Like he always does when he's passionate about something, he talked, thought and dreamed about baseball incessantly. He even convinced two of his buddies at school to try it out. This may not sound like much of a feat, but considering that most French children have never even heard of baseball, it seemed like a pretty good sales job to us.

The boys and girls on Joe's team ranged in age from six to twelve and came in all sizes. The six year old was almost too tiny for T-ball, but when he hit he'd run as if he'd been shot out of a pistol. Most of the kids were pretty uncoordinated, though three or four of them, Joe included, had a real passion for the game and played it seriously. The twelve-year-old was lanky and languid, and there were several boys who were there because their parents needed to have them out of the house. Needless to say they played poorly. Most of the players would drift off into dreamland when playing in the outfield, and Joe was no exception. To avoid it as much as possible he decided to become a pitcher. He loved it, and still considers pitcher and catcher his favourite positions.

The baseball season in France lasts from September to July, and to celebrate the end of what had been a very entertaining experience we organized an American-style baseball picnic. We invited Joe's team and their families – whom we didn't know well at all – as well as several friends. By the time everyone showed up we had enough people for four teams. That half of them knew nothing about baseball didn't matter.

The start of the day was a study in cultural contrasts. We and our friends arrived at about noon, parked our car at the entrance to the area and hauled our picnic things through the beautifully maintained soccer fields and past the cosy little soccer clubhouse. The baseball field was the poor sister by comparison, with just four bases and a pitcher's mound established, and a high fence to close it in on one side. It didn't matter because all we needed was space and shade, provided by a row of trees that bordered the field.

The parents of the French children on Joe's team didn't walk through the soccer field, they drove their cars through it, parked under the trees, unloaded their things and left their cars there. Then the French mothers, three of whom were cheerful, authoritative sisters, set about erecting collapsible picnic tables on which they settled tablecloths and composed rice salads, plates of cucumbers and cream, and gorgeous beef roasts. One of the French dads, the thinnest, most wiry man I've ever seen, who was married to one of the three sisters and was extremely serious and competitive about baseball, lit up a tiny barbecue and prepared to grill kebabs.

Meanwhile the American moms laid out blankets on

the grass. There was Deborah, an American married to a Frenchman for twenty years and the mother of three teen-age children. Despite her sojourn in France she remained very American, always up for everything, great at a picnic. I'd thought maybe we would all arrange our food on the French team's tables, but when I glanced at them they were already set for eating, so with Babette and Marie-Laure, Frenchwomen and good friends of ours, Deborah and I set about arranging food on the blankets. I had made a platter of barbecued chicken and a big bowl of potato salad; Deborah contributed roast pork loin and potato salad, we had Babette's version of coleslaw, sea-soned with mustard seed and grilled cashews. Marie-Laure piled her cheese sandwiches in the centre of the blanket. Deborah has an immense garden and she brought baskets of gorgeous Napoleon cherries (we call them Queen Anne) and a big plate of fat red gooseberries. There were bunches of garden radishes and bowls of marinated olives and some potato chips. Michael contributed a gorgeous loaf of sourdough bread, others had brought baguettes, and there were several bowls of lettuce ready to be dressed with vinaigrette.

When all the food was out and the first game was over it seemed like a good time to dig in.

'But we must have our aperitif first,' said one of the cheerful authoritarian French mothers.

'Oh, of course, of course,' I said, gently elbowing an American friend who was filling her plate.

Out came bottles of rosé, Pastis, beer and Orangina and we all clinked glasses and stood around sipping, every-one a bit shy. I looked at the segregated food camps. I had imagined that all the food would be shared by every-one, but once the aperitif hour was over the French con-tingent and their multitude of children retreated to their carefully set-up tables. Our group filled their plates and sat on blankets.

There was some crossover. A few of the friendlier, braver French came over to try the barbecued chicken and the potato salads, and one French mother hesitantly offered us some of her rice salad, which we accepted with pleasure. I wanted to go over to their table and try more of their salads, but the ambience didn't allow for that, so I resisted. The situation remained pretty much a cultural stand-off. Oh, we poured them some of our wine and beer and they poured us some of theirs, and we joked back and forth a bit. Mostly, though, things didn't relax until the chocolate chip and peanut butter cookies I'd made came out. Pretty soon everyone was munching, laughing and getting ready for game number two.

The games were pure fun and everyone played, from the littlest boy who was about four to the most uptight Frenchman who, it was obvious, had been coerced to attend by his wife. He stood stiffly in the outfield at first, looking around to see if anyone was watching, rolling his eyes. By the end of the second innings, though, he was hunkered down behind his mitt like a pro. With more games and lots more beer, wine and cookies, we were all there until well into the evening.

We had successfully staged a very American event where we played for fun and not to win. The American attitude of including everyone in the games and playing purely for fun surprised the French parents, for it turned out that among themselves they play baseball, and they are very competitive. I wondered, too, if they were uneasy at first because they had assumed that the Americans present would all be good, ultra-competitive players. When they'd witnessed the reality and realized they had nothing to fear, they relaxed, let down their hair and had a great time.

As the group broke up we were already talking about next year's game, in what was one of those rare and beautiful moments of true cultural exchange. I received an email from a friend the next day, who wrote, 'I haven't had so much fun since 1962!' I knew exactly what he meant.

The following baseball season was more problematic. Some particularly active parents from the town of Vernon had done a lot of recruiting, and they had enough children to form their own, so they dropped out of the Les Andelys team, leaving it without enough players. This left Joe with all his passion intact, but nowhere to play ball.

He took the matter into his own hands. He made posters which read: 'Baseball? It's the most fun sport in the world!! If you want to be part of the best team, the really best team (which I advise you to do), come give it a try!!' and together he and I put them up in shop windows around Louviers. His effort netted a handful of players and the thanks of Mr Casazza, but there still weren't enough kids of Joe's age to make a team.

Joe was despondent but loyal, and he continued going to practise in Louviers and Les Andelys. Finally he came home nearly in tears. 'The big kids don't want to play with us, so all we do is stand around,' he said. 'I wish I could play for a team like Bois Guillaume.'

Bois Guillaume is a town near Rouen, a half an hour from Louviers. The head of their baseball club is an enthusiastic young man from Quebec who learned to play baseball as a child, and who has infused his club with a dynamism absent in the other teams we'd seen. Michael had got to know the coach a bit, and we called to see if Joe could join his team. He acquiesced immediately.

Two weeks later Michael drove Joe the thirty minutes to Bois Guillaume for his first practice. Joe was apprehensive. He'd played against the team throughout the last year and, though he knew the coach wanted him, he was afraid the players would think he was the enemy. When he got home from that first practice, though, he had stars in his eyes. 'Bois Guillaume is a *real* team,' he said. 'I loved Les Andelys and I wish I could have stayed playing with them, but it's so fun to be with Bois Guillaume!'

Since that first practice Joe hasn't looked back and neither have we, except to realize we are now like American 'soccer moms', driving our son to faraway places to practise and play the game. The good definitely outweighs the kilometres, though. Michael has become a baseball nut right along with Joe, and he is now the assistant coach of Joe's team. A natural athlete, he was recruited to the adult baseball and softball teams with a bunch of surprisingly enthusiastic but pretty disorganized men and women. The average age of these players is probably forty and they come from all walks of life. There is a history professor and a professional cook, a primary school teacher and an engineer. I am often a weekend baseball widow as Saturday afternoons are devoted to Joe's playing and Michael's coaching, and Sundays to Michael's coaching and Joe looking after the equipment as batboy. There are those weekends when Fiona and I are caught up in it, too, as cheerful supporters, and Fiona says she wants to play when she 'has *cinq ans*,' is five.

What I love about it all is that here in this country of soccer and tennis players, croissant eaters and wine drinkers, Joe managed to hit on the one passion that would keep him in touch with his cultural roots. By becoming passionate – and I don't mean just interested, I mean passionate – about baseball, he has ensured himself the most American-possible childhood he can have while still living in France. And he has assured us all lots of gorgeous afternoons outside watching cute kids play a game they love.

The repercussions of his passion are fascinating. Joe comes home from school with a quick 'Hi!', and heads for the newspaper, which he opens to the sports page. He reads whatever interests him, then he and Michael have a deep and informed conversation about baseball. Joe sits right down to do his homework, then either goes outside to hit balls off the T-ball he got for his birthday, or toss the ball with Michael, or watch baseball videos on the television. When Michael isn't working he is reading baseball books, learning as fast as he can. He and Joe pour over baseball equipment catalogues, and Joe writes and rewrites his wish lists. Naturally, we ask anyone coming to visit us from the States to bring equipment with them, since the choice in France is limited and outrageously expensive.

Sometimes when Joe is desperate to play catch and Michael isn't home, he will ask me. I love it and Joe is a very patient teacher, rolling his eyes only when he thinks I'm not looking. Try as he might, he cannot hide the relief in his face when Michael turns up. 'Uh, mom, I hope you won't be insulted or anything, but Papa's here and, uh, well, uh, I think maybe he'd like to play catch with me,' he says. Joe returns to the United States each summer and he always has such fun that to him paradise and the US are synonymous. He went to his first serious baseball camp there last summer and we were all curious to see where he stood compared with American boys his age. It turned out that, unlike in France where he is the best player of his age in our region, in the US he was simply a good player. Joe took the camp experience as he takes much in life, with an equanimity that I find admirable. 'After all,' he said, 'I started playing baseball when I was ten. Americans start when they are five.'

Joe does wish that his life in Louviers corresponded

with the vision he has of life in the States, where he thinks pick-up baseball happens on every street in every neighbourhood at every moment of the day. He petitioned his aunt and uncles to convince us to let him go to high school in America so he could play baseball all the time. Naturally, we refused.

He also thinks it is stupid that he's studying Latin, German, English and a host of other serious subjects, so that he doesn't have much time to hit the ball during the week, and he gets really frustrated that he can't share his enthusiasm with his friends at school since they know nothing about baseball. But he deals with it. And, in dealing with all of this, which is his biculturalism, his mind is stretching in ways most children his age don't experience.

Reality doesn't affect Joe's hopes and dreams, nor his ambition. As he practises here with Michael and his team, plays games, participates in select teams and regional play-offs, he dreams of his life in the pros. He has already designed the house he's going to build then. It has many rooms including, I'm happy to notice, a large and well-designed kitchen. I am also gratified to see we all have rooms there, along with an indoor pool, batting cage and gym, an outdoor pool and a Jacuzzi, and a small stream running through the property, just like the one at the estate of friends who live in the valley below Louviers. He currently thinks he'd like to play with the Seattle Mariners, though he admires the Arizona Diamondbacks too.

Regardless of what team he decides upon, though, he's got his future tracked. Get through high school, get a scholarship to university in America, then head for the big leagues. It's as simple as that for a twelve-year-old American French boy!

ROAST PORK WITH SALT AND SPICE CRUST
Rôti de Porc en Croute d'Épices

— ↭ —

This roast pork dazzles, with its aromatic crust and tender, succulent interior. It is so easy to prepare, you'll find yourself making it often. And it is so elegant, you can serve it to the most discerning group without hesitation.

2 dried, imported bay leaves, ground
4 tsp fresh thyme leaves
½ tsp ground allspice
½ tsp freshly ground black pepper
1 tbs coarse sea salt
One 2 lb (1 kg) pork loin, wrapped either in barding fat or side pork and tied
Fresh thyme and parsley sprigs – for garnish

1. Coarsely grind the bay leaves in a coffee or spice mill. Mix all of the spices with the salt in a small bowl, and press the mixture as evenly as possible into the pork loin. Some of the spices will fall from the pork loin – simply press them onto the top, where the mixture will be thickest. Place the pork in a dish, cover, and let sit at room temperature for at least one hour and up to 3 hours.

2. Place the pork loin in an earthenware baking dish. Preheat the oven to 375°F (190°C). Pour 1 cup of water around the pork, and roast it in the centre of the oven until it is golden on the outside and cooked to your liking on the inside (it will be properly cooked and at

140°F on the interior after 1 hour). Check the loin occasionally as it roasts and add additional water as necessary to keep the bottom of the roasting pan moist.

3. Remove the pork loin from the oven and let it sit for at least 30 minutes before slicing, so the juices can retreat into the meat.

4. Remove the pork from the roasting dish and slice it on a cutting board that will trap any juices that run from it. Pour the juices back into the roasting pan, and set the pan over a very low flame to heat up the juices. Scrape up any caramelized juices from the bottom of the pan and transfer the juices to a warmed sauce dish. Arrange the slices of pork loin on a warmed platter and garnish with fresh thyme and parsley sprigs.

Serves 8

Cultural Differences/Cultural Sameness

When we opened our home to strangers who come for lunch or to take a cooking class, I expected lots of questions about France, agriculture, food trends, cooking and restaurants, along with the laughter and good times. I, naively perhaps, didn't expect to delve into the personal, so I wasn't entirely prepared for questions about what it was like raising children in France, how we'd been accepted, how our habits in France differed from our habits in the United States, whether or not we liked the French and living in France.

My instinct was to field these questions with demure yeses, noes and maybes, but I knew this wouldn't suffice. We'd opened up our front door to the world and they wanted to know what it was like to live our life. I found myself wanting to answer their personal questions.

The most frequently asked question was how Joe fitted in at school, and whether or not his adjustment had been difficult. The answer to that was easy. Joe has always felt fiercely American, but hardly anyone at school knows or

311

cares about his nationality. Almost from the start he fitted in seamlessly. The transition period was difficult as he tried, in his nearly three-year-old way, to figure out just exactly why his little world had turned upside down, but once he began to understand French he relaxed and settled in.

There were other questions with easy answers: Are the French nice to you?; do you pay your taxes in France?; was it hard to buy your house? The answers? Yes to the first two. To the third, no – French banks like money, no matter where it comes from.

Harder questions followed.

Do you think you'll ever move back to the US? Do you have family in the States and do you miss them? What makes life in France so much better than life in the US?

All of these questions touch at the heart of our beings, the meaning of our lives and our actions, and I found them all thought-provoking and not so easy to answer. I had made a decision to return to France for two main reasons: I loved the lifestyle and I wanted to raise my children in its midst, and I wanted to exercise my profession in a country where excellence in food production and preparation prevailed. I felt strongly that the world wanted and needed to see how the French revere food, and how farmers and other food producers have vital and immediate relationships with consumers. I saw my role in reporting all of this as important.

There were plenty of little reasons I wanted to live in France, too. I love eating out in restaurants where the service is sublime and the food is exceptional. I wanted to perfect my French; I wanted to be part of the society of the friends I'd made in France who all had an innate style that I loved. I wanted to wake up to air that smelled of butter and fresh bread, shop at little shops, go to the farmers' market on a regular basis, visit *brocantes*, second-hand markets, and find little old French treasures. I ignored the outrageous things like the cost of petrol, electricity and building materials, and the mountains of paperwork involved in establishing a life in France. What did I care about reality? Since moving to France and discovering the outrageous along with the sublime, however, Michael and I have had moments of extreme frustration and our fair share of doubts. We had begun the adventure on a wing and a prayer, and often it was much more prayer than wing, so that we'd find ourselves wondering just how we would actually make it through the next month of '*factures*' – bills. Part of the reason we were caught so short was that I had thought, after ten years as a successful freelance writer, that work would simply flow my way once I was in France. I couldn't have been more wrong. The freelance life seems as if it should be made for flexibility and change, but the opposite is true. It was as if by changing countries I'd suddenly dropped off the face of the earth. I needed to build back my business, recreate myself as a food writer from France.

So Michael and I would look at each other and wonder just why we were struggling so much. Occasionally we would think about moving back to the States, thinking about how much easier life was since we understood it and its systems and routines. We would reminisce about the efficiency there, the freedom of information about everything – from building techniques to food. We would compare it with France, where you have to rattle, shake and stomp your feet to get any information at all. Financially our lives would have been easier in the US, too, for there Michael could always find work to supplement his earnings as a sculptor. He didn't feel like he could do that in France.

I would think about my parents and brothers and sisters

and miss them terribly, knowing how helpful and comforting it would be to be near them. I would particularly miss them around holidays when the French retreat into their immediate families.

Sometimes when I got really discouraged, I would visualize moving back to our former house in our old neighbourhood in Seattle and heave a virtual sigh of relief. How easy life was there, how comprehensible. There were none of the mysteries and complexities of life in France that keep you awake at night, nor the constant shock at how expensive life was.

We worked much harder in France than we'd worked before, in part because our overhead had ballooned compared with what it had been in America. And we worked harder because we're foreigners, for as a foreigner one must work harder simply to stay abreast of what is going on. It seems as if, no matter the subject, there is always one more thing to know. Though I love the daily challenge and the constant and graphic learning, it is wearing sometimes, for no matter how integrated we become, we remain on the outside. For instance, we cannot vote, which goes against my democratic grain. Because we don't vote we aren't on the mayor's mailing list, so we aren't informed about neighbourhood meetings and other interesting town-wide events. I've asked a hundred times to be put on the mailing list anyway, and each time the mayor's right-hand man assures me he will take care of it. But it hasn't happened and now, after nearly ten years, I doubt it will. So I have to keep my ear to the ground, work harder, to get the information.

Despite the difficulties, which I refer to as 'uptown hardships', I've never missed life in the States. I miss the individuals down to my fishmonger, who became a close friend, but I don't miss having to get into my car to buy fish from his store, nor fight the traffic in an ever-growing city, nor the lack of access to incredibly flavoured ingredients. I also don't miss the violence of life in the US, which troubled me every day I lived there. I was never personally touched by any of the shootings or muggings or rapes or other common occurrences of life in a US city, but I observed them and feared. France is far from perfect, but for now it remains a safe place to live, for us and for our children. I don't worry about drive-by shootings the way my sister had to when her children were in high school, and I don't worry about Joe having to beware of weapons at school. For now, all of that is still at a distance in France, at least where we live.

One of the things I love most about life in France is its immediacy. It is tactile, charming, filled with real people who share themselves in a hundred little ways. It isn't efficient, but I've learned that efficiency can erase warmth, so I'm glad for certain inefficiencies. Take shopping. It takes a lot of my time and energy because as I do it I become caught up in myriad little conversations with shopkeepers and people I run into on the street. Part of this is life in a small town, though it happens to me in Paris, too.

As I walk past our pâtisserie, which features a new cake almost every week, like the one on the shelf now made with apples, almonds and toasted hazelnuts on top, I think to myself that, with such delicious food made with such care all around me, I couldn't live in a better place. I feel it again when I pick up the country's major newspaper and read on page three that Pierre Hermé, France's current pastry darling, has just created a newsworthy macaroon made with olive oil, or when I walk past the charcuterie and see from a sign in their window that they've just been given an award for the best *boudin blanc* white pudding, in Europe. These things are important, and not just to a small percentage of people who think food is important, because everyone in France thinks food is important. And fundamentally, this is why I love it in France so much. Here I can commune with just about anyone on the subject of my passion, food; here its appreciation and quality isn't reserved for an elite, it is the province of everyone.

This differs strongly from the US, where food is a complex affair. Like nudity or sexuality, both comfortable topics of conversation in France, food in America is something to feel guilty about, not something to celebrate. Which leads me to the next question, the one I am asked perhaps more than all the others. How do I, and the French, stay slim?

I like this question because it gives me a chance to air my observations and analyses of food and its place. I stay thin despite my large appetite in part because my metabolism is on overdrive. But I, like all my French friends, also stay thin because we eat really delicious food that is well-prepared, and we don't eat too much of it. We take time to eat, and we tend not to eat between meals. We don't eat prepared foods unless they come from the charcuterie down the street, whose food is like home cooking. Soft drinks aren't part of our lives; pastries from the bakery are, but not every day. I make desserts and cookies, but not all the time. We eat cheese, but not every day. We always eat salad, and lots of wonderful bread. We eat butter or olive oil on our bread in the morning and the children eat it on their bread at four o'clock, but otherwise we eat our bread plain. We drink wine with dinner every night, though just a glass or two. I think that what counts most in all of this is that the food we eat is wholesomely delicious because the ingredients are so fine, and if I've learned anything in all my years of cooking and living in France it is this: excellent ingredients make excellent food, no matter how simple it is, and when you eat excellent food you are satisfied.

As I consider these questions and try to formulate intelligent answers I don't want to sound smug, because I don't feel smug. I feel, to the contrary, that in moving to France we opted out of a great deal of what has become so important to the American psyche: money, swift career advancement, the possibility of deluxe private schools for our children. We've opted out of the competition that is so rife in our society, which at times seems more concerned with the competition itself than with what I find important, like quality, excellence and time.

By opting out we don't participate in the energetic creativity that goes on in the US, either, which we miss since we both have our competitive sides, and we both want to excel in our professions. By opting out we've had to be ever more creative about supporting our lifestyle, and I have needed to make sure that my colleagues and readers do not forget who I am. This means doing regular freelance articles in widely read publications, travelling to the States at least once a year to teach cooking classes, to meet with editors and colleagues, to keep myself and my name 'out there'. Having a cooking school for an English-speaking audience would only make this that much more vital. 'Opting out' has meant working harder, but we consider the trade-off worth it for the quality of life we've been able to create.

I've always been attracted to people who have a passion for what they do connected to food, whether it be working the soil, fishing, farming or cooking, and those kind of passionate people abound in France. Take the young cheese *affineur*, or ager, in Rouen, who takes time out of his incredibly hectic schedule to talk to groups I bring about what he does, because he's driven to make people understand how the quality of the cheese they eat is no accident, how it comes about because of the effort he and others put into it. Take our local baker, who is always ready to talk about what he does and why his bread is more crusty one day than the next, or the local *épicier* who spends so much time finding the best quality produce and products for his clientele. Food is such a part of daily life in France that you cannot avoid it, ever.

I do miss the diversity of the food in the US, particularly when I hear our American visitors talking about their favourite restaurants, which might as easily be Afghani or Egyptian as Italian, French or Spanish. I miss the pace and the energy, the ability Americans have to say 'Why not?', whereas the French response tends to be 'Why?' We are so fortunate because we can have the best of both worlds, by living in France and visiting the States, and by having the US visit us.

I read about American food trends and see how far people stretch, and how easily American chefs incorporate outside influences into their food and I admire their openness, creativity and willingness. On the other hand, when I lived in the US those same characteristics sometimes confounded me, because I felt that culinary trendsetters weren't looking at their own history, their own wealth, their own traditions; they wanted to be famous instantly, and were always referring to something outside rather than inside. The results may have been dramatic, but they weren't excellent. They couldn't be because they weren't based on experience and tradition.

In France the creation of food is based on experience and tradition, which means that the young learn from their elders until they have a good solid foundation and experience. Then they begin adding olive oil to their macaroons, or rose petals to their ice cream, or star anise to their poaching liquid, and coming up with food so delicious and well balanced that it makes sense and tastes divine.

I am often asked what the French think of me, an American woman, trying to unlock the secrets of their traditional cuisines. It's an interesting question. I've had tough moments when I'd find myself at the table in a farmhouse, the only American within miles, and have to answer for American foreign policy, agricultural subsidies or political domination. I would hear a French person say, 'All Americans are obese, or rich, or ugly,' and I would respond simply by asking them how they could possibly generalize about a population of 300 million individuals whose origins are in every country in the world.

Aside from the sticky times, I have mostly had great moments when people thank me for being interested in what they do. They express their admiration for the way Americans are always so eager to learn, and their humble surprise that Americans would be interested in their food. I gather that I am perceived as strong and independent by the French people I know, a woman who knows what she wants and has figured out how to get it. I lose points in seductiveness, though, something my French female friends, working women or not, are experts at. I'm too much a 'northerner', a 'Puritan' to excel here, though I'm a willing learner and my French friends are willing teachers!

It is so great to be with Americans who ask such frank questions, and who express themselves so openly. As a nation we are very inquisitive, and we think that information is free and to be shared. The French don't feel this way. Because of my job as a journalist I naturally ask

319

a lot of questions and I didn't realize that it was odd until some French friends told me how un-French it is. 'We think your habit of asking questions is charming, because we know and love you,' a French friend told me. 'But most French people don't like to answer questions or give out information. They like to hide it.'

The French will talk openly about sex, food, relationships, politics and literature, but it is true that when it comes to finances, work, or family affairs they are like Fort Knox. It takes getting used to.

We are also often asked, 'How do you like living in a small town?' I surprise myself when I say I like it, for I love the beat of the city and all it offers, and my one experience of living in a small town in the US was excruciating. Louviers offers nearly everything we need in a very accessible manner, from a multiscreen cinema to fabulous bakeries on every corner. There is theatre and music, and we have a group of nice friends. With five minutes of vigorous bike-riding we are out in the flax and corn fields, and yet an hour in the car driving southeast puts us at the foot of the Eiffel Tower.

So, life in Louviers is good, but it hasn't just happened. We work hard to make it good, interesting, stimulating. And now, with the cooking school, we share it with an increasing number of people. It is so gratifying to see the messages I've worked very hard to transmit over the years, about supporting and getting to know local producers, eating locally and seasonally, taking time at the table to savour and enjoy food getting across in a very immediate way.

I was in a small restaurant in Rouen with my cooking class and we were having lunch with the young cheese *affineur*. He asked for a moment of silence so he could speak.

'I'd like you all when you go home to do something for us,' he said. 'I'd like you all to make something delicious and take it to work with you for your lunch. Ask your colleagues to join you, and take an extra fifteen minutes to enjoy it. Think of us, of me and Susan and the others you have met while you've been in France. If you do this, you will make us extremely happy.'

His suggestion, made to a table filled with highly placed professional women, was met with silence. Then a small ripple started at one end of the table. 'I'm going to do that,' said one woman, then another, until everyone agreed they would.

By following his suggestion they would take a valuable part of the French culture home with them and make it part of their own. And that, for me, is the point.

MUSTARD CREAM WITH FRESH VEGETABLES
Crème de Moutarde aux Legumes

───────── ⌇ ─────────

This is a favorite aperitif at *On Rue Tatin*, simple to put together and appealing at any season.

1 cup (250ml) crème fraîche
3 tbs (45ml) Dijon-style mustard, or to taste
Seasonal vegetables such as small carrots, turnips, broccoli, cauliflower, fennel
Chive points, chervil, or fennel fronds

1. In a medium-sized bowl whisk the cream until it is thick. Whisk in the mustard and reserve.
2. Bring salted water to a boil in a large kettle. Blanch the vegetables, beginning with the carrots, then the turnips. Once the vegetables are blanched, refresh them in ice water then let them drain on tea towels. Change the water, bring it to a boil and blanch the broccoli and the cauliflower.
3. Place the mustard cream in an attractive serving dish, and serve the vegetables alongside.

6 appetizer servings

THREE NUT BISCOTTI
Biscotti aux Amandes, Noisettes, et Noix

⌐⌐

This recipe is based on a traditional Tuscan biscotti called *cantucci,* where almonds are used. I love the deep, golden flavour of the combination of nuts, which are lightly toasted before being added to the dough.

1¾ cup (230 g) all-purpose flour
1 tsp baking powder
½ tsp fine sea salt
4 tbs (60 g) unsalted butter, at room temperature
½ cup (100 g) vanilla sugar
2 large eggs, at room temperature
1 large egg yolk, at room temperature
⅓ cup (50 g) almonds, skinned, toasted,
and coarsely chopped
⅓ cup (50 g) hazelnuts, toasted, skinned,
and coarsely chopped
⅓ cup (50 g) walnuts, toasted and coarsely chopped

1. Preheat the oven to 350°F (175°C). Line 2 baking sheets with parchment paper.
2. Sift together the flour, baking powder, and salt onto a piece of waxed or parchment paper.
3. In a large bowl or the work bowl of an electric mixer, beat the butter until pale yellow and light. Gradually add the sugar and mix until thoroughly combined. Add the eggs, one at a time, then the egg yolk, mixing well after each addition. Add the flour mixture and mix just until combined. Fold in the nuts.

4. Divide the dough into quarters and shape each quarter into a 6-inch (15 cm) log about 1½ inches (3.75 cm) thick. Place the logs about 1½ inches (3.75 cm) apart on the prepared baking sheets.
5. Bake the logs in the centre of the oven until they are puffed and golden, about 25 minutes. Remove from the oven and let cool on a wire rack for 10 minutes. Leave the oven on.
6. With a sharp knife, cut the logs on the diagonal into ½-inch (1.3 cm) thick slices. Place the slices, cut side down, on the parchment-lined baking sheets and bake until they are golden on one side, about 15 minutes. Turn the slices and bake until they are golden on the other side, 5 to 10 minutes more. Remove from the oven and let cool on a wire rack.

About 48 biscotti

Home Away from Home –
September 11

I'd been to Chez Clet, our neighbourhood *épicerie*, buy-ing fruits and vegetables, and was returning home with my baskets full. I had just turned from rue Pierre Mendès France onto rue Tatin and, as I approached our courtyard door, André from across the street came hurrying across the street, his face red, his arms flying.

'*Je vous cherche depuis toute à l'heure. Le World Trade Center à New York a été détruit,*' he said, so fast I could not under-stand him. '*Pardon?*' I said, fearing he was giving me bad news about his wife or sister-in-law.

'*Chez vous, aux Etats-Unis, à New York, deux avions ont detruit le World Trade Center,*' he said, shaking his hands, almost shaking me.

I understood his words this time, but they made no sense to me. The World Trade Center destroyed by two airplanes? What was he talking about?

By now he was close to apoplectic. '*Allez, allez dans votre maison et disez à votre mari, écoutez votre radio,*' he said. 'Go, quickly, into your house and tell your husband, then listen to your radio.' He touched my back, turned, and walked slowly back to his apartment. I rushed into the house, stunned and confused by what he'd told me.

I turned on the BBC and there heard confirmation of what he'd said. I was filled with such fear, such horror that I thought I would be violently ill. Michael was outside working in the courtyard and I called to him.

He came in. I told him. 'I know,' he said. 'I know.'

I looked at him. 'You already heard?' 'Yes,' he said. He had heard just moments before but, as with me, it made so little sense and had so little to do with reality that it hadn't sunk in. We stood there, dumbstruck, barely attached to our bearings.

Then I panicked. 'The kids, we have to get the kids,' I said, as if they were in some danger.

'They're OK, it's all right,' Michael said, but I wasn't convinced. If someone could blow up the World Trade Center, someone could reach right into their safe little niches and hurt them too.

The radio was broadcasting barely controlled hysteria. We listened and heard about the Pentagon, then about the plane in Pennsylvania, as though the horror wouldn't stop. The radio announcer was spurting out facts as he heard them, as they occurred. People jumping, people fighting for their lives, people armed with paper cutters committing senseless acts of destruction. The more news that emerged, the more bizarre and horrific it was.

Michael left to pick up Joe from school and I went to collect Fiona from the babysitter, so queasy I could hardly drive. There was an unnatural brightness to things, a feeling of falseness, as though the fields I was driving through weren't real but part of a movie set. I clutched Fiona when I saw her, so grateful she was safe and beautifully sound.

When we were home our neighbour, Marie-Odile,

knocked on the door and walked in, her face crumpled with sorrow. She stood there, twisting her fingers, then said we could come watch the news on their television if we wanted to, since our television wasn't hooked up. I declined, but said that I thought Michael and Joe would when they returned. I didn't want to see images, and I certainly didn't want Fiona to see them. I was already more afraid than I'd ever been in my life and I didn't want her to be afraid too. Michael and Joe came home and we all just hugged each other. Joe had already heard the news at school, though he didn't really understand. 'What is everyone so upset about?' he asked.

He and Michael went to the neighbours, and Joe returned much chastened. 'Oh mama,' he said hugging me, 'are we safe?'

Were we safe? The question ran through my mind as I was sure it ran through the minds of every American everywhere. Were we safe, in our little town in France? Chances are we were, but we didn't know. No one knew. No one knew anything. I assured Joe we were safe, and hoped he believed me.

We got through dinner and putting the children to bed that evening, their fears allayed but not ours. I called my parents in the United States and, to my horror, heard a recorded message saying no calls were going through. From the news we knew the country was on a high state of alert. I knew about alerts: how many nights had I gone to bed as a child knowing my father had been called away because he and the men he commanded were on alert?

I called again and again and nothing went through. It was my worst fear brought to life. I had had infrequent but regular nightmares the first years we lived in France, where I heard jackboots echoing on our narrow street at night as we hid in the house, fearing for our lives. In my dream I couldn't contact family, couldn't get calls through, couldn't ever return to my country. I recognized the nightmare, which never varied, as the product of an active imagination and the holocaust literature I had steeped myself in as a teen-ager, but that didn't make them any less terrifying. It had been years since I'd had the nightmare, but my fear now came from the same source as those dreams. 'Could it be happening?' I asked myself many, many times.

The phone rang and it was Edith, crying, saying how sorry she was, asking if we had news of anyone. She was panic-stricken because Bernard was in Atlanta, Georgia, for a meeting, and he'd called her on his cell phone to say he was fine, but that he didn't know when he would be home. She wanted to come over and see us, but she didn't want to leave her house or her son. We talked for a while then said tearful goodbyes.

I tried again to get a call through to the States then gave up and sent emails. Miraculously, they went through.

The following morning I remember awakening with a start, thinking I'd just had a terrible nightmare, then remembering it was all true. I turned on the radio and the news was horrible. I went to the computer and thank-fully found some messages from friends in New York say-ing they were safe. I went downstairs, walked into the kitchen and burst into tears.

That was the last time I cried, at least in front of anyone. I didn't want the children more alarmed than they already were. But I felt like crying all the time, from fear and the frustration of being so far away from our home. These horrible things were happening in places we knew so well, places we'd walked, eaten, had meetings, driven by any number of times. Here was our country, our strong, impenetrable country, violated by the unthinkable – air-planes, carrying passengers, diverted by a handful of poorly armed, angry men. Families had been destroyed, our friends and countrymen traumatized, and here we were in our comfortable house in our comfortable adopted French town absolutely useless, unable to contact our loved ones, dependent for news on one thin radio antenna and the internet. It was enough to make a person want to jump out of their skin.

We were glued to the radio most of the day, picking up whatever information we could. I'd called some American friends in Paris just to hear their voices. I kept running to the computer to get news, to check emails, wanting everyone we knew to be accounted for. An American friend who lived in a village not far away called me. We made plans to get together with our other American friends in the area. We needed to see each other.

Our phone rang incessantly that day as French friends called to express their sorrow. We received a flowering plant from a friend of Michael's with a note expressing solidarity and friendship. I was astonished at the outpouring, the formal declarations of warmth and sadness, the shared incredulity.

I called Edith to check on Bernard. She'd spoken to him and he was fine, in awe of the way Americans were rallying, the response by the air force, the atmosphere. He wanted to come home but no planes would be flying for days, so he had to sit tight.

My tendency that first day was to keep the children home, to huddle. I was actively concerned for their safety as it was impossible to predict how anyone, anywhere would act. If indeed this was a question of Arab versus American, we in Louviers were surrounded by Arabs, just as Joe would be in the town where he went to school. We've always appreciated the mix of cultures we find around us here, the North African groceries and butcher's shops, the cafés that are filled with men from dawn to dusk, the Turkish restaurants, the kebab shops, the market vendors. It makes for colourful diversity. My fears were unfamiliar and I felt they weren't appropriate, yet when I examined them and the situation I understood them. The world was turned upside down, and so were my feelings.

We sent Joe to school, and Fiona went to the baby-sitter's. We tried to pursue our lives, our ears glued to the radio and the telephone.

Everywhere I went in Louviers people stopped me to say how sorry they were. And everywhere I went I carried the news with me as though it was my personal grief. Michael did too. We both felt grey with sadness and sorrow.

I believe it was the following day that Joe returned from school and told us that he'd sung the national anthem in front of his class. 'My English teacher asked me if I would,' he said. 'I felt so good standing there singing it.' Joe had been cast as a hero that day, and we talked with him about it, about what it meant to him to have sung that song. 'I'm American, and I'm so glad to be American,' was his response.

I was walking down our pedestrian walkway a day or two afterwards, having just bought freshly roasted coffee beans at our little local roaster, and a journalist from the local paper greeted me. 'Madame Loomis,' he said, 'may I come and interview you about what has happened?'

I stared at him. He's interviewed me before about many things, but this time I knew I had nothing to say, to him or anyone else. I felt as though I was grieving for a personal loss, and that his request was inappropriate. I wanted to tell him to leave me alone, to let me be. Instead I told him I simply had nothing to share. 'But surely you have impressions, feelings, something to say,' he said, as though

330

it could come out in a coherent, reasoned way. I told him it was too fresh, too immediate. What I didn't tell him, but what I felt as well, was that now was not the time to step forward as an American. We were all, everywhere, far too vulnerable. I told the reporter to call me in a week, that perhaps then I would have something to say. He did, and I was ready to talk. The story he wrote was on the front page of the local paper, with a big photograph of me sitting in the reporter's office, reading the issue of *USA Today* from September 12 that Bernard had brought home. I refused to be photographed at home, and refused to let him use our address. He wrote a heartfelt piece, and quoted me saying several things, among them that we didn't have a television and thus had been spared the footage that ran continuously and contributed to the horror.

The day the article ran I received a phone call, from a man I didn't know. 'Madame Loomis,' he said, 'I read in the paper that you don't have a television. I'm calling to tell you that I've got one for you, and if you'll tell me where you live I'll come over and hook it up for you.'

I held the phone away from my ear and looked at it. Was this a hoax? I wasn't in the mood to give out our address. 'Thank you, Monsieur,' I said. 'We actually do have a television screen, it just isn't hooked up.'

'Well,' he countered, 'I've already recorded all the newscasts of September the eleventh, and I want to bring them to you so that you can see them.' Then he added 'You don't have to be afraid, Madame Loomis, I and my whole family love Americans.' Then he told me his name, which I recognized from knowing his father. I gave him our address.

I hung up, wondering if I'd done the right thing. Within a half an hour a friendly young man was at the door, a stack of videotapes in his hands. He had a baseball cap on, and an American flag in his lapel.

'Bonjour, Madame Loomis,' he said. 'I felt so bad that you didn't have a television and weren't able to see what is happening that I got one of the stores here to loan me one, for you.' He went on to tell me the story of his life, that his father had been in the French legion and worked with Americans, had travelled extensively in America, and had many American friends. 'I've always loved America, and I love Americans,' he said, with tears forming in his eyes. 'You take these and look at them, and I'll record more, every day, and bring the tapes to you.'

He left me standing with the tapes in my hand, and tears in my own eyes. His motivation was sheer goodness. He did a lot to restore our confidence in the basic goodness of people, with his daily gifts of tapes and goodwill. So did our neighbours, the florists, who were also recording for us. They faithfully brought us tapes whenever there was something they thought would be of interest.

A week after the event they asked us to come watch a television special on the disaster. It was the first time I'd seen the images and they struck me full in the chest. I understood the horror even better, the brazenness of the act, the crushing reality that life would never be the same, for anyone. This was our New York, our Trade Center, our hallowed ground that had, in a matter of moments, been destroyed. Like any senseless act or occurrence I've experienced, this one left me feeling completely empty.

After about fifteen minutes of footage and interviews, talking heads and people on the street, I realized how much speculation there was, how little hard information was at hand. It was frustrating and, it seemed to me, dangerous to be filling the airwaves with empty speculation.

That Friday the world declared three minutes of silence for the victims. In France, the silence was scheduled for 3 p.m. I knew that at Joe's school they were observing three minutes of silence for victims of terrorism world-wide, which we thought a very wonderful way to teach the children about all the world's victims. In Louviers the three minutes of silence passed, then the American national anthem came belting out of the town's loud-speakers, not just once, but twice. I'd been out running an errand and I walked into the courtyard with tears streaming down my face, to find Michael standing in the courtyard, his face wet too.

The United States has never once ceased to be home for Michael, nor for me. We don't even consider ourselves expatriates for, though we've withdrawn from our native land, our patriotism hasn't changed. We've just found a new home, but that has never meant we've given up our country, or ceased to think of it as home. We are both American through and through, and our allegiance never wavers. Never had we felt more like being there than now. We wanted to be home with our own people, to touch them, see them, share this horrible time with them. It was an extremely, exceedingly lonely and vulnerable time, throwing into question the very notions of patriotism and allegiance, independence and connectedness. I, particu-larly, remain extremely close to my family, and manage to see them all at least once if not twice a year. Together, Michael and I are close to a group of friends who live in the US and whom we've known for almost twenty years. We now wanted, more than just about anything in the world, to be with all these people we loved. And we wanted to be in New York, helping.

None of these feelings belittled our attachments in France. They simply pointed out that, as the death of a close relative propels you into the bosom of your family, so this tragedy propelled us towards our own.

The morning of the national anthem in Louviers there had been a mass at the church across the street to observe the tragedy. It was heavily attended, and when the people had dispersed, many of them walked down our street to get to their cars. I went to get the mail and found two envelopes in the mailbox without postmarks. One was labelled simply '*Témoignage de Sympathie*', 'Gesture of Sympathy', in a clear and careful hand. Inside was a handwritten card that spoke of victims and heroes, of inalterable occurrences, of everlasting feelings of friendship. It ended with the simple phrase '*Vive l'Amérique, qui a tant donné à la France.*' 'Long live America, which has given so much to France.' It was signed, 'A loyal reader, and admirer of your house.'

The other envelope contained two cards, each written in beautifully decorous French handwriting, from the florists. One spoke of the sixty years they had harboured a heartfelt thankfulness towards the Americans who had given them their freedom, and towards the many who had lost their lives doing so. She said she was with us in our pain and admired the courage we had in overcoming the sorrow and horror of September 11. The other declared the friendship of the entire family, and her sorrow for the Americans who had come to their aid on the Normandy Coast. '*Combien nous voudrions les aider, dans ce grand malheur,*' it ended, 'How we would like to help them, during this horrible ordeal.' These notes were not for us, but for all Americans; we were simply witnesses. Yet at the same time they were heartfelt and sincere personal testaments. As if I hadn't cried enough, the tears streamed out of my eyes again at these touching declarations. They came from a generation of French who innocently and

334

without question believe in the greatness of the United States of America.

The following week, about three weeks after the event, Joe came home from school, crestfallen. 'Some kids called me a dirty American,' he said.

We were upset and a bit shocked, but not surprised. This time was like no other for us, and for the world. The US was thumping its chest, trying to find its way out of its pain, talking about war and evil, and not everyone was on our side. We explained to Joe that the children who said that to him didn't understand what they were saying, that no one really understood what they were feeling. We told him that not everyone loves Americans, and why. We talked about ostentation and humility, about haves and have-nots, about civil rights and freedoms. We had already told him, gently, that simply being American didn't make any of us heroes. Now we told him that simply being American didn't mean we were going to be sheltered from criticism, or racism, or any other kind of hurt.

It took many months to feel a semblance of normalcy about the world, and still it is shaky. As many have said before me, nothing in our world will really ever be the same. Nothing in our lives will really ever be the same. The disastrous event has had some positive repercussions in that I think we have become more sensitive about others, more tolerant. We assume much less than we did before, because we saw how quickly innocent realities and assumptions can be destroyed, and we learned how fragile and vulnerable every single individual in this world has become.

Our good friends Dalila and Salah are Muslims originally from Algeria, and they had called us to express their sympathy. A month or so later, I called to invite them over. I'd wanted to learn to make couscous from Dalila, and no time seemed better than now, when we all needed a happy diversion.

Dalila moved to France fifteen years ago to marry her husband, Salah, who was raised in France. We met when their bright and beautiful daughter Lydia, and our son Joe, became friends in pre-school. Our backgrounds couldn't be more diverse, yet Dalila and I have become close friends. Much of our commonality is food. While Dalila is a nurse's aide during the day, once home she turns into a passionate cook. She tries different recipes at times, yet she refers most often to dishes she grew up with, making them with a sure hand, and serving them with obvious pride.

Salah is a former plumber turned prison guard. What he does for a living has nothing to do with who he is, however, for he is as passionate about the world as Dalila is about food. He loves art and writing, and I have never seen more beautiful handwriting than that on the cards Salah sends us when the family goes on holiday.

The Bouferchas live in a charming village of stone houses and verdant pathways on the flank of the Seine River. Divided between wealth and poverty, it has a narrow slice of comfortable middle-class families like the Bouferchas, who were delighted with it when they first moved there. There have been some unsettling racial incidents since, which have tempered their affection, but they still love their home and have made it their policy to go about their lives ignoring what others say.

We'd missed seeing them during Ramadan, which had fallen right before Christmas. Usually Dalila invites us over once or twice to participate in an evening break-the-fast meal, but this year she'd been silent. I waited until Ramadan was over to call her and she admitted she'd had a hard time throughout the holy period. 'Usually I feel happier,' she said. 'This year I couldn't, I was down-hearted. I didn't even feel like cooking.' We both knew why. Dalila and Salah are Arabs. They were heartsick about the terrorist attacks, as we all were. But while we had been the recipients of warm and loving testimonials, the Bouferchas's experience had been different. 'There have been incidents,' Dalila said, 'anti-Arab incidents. We haven't felt like celebrating and we haven't gone out. The children are going to school, we are going to work, but that is all, nothing more.'

I was so sorry to hear this. It didn't seem fair. We hadn't noticed any difference in the way our Arab neighbours had treated us, except for one man who was the father of a former schoolmate of Joe's. Always friendly and very polite, he simply came up to us in the street one day, after separating himself from the group of Arab men he was with, and clasped our hands and our shoulders, wordlessly.

I was so happy that the Bouferchas were with us for the evening. It was such fun to be in the kitchen, cooking together. Dalila's and my first task was to make *Chorba*, a typical soup eaten during Ramadan. 'I can't imagine Ramadan without *Chorba*,' Dalila said. She gathered together the appropriate quantity of ingredients and I measured and weighed them carefully before dicing, slicing and sautéeing. For a cook who is used to simply assembling ingredients, my methodical approach made her giggle, and soon we were laughing our way through the dishes.

We made several other dishes before Dalila's family arrived, and we all sat down to a feast. When the couscous we'd made came to the table, Dalila inhaled, deeply.

'This is the aroma of my grandmother's kitchen,' she said. 'How did we do this? I can't even make it this way at home.' The couscous grain that went around the table was the most fluffy and full of flavour that I'd ever had, and Dalila agreed.

We were all sated. Gradually the children left the table to play together, Michael and Salah went outside to smoke a cigarette, and Dalila and I stayed at the table to discuss our culinary efforts. Each dish we'd made had been exceptionally delicious, a result of concentrated effort I knew, but also the sharing that had gone on. While cooking and explaining, Dalila had given me the secrets of her childhood and her family. I had opened up my kitchen to her, and together we'd made a wonderful meal. It might have been a night like any others with the Bouferchas, but instead it was significant, a moment of detente between people of different beliefs and cultures. If only we could make one world meal and set it on a table for all peoples to share. We'd soon discover that, in fact, our differences are less remarkable than our points of commonality.

It's been almost two years since that dark September. Worldwide, everything is in upheaval and big changes are imminent. We can only hope they will be positive for someone, for at the moment the world powers seem at odds, the world mood fearful, aggressive and uncompromising. We've seen the French come way too close to electing a Fascist President, then seen them muster their convictions and send him away in a rout. We've seen America vulnerable and incoherent. We've seen Joe through hard times at school as he experienced racial slurs and came out the other side strong and, we hope, wiser to the ways of the world. We've welcomed Americans who, despite travel-warnings and fear, decided that their dream to attend cooking classes in France was worth the risk.

We won't ever forget the first class we held less than

two weeks after September 11. We'd had seven guests signed up but four cancelled, which left the three who showed up that Sunday evening for dinner bubbling with excitement and with news. Marie, a high-strung, hilariously funny Italian New Yorker from Queens who worked in an office building in central Manhattan, told us how she had seen the first plane hit the Trade Center. 'I realized immediately what was happening, then I thought "Oh my God, our building will be next." I made everyone evacuate.' Joan, from a small city in Texas, had been the most nervous about travelling and had emailed me before coming to see whether I felt she should risk it. I had no crystal ball, but I told her that we'd already had visitors who had come and gone, and that they had experienced no problems. That helped her make up her mind. She and Marie had become instant friends and they both agreed that they were right where they wanted to be, away from all the news, doing something they'd dreamed of doing. Our third guest, Delia, simply seemed shell-shocked, and didn't talk much at all.

We usually serve homemade orange wine as the welcome aperitif, but for these brave women we pulled out our best champagne. 'To you, for your courage,' Michael said, as he toasted them. With that we began one of the warmest, funniest weeks we've ever had. Marie and Joan, particularly, kept us all in stitches as we sautéed and steamed, poached and roasted our way through a delectable series of menus. We cried together, we laughed together as we all – children included – sat at the table together. We took enormous comfort from each other, and bonded in a way that has made us friends for life.

Looking back on that week I am amazed those women had the courage to fly, and I thank them in my mind over and over, for they helped us get through a horrible time.

They say we helped them too. It was the antidote of laughter, food, cooking, friendship and exchange that helped us all.

Since then our house has changed, with the addition of a beautiful new brick courtyard off the kitchen, whose wall Michael built of old, white Norman stone. We recently had our first large al fresco dinner there with French friends, a magical event which will be repeated often with cooking school guests. Like all improvements Michael makes, this one signals our continued attachment and commitment to this small town in the Normandy countryside where, since September 11, we have discovered a well of warmth and something deeper than acceptance, something closer to the feeling of home.

September 11 caused us to reconsider our definition of who we are. Before, we knew we were Americans but we didn't feel that we necessarily belonged to a people. Now we do. We feel at home here in Louviers, in these beautiful surroundings with the friends we've made, yet we feel more attached than ever to our other home across the Atlantic, there with our family and our people.

The feast of Thanksgiving in the year 2001 was poignant as we worked our way through so many new and different emotions and sentiments. It took on a new and deeper meaning for us all. I had invited a Franco-American couple, Deborah and Olivier, with their three children, and my American assistant, Kerrie, as well. I'd also invited Bernard – Edith was out of town, our neighbour, Patrick, our young friends Eloise and Nicholas and Joe's friend Florian.

Kerrie made her sweet potatoes with maple syrup and pecan topping and Deborah brought cornbread and pumpkin pie. I roasted a lean, flavourful turkey that I had ordered from a farmer at the market, and I stuffed it with our favourite mushroom and bread stuffing. I creamed pearl onions and shallots, steamed Brussels sprouts then sautéed them with chestnuts and garlic butter, baked my grandmother's ethereal crescent rolls, and mashed potatoes with garlic. Kerrie and I hollowed out a *potimarron*, a small, sweet-meated squash that tastes much like a Delicata, for each person and filled them with leeks and cream then baked them until the squash was tender. Just before everyone sat down we sautéed wild mushrooms, put them inside and served one to each guest.

But before we did that we had toasted almonds with fresh lemon thyme and honey, delicate cheese crackers and herbed *gougères* – cream puffs – and Michael poured champagne. We all toasted each other, then both Eloise and Nicholas spoke at the same time. 'What is Thanksgiving?' they asked. 'I have heard about it and I know it has something to do with the harvest, but why is it so important?' Eloise continued.

I explained about the first harvest and the gratitude of the Pilgrims for all the help they'd received from the native tribes. I spoke of Squanto, the Native American ambassador to the Pilgrims, and explained what a diplomatic success that first harvest meal had been. I talked about how important the Thanksgiving meal is, and how significant each and every ingredient is, for each represents the beginning of our country. As I spoke, everyone down to Joe and his friend were very, very quiet. There was a palpable sense of history in the room, a sense of warmth and emotion. Patrick had tears in his eyes; Eloise and Nicholas were holding hands. Even Bernard, never at a loss for the appropriate remark, remained silent.

'We don't think of Americans caring so much about food or a meal,' Eloise said. 'It is so simple yet so meaningful, and such a beautiful story.'

341

I think I was surprised at my own telling of the story, too, because I realized as I told it how significant Thanksgiving, which is consecrated to the careful preparation and enjoyment of delicious and indigenous foods is, not only to our history but to Americans everywhere. This year it had a very special significance, for in celebrating we were expressing a declaration of hope, solidarity and love for our people out there, and for these people right here.

We sat down to our individual *potimarrons* and I glanced around the table. I felt so humble and so thankful for the luxury of our home, our family, and our friends. Without any of us saying so, I knew that we were all grateful to be here safe and sound, and grateful to be together, two cultures mixing in harmony. The scene couldn't have been more American, yet the sentiment was universal. We were all at home together.

PUMPKINS FILLED WITH LEEKS AND WILD MUSHROOMS

Potimarrons Farcis avec des Poireaux et des Champignons du Bois

———————— ～ ————————

4 small (1 lb-ish; 500g) pumpkins
1 medium-sized leek, sliced thinly
1 cup (250 ml) heavy cream or crème fraîche, plus 1 tbs sea salt
Heaped quarter teaspoon freshly ground nutmeg
About 1 cup (250 ml) water
1 lb (500 g) wild mushrooms such as chanterelles
(may substitute an equal amount of cultivated mushrooms,
such as oyster mushrooms)
Sea salt and freshly ground black pepper
Flat leaf parsley or chervil, for garnish

1. Preheat the oven to 350°F (175°C). Cut the stem ends off the pumpkins, about 1-inch (2.5cm) down the side of the pumpkin to give a nice 'hat', preferably with a bit of stem on it, to use as a handle. Scoop out all of the seeds and the stringy pith of the pumpkin, and discard. Trim the other end of the pumpkin just enough so it sits flat, without tipping.
2. Evenly divide the leeks among the four pumpkins. Add ¼ cup (60 ml) of the cream to each pumpkin, season with salt and the nutmeg, replace the top, and place the pumpkins in a baking dish large enough to hold them without being crowded. Pour ¾ cup (180 ml) of the water around the pumpkins, and place the pan in the centre of the oven. Bake the pumpkins until their flesh is nearly but not quite tender through, about

45 minutes. Remove the pan from the oven, and remove the top from each pumpkin. Carefully scrape some of the flesh from the sides of the pumpkin, leaving it inside the pumpkin, return the tops, and return the pumpkins to the oven to bake until they are tender through, an additional 15 to 20 minutes. While the pumpkins are baking, check them occasionally to be sure the pan hasn't baked dry, adding additional water if necessary.

3. If using wild mushrooms, about 5 minutes before the pumpkins have finished baking, place them in a non-stick skillet over medium high heat and cook them until they have wilted but are not soggy, and have given up a fair amount of liquid, 4 to 5 minutes. Remove the mushrooms from the pan and continue cooking the liquid until it has nearly evaporated, about 1 minute. Return the mushrooms to the pan, add the remaining tablespoon of cream, stir, and cook just until the mushrooms and cream are hot through, 2 to 3 minutes. Season with salt and pepper and remove from the heat. If using cultivated mushrooms, begin cooking them about 10 minutes before the pumpkins are cooked, and follow the same procedure.

4. To serve the pumpkins, remove the tops and evenly divide the mushrooms among them. Garnish each pumpkin with the chervil or parsley, place the tops on the pumpkins leaving them somewhat askew so the mushrooms show, and place one in the centre of each of 4 warmed dinner plates. If there are extra mushrooms, arrange them at the side of the pumpkin. Serve immediately.

4 servings

WINTER FRUIT TARTE TATIN
Tarte Tatin aux Fruits d'Hiver

———————— ʗʑ ————————

This is a sumptuous variation on Tarte Tatin using a combination of apples and pears. I occasionally add quince, as well, cut in quarters. This is delicious, and so gorgeous once the fruit is caramelized and the tart is turned out onto a serving platter.

1 recipe *On Rue Tatin* Pastry
2 cups (400g) sugar
8 tbs (4 oz.; 120 g) unsalted butter
9 medium, tart cooking apples, such as winesaps or cox orange (about 2.5 lb; 1.25kg) cored, peeled, seeded and cut in quarters
8 good-sized, not quite ripe pears (about 2.5 lb; 1.25kg) cored, peeled, cut in quarters

1. Line a baking sheet with parchment paper or lightly flour it.
2. Roll out the pastry on a lightly floured work surface to form an 11 ½ inch (29 cm) round. Transfer the pastry to the prepared baking sheet and refrigerate for at least 1 hour.
3. Spread the sugar evenly over the bottom of a very heavy 10-to 10½-inch (25 to 26½ cm) oven-proof skillet; a simple cast-iron skillet is perfect. Place the butter slices evenly over the sugar, then arrange the apple and the pear halves alternately on top of the butter. If the pears are longer than the apples, lay the pear halves on their sides, with the narrow, stem end towards

345

the centre. Do the same if using quinces if they are longer than the apples. Begin at the outside edge and stand the halves on their sides, facing in one direction with stem ends toward the centre. Pack the apples close together so they are held standing by pressure. Make a second circle of apple halves inside the first, packing them in on their edges as well. Place one apple half right in the centre of the second circle to fill in the small space that remains. The idea is to get as many apples into the pan as possible, while keeping them nicely arranged.

4. Place the skillet over medium-low heat and cook the apples in the butter and sugar, uncovered, until the sugar turns golden brown; this will take about 50 minutes. Watch the apples closely to be sure they don't stick; you may want to adjust the heat now and then, to slow down or speed up the cooking. As the sugar and butter melt and the apples give up some of their juices, baste the apples occasionally with a turkey baster. Gradually, the sugar will caramelize the apples nearly all the way through, though they will remain uncooked on top.

5. Preheat the oven to 425°F (220°C).

6. When the cooking juices are deep golden and the apples are nearly cooked through, remove the pastry from the refrigerator and quickly and carefully place it over the apples, gently pushing it down around them, simultaneously easing it toward the centre so that if it shrinks on the sides there will still be enough of it to cover the apples. Using a sharp knife, trim off and discard any extra pastry.

7. Place the skillet on a baking sheet. Bake in the centre of the oven until the pastry is golden, 25 to 30 minutes. Don't be concerned if the juices bubble over; the tart

will be more or less juicy, depending on the variety of apple you've used.

8. Remove the skillet from the oven. Immediately invert a serving platter with a slight lip over the skillet. Quickly but carefully invert the two so the crust is on the bottom, the apples are on top, and the juices don't run off onto the floor. Remove the skillet. Should any apples stick to it, gently remove them and reinsert them into their rightful place in the tart.

9. Serve generous slices as soon as the tart has cooled slightly, but is still very warm through.

One 10-inch (25 cm) tart; 6–8 servings

Afterword

The month between Thanksgiving and Christmas is one of my favourite times of year. It is traditionally a slow work period, allowing me the luxury to indulge in Christmas preparations. The children and I make batches and batches of cookies which we package in fanciful bags and deliver to the neighbours, and Michael bakes loaves of his *pain au levain*, sourdough bread, which are delivered too. He and I take a day or two together in Paris to wander, eat oysters on the half shell at Le Dôme near Montparnasse, shop for Joe and Fiona. We like to take the children to a performance, too, which might be a concert at the gorgeous old church in Acquigny, a village near us, or a circus performance at the Cirque d'Hiver in Paris.

Each year the town of Louviers does something a bit different for Christmas, and we woke up on the first of December 2001 to find a gorgeous, old-fashioned *manège* or merry-go-round installed right across the street in the church plaza. Fiona was beside herself, dying to go out and ride it. Since it didn't open until the afternoon, she spent the first several mornings standing at the hall window, her finger on her bottom lip, just staring at the baroque horses, ducks, elephants and lions, waiting for them to come to life. The minute she heard the *manège*'s tinkling music she'd come find me and out we would go. Joe often came, too, and the three of us would spin on it under the gaze of the gargoyles.

Each year garlands hang high across the streets of Louviers and a series of lanky, life-size Santa figures that look astonishingly real are arranged in strategic spots around town. One perches high on a rooftop at the edge of a chimney, as though preparing to descend; another balances on a string ladder hung from a balcony, another hangs on the side of a building and peers in a window, and there are more. The first year they went up, the police received hundreds of calls from elderly people who thought the Santas were real people up to no good!

Michael has always taken great pleasure in decorating for Christmas, and he outdoes himself in Louviers. We all participate by going into the woods that belong to our friend John-Pierre to cut pine boughs, which Michael fashions into garlands to hang from the eaves and put on the exterior window sills. Once these are in place he winds yards of tiny white lights through them, and through the branches of our old apple tree in the middle of the garden. The children and I hang ornaments in it, and in the espaliered trees that line one side of the property. I make a huge wreath for the courtyard gate, and we put candles at all the windows. The result is a fairy wonderland. It is also very American because, while the French decorate ' their homes, they do so in a more muted way.

Inside we put up our collection of nativities, hang glittering garlands and line the chimneys with fresh greens. I make an advent wreath for the table and we light the appropriate number of candles each night. We make an occasion out of choosing our tree from the selection at the florist's next door, carrying it home to set it up, then spending the evening decorating. Most years, when all is in place, I invite friends and neighbours in for mulled wine and appetizers. All of our Christmas efforts are traditions that we brought with us and that we like to keep alive. They are unusual to the French, which gives them a whole new and interesting dimension as we realize that what is normal for us is such a novelty to others.

We were looking forward to our annual mulled wine evening when a friend, Astrid, called to ask if I would host a tasting for the wine that her husband, Olivier, had begun to make two years before. We first met Astrid and Olivier several years ago when they lived in Normandy, where Olivier made wonderful cider, Calvados and Pommeau. I did a story on their production for *Bon Appétit* magazine, and I liked them and their products so much that I began bringing cooking school students to their orchard. Through the course of these visits we became good friends, and when they decided to move south to Gaillac, near Toulouse, to make wine instead of cider, we cheered them along and have kept in close touch since.

The wine Astrid wanted to serve was their first vintage, which showed enormous promise. She had decided one of the best ways to create a market for it was to do private tastings, and to that end she travelled frequently to Normandy while Olivier stayed in Gaillac supervising the vineyards and taking care of their four young sons. I couldn't have been more delighted to do a wine tasting evening for them, and Christmas was the perfect season.

Along with my assistant, Kerrie, I spent the day of the tasting preparing for what I knew would be an entertaining evening. I carefully melted leeks and cream together and wrapped the mixture in strips of filo dough to make crisp, mouth-melting bites. I toasted almonds and tossed them with honey and lemon thyme, wrapped small cubes of feta cheese with air-cured ham and marinated them in extra-virgin olive oil and sage. I blended smoked and fresh salmon with butter, lemon and chives to make salmon rillettes, and I made savoury breads seasoned with parsley and shallots, and with red peppers and parmesan cheese. I set bowls full of clementines on the table, and had chestnuts from the woods roasting in the fire.

More than thirty friends and acquaintances, wine enthusiasts all, came for the tasting and to spend an evening together. Candles flickered, decorations sparkled; American and French Christmas music added to the festivity.

'We all needed this,' a friend came up and whispered to me. 'Thank you.'

I agreed. We all need celebrations like this every year. This year, in particular, the gathering had a certain resonance, as though each person was more grateful than usual for the opportunity to be together.

When everyone had left, including a very satisfied Astrid who had sold twice the amount of wine she'd expected, Michael and I sat in the kitchen and did a post-mortem. I'd cooked all day in the kitchen, which, even in the dark December weather, had been infused with light. We'd all helped decorate, so there had been something for everyone, children included. Michael and I had enjoyed being guests in our own home as Astrid poured her wine and entertained.

As we sat with our backs to the marble-topped counter and looked out through the paned windows of the front door to the church, whose gothic gargoyles and arched Romanesque doorways were in deep shadow, I thought how simply fortunate we were. When we bought this house it was beautiful though somewhat austere. Any austerity has long since been banished as we've lived our lives under its roof with our children, our singing, our laughter, our friends, our dinner conversations and our parties. It has become a shelter, a place of happiness, security and comfort for us and for our multi-dimensional group of friends. It is stretching further now, to accommodate an ever-increasing number of cooking school guests who will come to experience life, learning, food and sharing within its walls. We have, in the truest sense of the word, created a home.

LIST OF RECIPES

Allspice Ice Cream	157
Belgian Endive with Lemon and Garlic Vinaigrette	69
Cepes Omelette	252
Chicken with Sorrel	67
Chocolate Ice Cream	253
Corn Loaf	49
Fishmonger's Favourite	119
Ginger Madeleines	155
Grilled Rabbit with Mustard and Bacon	233
Hot Chocolate the Way We Like It	211
Marvellous Berry Dessert	266
Michael's Sourdough Bread	293
Mustard Cream with Fresh Vegetables	322
Olive Cookies from the Drome	15
On Rue Tatin Pastry	97
Onion, Bacon and Cream Pizza	211
Orange Wine	16
Oxtails with Cinnamon	153
Pear and Cream Tart from the Market in Louviers	95
Pumpkins Filled with Leeks and Wild Mushrooms	343
Quiche from the Louviers Market	96
Raw Beet Salad	50
Roast Chicken	98
Roast Pork with Salt and Spice Crust	309
Roasted Cockles with Saffron and Lemon	70

Rosemary Baked Potatoes   121
Salted Spanish Almonds   186
Savoury Beef Stew from the Florist   122
Scallion Bread   234
Skate Salad   276
Three Nut Biscotti   323
Tuna with Pine Nut and Anchovy Sauce   275
Winter Fruit Tarte Tatin   345
Wood Fire Grilled Lamb Chops   185